WASTEBOOK 2012

Table of Contents

Introduction 1

1. The most unproductive and unpopular Congress in modern history – (Congress) $132 million 4

2. Professional sports loophole – (Taxes) $91 million 7

3. OH SNAP! Junk food, luxury drinks, soap operas, and billions of dollars in improper food stamp payments – (Department of Agriculture) $4.5 billion 10

4. Oklahoma keeps unused airport open to collect federal checks – (OK) $450,000 13

5. Moroccan pottery classes – (U.S. Agency for International Development) $27 million 15

6. Out-of-this-world Martian food tasting – (HI) $947,000 17

7. When robot squirrels attack – (CA) $325,000 20

8. USDA's caviar dreams – (ID) $300,000 22

9. Bailed out tourist boat sinking private business – (AK) $3.3 million 24

10. Phantom, unused grant accounts draw fees – (Department of Health and Human Services) $2 million 28

WASTEBOOK 2012

Dear Taxpayer,

Times remain tough in America. The number of people working has dropped to the lowest level in decades. More than 23 million of our fellow citizens do not have good jobs, and wages for many others are stagnant and even declining.[1] Families are struggling to do more with less.

But not everyone in America is living on a smaller budget. Washington politicians don't even bother to give themselves a budget anymore. For the third consecutive year, Congress failed to pass a budget. And, for the fourth straight year, these compulsive spenders charged more than $1 trillion to our national credit card, pushing us to a $16 trillion debt.

Some try to rationalize the excessive borrowing and spending as necessary until the economy gets back on track. But the increased demand for help is precisely why Washington must be more careful how tax dollars are spent to ensure we can care for those who are truly in need. To do this Washington must set priorities, just like every family. The problem is Washington has all the wrong priorities.

> As you read each of the 100 projects costing over $18 billion outlined in this report, ask yourself:
>
> - **Can we can afford this at this time?**
>
> - **Could this money have been better spent, or not spent at all?**
>
> - **Is this a national priority or is this something benefiting a special interest?**
>
> - **Does this fit the role of the federal government, as outlined in the U.S. Constitution?**

Thousands, millions and even billions of dollars in an annual budget in excess of $3.7 trillion may not seem like much to Washington politicians, but these days a dollar can make a big difference for families on fixed budgets. How many of our friends, families and neighbors could be fed with the nearly $1 million the government spent taste testing foods to be served on the planet Mars? How many nutritious school lunches could have been served with the $2 million in financial assistance provided to cupcake specialty shops?

Washington priorities are backwards. This is why important programs go bankrupt while outdated and outlandish projects continue to be funded.

WASTEBOOK 2012

The Highway Trust Fund, which has been bailed out several times over the last five years, is a good example, as billions of dollars intended for transportation are wasted on questionable projects that do little to fix congestion or other transportation problems. An unused Ohio bridge — not even connected to a road or trail — received a half-a-million dollar makeover this year. An Oregon town will pay $388,000 for just five bus stops – enough to buy two houses in the same town! And in West Virginia, thousands of dollars were spent to reconstruct a historic streetscape... out of Legos. Would the dollars spent on these transportation projects not have been better spent to fix some of the 22,158 deficient bridges plaguing our national highway system?[2]

> **Washington priorities are backwards. This is why important programs go bankrupt while outdated and outlandish projects continue to be funded.**

Perhaps nothing demonstrates just how out of touch Washington is more than the $300,000 USDA is spending to tell Americans to eat caviar, one of the world's most expensive delicacies, at a time when millions of Americans are struggling just to put the basics on the family dinner table. It echoes back to the fabled proclamation of the callous royal who, when asked about the hungry and poor shortly before the French Revolution, replied "let them eat cake."

This "let them eat caviar" attitude in Washington is evident in countless instances as the well-off are rewarded with the taxes paid by other hard-working Americans: In Los Angeles, a yacht used by city officials, celebrities, and other VIPs was upgraded for nearly half a million dollars. In Indianapolis, the costs of providing free bus service for the ticket holders attending the Super Bowl totaled almost $150,000. Wealthy tax cheats collected hundreds of millions of dollars in payments from a health care program for the poor, professional sports leagues were exempted from paying taxes, and the world's largest snack food company benefitted from over $1 million in governments grants to support the multi-billion dollar company's new Greek yogurt facility in New York.

> **This "let them eat caviar" attitude in Washington is evident in countless instances.**

These and the other examples of mismanagement, wasteful spending and special interest deals highlighted in this report represent missed opportunities to assist those in need and to shore up the nation's finances. Washington spent much of the year deadlocked over whether to cut spending or increase taxes to address our fiscal crisis, all the while, allowing or even supporting these questionable projects. Each of the 100 entries highlighted by this report, therefore, is a direct result of Washington politicians who are preoccupied with running for re-election rather than running the country, which is what they were elected to do in the first place.

As you look at these examples, put your personal political persuasion aside and ask yourself: Would you agree with Washington that these represent national priorities, or would you conclude these reflect the out-of-touch and out-of-control spending threatening to bankrupt our nation's future?

Sincerely,

Tom A. Coburn, M.D.
U.S. Senator

1) The most unproductive and unpopular Congress in modern history does nothing while America struggles – (Congress) $132 million[3]

Persistent unemployment. Insurmountable debt. Mounting war casualties.

The challenges facing our nation have rarely been so dire for so long. Yet, never before in recent history have our elected leaders in Washington worked less and been more lax in addressing our nation's problems.

Congress is "on pace to make history [for] the least productive legislative year" since 1947, with just 61 bills passed and made law in 2012 to date.[4] "Even taking into account bills the House and Senate are expected to pass in the upcoming lame-duck session, the current Congress could easily have the lowest level of legislative activity since statistics began being tabulated," according to the Capitol Hill newspaper *Roll Call*.[5]

Senate committee rooms like this one were largely vacant and unused for most of 2012, as the most unproductive and unpopular Congress in modern history chose to avoid addressing the multitude of issues facing our nation.

The inability of Congress to get things done has resulted in the lowest public approval in the nearly four decades the rating has been measured by Gallup. A stunning 83 percent disapprove of "the way Congress is doing its job."[6] The poor ratings given Congress are consistent across the political spectrum with approval from only nine percent of Democrats, 11 percent of Independents, and 10 percent of Republicans.[7] During these contentious times, Americans find so much to disagree about, yet almost everyone agrees Congress is failing to do its job.

With the House and Senate controlled by opposite parties, partisans point fingers of blame at the party in control of the other chamber. But, the stalemate is not simply the product of split-party control between the two chambers.

The Senate has cast fewer votes in 2012 thus far than any year in decades.[8][9][10] More than 20 of the 100 senators — on both sides of the aisle — have not had a single amendment considered on the Senate floor in 2012.[11] And after blocking senators from offering fixes to bills throughout the year, the Majority Leader of what once was the world's greatest deliberative body publicly announced from the Senate floor, "I will say this so it will save a lot of trouble for anybody. ... Amendment days are over."[12]

A number of important committees within both the House and the Senate are failing to do the important work for which they are responsible.

Perhaps the most striking disappointment is the Senate Budget Committee (see appendix for complete lists). Since the last budget was passed on April 29, 2009, Washington has spent $11.2 trillion and added more than $4.8 trillion to the national debt.[13] With the national debt now over $16 trillion, never before have taxpayers needed a budget blueprint more to guide our nation away from fiscal ruin. Yet, the Senate Budget Committee has failed to produce a budget – which it is required to do by law – in over 1,200 days.[14] In addition to not producing a budget resolution, the committee has also failed to hold many hearings, a key tool for Congress to conduct oversight, investigate problems, seek solutions, initiate conversation and debate, and advance an agenda. The Senate Budget Committee held a mere 12 hearings in 2012 – fewer than all but five other congressional committees from both chambers.[15][16]

Likewise, the Senate Finance Committee, which oversees about three-fourths of the federal budget including all of the major health care and retirement entitlement programs and the federal tax code has done little in 2012. Despite its broad jurisdiction, the Finance Committee reported out and discharged only 11 legislative measures.[17] These included a non-binding resolution supporting the goals and ideals of "National Save for Retirement Week" and a resolution authorizing the committee's own expenditures. The Senate Finance Committee held just 28 hearings this year (as of September 1).[18] Overall, the committee places in the top ten *least* productive of all congressional committees in terms of approving legislation and the top ten Senate committees holding the *fewest* number of hearings.[19][20]

Despite the importance of small business to our nation's economy and their recent struggles, the small business committees of both chambers tied for first place as the committee approving the least amount of legislation in 2012. The Senate Small Business and Entrepreneurship Committee held only four hearings and passed out just three measures, one of which authorized expenditures for the committee itself.[21] Likewise, the House Small Business Committee reported out just three bills and held 31 hearings, which is significantly more than its counterpart in the Senate, but fewer than most of the other committees in the House.[22]

Two other committees have been largely idle this year: the Senate's Agriculture, Nutrition, and Forestry Committee and Special Committee on Aging. The Senate Agriculture, Nutrition, and Forestry reported out and discharged just seven measures, one of which was to provide for its own budget, and held a mere nine hearings.[23] [24] The Aging Committee reported out a single measure, which was to provide for its own budget, and held just nine hearings.[25] [26] [27]

Whether it was failing to hold oversight hearings, pass laws, cut unnecessary spending, or simply cast votes on amendments, the U.S. Congress let taxpayers down in 2012. In fact, many high school student councils have been more deliberative than the U.S. Senate.

All that follows in this report can be traced right back to what Congress has and has not done. Article 1, Section 9 of the U.S. Constitution entrusts Congress with the responsibility to approve how money is spent out of the Treasury and to account for such expenditures. Congress approved every cent spent to fund the projects outlined in this report and did nothing to stop any of these expenditures. In fact, in many cases members of Congress actually took credit for the projects with no shame. All of the outrageous and wasteful contents of this report were made possible by either the action or lack of action of Congress, earning it the well-deserved but unwanted distinction as the biggest waste of taxpayer money in 2012.

2) Professional sports loophole – (Taxes) $91 million

The National Football League (NFL), the National Hockey League (NHL), and the Professional Golfers' Association (PGA) classify themselves as non-profit organizations to exempt themselves from federal income taxes on earnings. Smaller sports leagues, such as the National Lacrosse League, are also using the tax status. Taxpayers may be losing at least $91 million subsidizing these tax loopholes for professional sports leagues that generate billions of dollars annually in profits.[28] Taxpayers should not be asked to subsidize sports organizations already benefiting widely from willing fans and turning a profit, while claiming to be non-profit organizations.

Touchdown! Grass is always greener when a sports league can score with loopholes to avoid paying taxes.

In 2010, the registered NFL nonprofit alone received $184 million from its 32 member teams.[29] It holds over $1 billion in assets.[30] Together with its subsidiaries and teams – many of which are for-profit, taxed entities – the NFL generates an estimated $9 billion annually.[31] Each of its teams are among the top 50 most expensive sports teams in the world, ranking alongside the world's famous soccer teams. Almost half of professional football teams are valued at over $1 billion.[32]

The PGA generated over $900 million in revenue, mostly through television rights, tournament earnings and sponsorships, and royalties.[33] In 2009, the NHL received nearly $76 million from its member teams.[34]

League commissioners and officials benefit from the nonprofit status of their organizations. Roger Goodell, commissioner of the NFL, reported $11.6 million in salary and perks in 2010 alone.[35] Goodell's salary will reportedly reach $20 million in 2019.[36] Steve Bornstein, the executive vice president of media, made $12.2 million in 2010.[37] Former NFL commissioner Paul Tagliabue earned $8.5 million from the league in 2010.[38] The league paid five other officials a total of $19.2 million in just one year.[39] In comparison, the next highest salary of a traditional nonprofit CEO is $3.4 million.[40]

Tim Finchem, commissioner of the PGA Tour, earned $5.2 million in 2010.[41] The NHL's commissioner, Gary Bettman, received $4.3 million in 2009.[42]

These organizations are taking advantage of the provision of the tax code that allows industry and trade groups, such as the U.S. Chamber of Commerce or the Natural Resources Defense Council, to qualify as non-profit and tax-exempt. None of these groups can promote a specific brand within an industry but each may promote an industry as a whole. Qualifying organizations pay taxes on few types of income and expenditures, including lobbying. State and local governments usually exempt these organizations from state income and sales tax as well, a boon worth an estimated $10 billion to the nonprofit sector.[43]

Seeing the advantage in operating largely tax-free, the NFL, NHL, and PGA are registered with the Internal Revenue Service (IRS) as nonprofit organizations. These leagues assert they help the professional sport in each of their leagues. For example, on its 2010 tax return, the NFL described itself as a "trade association promoting interests of its 32 member clubs."[44] The NHL said its mission is "to perpetuate professional hockey in the US and Canada."[45] These benign statements aside, major professional sports leagues are hardly in the business of simply promoting the hockey, football, or golf industry. They are in fact businesses – designed to make money.

The history of the NFL's tax exemption status stems from the 1966 merger of the then-American Football League and NFL. Congress passed a law granting specific antitrust exemptions to the new NFL.[46] At that time, it also added "professional football leagues" to the list of entities eligible for nonprofit status.[47] According to the IRS, "Section 501(c)(6) of the Internal Revenue Code provides for the exemption of business leagues, chambers of commerce, real estate boards, boards of trade and *professional football leagues*, which are not organized for profit and no part of the net earnings of which inures to the benefit of any private shareholder or individual" (emphasis added).[48]

One major sports league – Major League Baseball – filed as a nonprofit for years, but chose to become a for-profit limited liability corporation in 2007. At least partly motivating the change was an opposition to the IRS' new salary transparency rules for nonprofits, which require releasing information on salaries above $150,000.[49] The NFL lobbied strenuously in Washington against an expansion of the disclosure reporting, but found little support.

Major professional sports leagues should no longer be eligible for general federal tax exemption. Removing them from federal nonprofit status may also benefit states and localities, which lose out on much needed revenue. For example, the NFL may have lived every taxpayer's dream at this year's Super Bowl in Indianapolis. According to the *Indianapolis Business Journal*, "Hotels and restaurants [did not tax] National Football League employees ... The NFL [used] its tax-exempt status as a 501(c)(6) to avoid paying taxes, in addition to fuel, auto rental and admissions taxes."[50]

Hardworking taxpayers should not be forced to provide funding to offset tax giveaways to lucrative major professional sports teams and leagues. Based on publicly available information about the NFL and NHL alone, barring major leagues from using the non-profit status may generate at least $91 million of federal revenue every year.[51]

3) OH SNAP! Junk food, luxury drinks, soap operas, and billions of dollars in improper food stamp payments – (Department of Agriculture) $4.5 billion

Starbucks drinks, Kentucky Fried Chicken, Taco Bell, soap operas, and alcohol were all purchased this year with federal food stamp funds. In Tennessee, food stamps paid for beer, diapers, and condoms. In three states, some individuals received more food stamp benefits simply because they smoke marijuana.[52]

About $80 billion will be spent to provide over 46 million Americans with federal financial assistance this year from the Supplemental Nutrition Assistance Program (SNAP, previously known as "Food Stamps").[53][54] With so many families struggling financially, this support can ensure many children who otherwise might go to bed hungry have healthy meals.

However, lax controls and mismanagement resulted in billions of dollars being spent not on healthy meals for hungry kids but instead wasted on questionable and, in some cases, illegal expenditures. Approximately $2.5 billion in improper SNAP payments are projected to be made this year, while millions of dollars more will be misspent on silly promotional

Supplemental Nutrition Assistance Program benefits can be used to purchase fast food at franchises like Kentucky Fried Chicken in California and Starbucks Frappuccinos at grocery stores in Oregon.

activities and food with little nutritional value.[55]

Junk food and sugary drinks. While the program was recently renamed the Supplemental Nutrition Assistance Program, there is no requirement for the food purchased to be nutritious. According to the U.S. Department of Agriculture (USDA), "soft drinks, candy, cookies, snack crackers, and ice cream are food items and are therefore eligible items."[56] Additionally, "energy drinks that have a nutrition facts label are eligible foods,"[57] even if they have little nutritional value.

More than $2 billion of beverages sweetened with sugar are purchased with food stamps every year, according to a study by the Yale Rudd Center for Food Policy & Obesity published in the American Journal of Preventive Medicine.[58] "Fifty-eight percent of all refreshment beverages purchased by SNAP participants were for sugar-sweetened beverages," such as soda pop and sports drinks.

Fast food. In California, many beneficiaries use food stamps to purchase not-so-nutritious fast food at Burger King, Kentucky Fried Chicken, Taco Bell, Pizza Hut and Dominoes Pizza.[59] In Los Angeles County alone, at least 141,000 people may use food stamps at fast food and other restaurants.[60] The city Social Services Director said "his department lacks the resources to decide whether restaurants offer enough healthful choices, and would need another agency to monitor that."[61]

Gourmet coffee. In Oregon, food stamps may be used to purchase luxury drinks, such as Frappuccinos, at Starbucks counters inside grocery stores. As "an added convenience to customers," Safeway allows the purchases of chilled Starbucks beverages, according to a spokesman.[62] "As long as the beverage is cold or an approved food, which includes sweets," the card can be used at the in-store Starbucks, but "certain additions, such as syrup, are not allowed."[63]

More money for the marijuana munchies. Marijuana has been linked to an increased appetite, known as getting the "munchies," so perhaps it is no surprise the states of Maine, New Mexico, and Oregon gave extra food stamp benefits to users of the illegal drug.[64][65][66] These states allowed some marijuana users to deduct the cost of the drug from their income when determining the amount of the benefits provided for which they are eligible. In Oregon, the deduction "[i]ncluded ... fees for obtaining a state-issued medical marijuana card, expenses incurred while cultivating marijuana and the costs of purchasing it from a third-party grower."[67] It is not known how many recipients claimed the deduction.[68] The director of the Maine Office of Family Independence does not know how many individuals received extra food stamp benefits as a result of marijuana use.[69]

Booze and other un-allowable items. Undercover reporters "witnessed customers leaving with beer, diapers and condoms" paid for with SNAP *Electronic Benefit Transfer* (*EBT*) cards at a Food Land store in Memphis, Tennessee.[70] Technically, the purchase of these items is not permitted, but the practice goes on. In Ohio, another local television station reported in February that food stamps paid not only for beer and cigarettes, but also guns and cars.[71]

In Florida, an exotic dancer who made more than $85,000 a year in tips also collected about $1,000 in food stamps a month between March 2010 and June 2012.[72] During that time, she spent more than $9,000 on "cosmetic enhancements."[73] She has pled guilty to food stamp fraud but claims the plastic surgery and "other splurges were all gifts from men she met working as a dancer at adult entertainment clubs."[74]

Soap operas and parties. The food stamp program wasted millions of dollars on promotional campaigns encouraging local SNAP offices to throw parties and producing radio soap operas and advertisements. One recommended way to promote the program according to USDA is to "Throw a Great Party. Host social events where people mix and mingle. Make it fun by having activities, games, food, and entertainment, and provide information about SNAP. Putting SNAP information in a game format like BINGO, crossword puzzles, or even a 'true/false' quiz is fun and helps get your message across in a memorable way."[75]

USDA also produced "a compilation of ten two-minute Spanish public service announcements in the form of radio novelas or miniseries" of soap operas to promote food stamp use.[76] "Each novela, comprising a ten-part series called 'Parque Alegria,' or 'Happiness Park,' presents a semi-dramatic scenario involving characters convincing others to get on food stamps, or explaining how much healthier it is to be on food stamps."[77] Episodes conclude "with the announcer encouraging the listener to tune in again to see if" the characters apply for food stamps or to learn the importance of SNAP benefits to their health.[78,79] USDA also spent between $2.5 million and $3 million for four months of radio ads this year to promote the program in California, Texas, North Carolina, South Carolina, Ohio, and New York.[80]

Dead, duplicate, and disqualified recipients. The USDA Inspector General found roughly 2,000 dead people are still receiving food stamps in New York and Massachusetts combined.[81,82] Additionally, its investigation revealed 7,236 people in these states are receiving duplicate benefits, while 286 are on state lists that should exclude them from receiving food stamps.[83,84] These unnecessary payments amount to $1.4 million every month.[85,86]

4) Oklahoma keeps unused airport open to collect federal checks – (OK) $450,000

The Oklahoma Aeronautics Commission (OAC) voted this year to keep a rarely used Lake Murray State Park Airport open simply to land more federal funds. The airport averages just one flight per month, has no planes based there, and is situated mere miles from two more heavily used airports.[87]

An Oklahoma airport receives one flight a month, but the state keeps it open just to land federal funds.

Yet, the airport lands an automatic $150,000 from the Federal Aviation Administration (FAA) every year. Much of that money is eventually used elsewhere in the state, making the Lake Murray State Park Airport a layover to land government money.[88]

In the last five years, Lake Murray State Park Airport has received $750,000 through the FAA program, of which the commission has spent only $5,546 on the airport itself – less than one percent![89] The rest of the funds were transferred to projects at other state airports or remain unspent.[90] Just this year, OAC sent $150,000 to two other projects across the state, both of which have already benefitted from millions of federal dollars.[91] The commission is now sitting on $450,000.[92]

Since 2006, the state tourism department—which co-owns the strip along with OAC—has recommended closing and razing the airstrip to pave way for better access to a state park lodge and golf course adjacent to the property.[93] Both are major draws in the area. By closing the airport, OAC would be "giving up the ability to accept $150,000 in federal money each year," commission members worried.[94]

The commission's own director recommended closing the airport, but the members instead voted unanimously to keep the airport open.[95]

The OAC has also accepted FAA Airport Improvement Programs grants (AIP) totaling more than $180,000 since 2002 that were specifically for improvements to the Lake Murray airstrip, including runway rehabilitation, updated runway lighting, beacons, and tree clearing.[96] Despite these grants, the strip has no electricity and thus, no lighting and the runway pavement is said to be "nearing the end of its useful life."[97]

Besides its ability to land federal funds, there is no other apparent reason to justify the airport's existence. Closing it would not inconvenience travelers or pilots and would allow for better use of the property.

If this layover boondoggle is happening in Oklahoma, is it happening elsewhere?

5) Moroccan pottery classes – (U.S. Agency for International Development) $27 million

In 2009, the U.S. Agency for International Development (USAID) began pursuing a four-year plan to improve the economic competitiveness of Morocco. A review by the agency's Inspector General (IG) found the $27-million project "was not on track to achieve its goals."[98]

A key part of the project involved training Moroccans to create and design pottery to sell in domestic and international markets.[99]

To accomplish this, an American pottery instructor was contracted to provide several weeks of training classes to local artists to improve their methods and teach them how to successfully make pottery that could be brought to market. Unfortunately, the translator hired for the sessions was not fluent in English and was unable to transmit large portions of the lectures to the participants.[100]

Participants in the program were also frustrated by the choice of materials. The colored dyes and clay the instructor used during the class are unavailable for purchase in Morocco, making it impossible for the trainees to replicate the methods they had learned.[101]

Trainees also claimed the instructor would frequently forget to bring the right materials to class.[102]

In one class, organizers reported 56 participants, but a trainee stated many of her classmates only signed in so they could receive the provided lunch, and estimated only around ten potters attended her class with any regularity.[103]

The instructor of a pottery class in Morocco used dyes and clays not available in the country, making it impossible for trainees to replicate the methods being taught. The translator for the class was also not fluent in English, making the lecture impossible to understand for participants, of which there were very few.

One of the chief goals of the project – "to focus on women and youth" – also went unfulfilled.[104] Women accounted for just 25 percent of trainees.[105] Even though USAID mission officials knew of the challenge to involve women, they "did not adequately ensure" the program met their needs.[106]

Project managers agreed with the IG's comments on the pottery training, admitting the training was "ineffective and poorly implemented."[107]

Moroccans have been making pottery since at least the fifth century B.C., with the earliest urban pottery made after 800 A.D.[108] Perhaps USAID could learn a thing or two about pottery making from Moroccans who have been passing knowledge of the ancient craft from one generation to another for centuries.

6) Out-of-this-world Martian food tasting – (HI) $947,000

Imagine pizza so out of this world, you would have to travel to Mars to have a slice.

That is the goal of the National Aeronautics and Space Administration's (NASA) Advanced Food Technology Project, which has already developed a recipe for pizza and about 100 other foods that could be served some day on Mars.[109]

Of course, NASA no longer has a manned spaced fleet and no current mission plans for human space flight to Mars, but some are hopeful a trip to the red planet could possibly be taken in the mid-2030s at the earliest.[110] [111] Even this goal is optimistic, however, due to budget constraints that have reduced the appetite for costly space missions.

Yet, NASA spends about $1 million annually "researching and building the Mars menu."[112] This year, NASA also awarded $947,000 to researchers at Cornell University and the University of Hawaii to study the best food for astronauts to eat on Mars.[113]

Six volunteers will head into a barren landscape in Hawaii to simulate a 120-day Mars mission. In exchange, they receive an all-expenses-paid trip, plus $5,000 each, for

NASA will spend almost $1 million to test what astronauts might eat on Mars.

completing the journey.[114]

Volunteers will perform the activities Mars explorers might do, including wearing space suits and taking "Navy showers," in order to see how different foods might affect their moods and health.[115] In keeping with the purpose of the food study, one of the stated primary procedures for the participants is to "consume only 'instant' foods and foods prepared from shelf stable ingredients...and rate these foods."[116] Preparation for this extreme food-tasting challenge starts before the 120-day "mission." Participants will attend a four-day workshop, and a two-week training exercise in the months leading up to the simulation, slated for early 2013.

Though anyone could submit an application, the research team was not looking for just anyone. They needed "people who are interested in food, who know how to cook."[117]

Ultimately, NASA wants to know what the best food options might be for long-term travel. The study organizers note "humans eating a restricted diet over a period of months

The millions of dollars NASA is spending to develop recipes for pizza and other foods to be served on Mars may be lost in a black hole since it could be decades before man sets foot on the red planet.

ultimately experience 'menu fatigue,' also known as food monotony."[118]

Astronauts currently have over 100 different food options.[119] Preparing meals on Mars, however, offers new culinary opportunities. In space, "the lack of gravity means smell — and taste — is impaired. So the food is bland."[120] Because gravity does exist on Mars, astronauts would be able to "chop vegetables and do a little cooking of their own."[121]

All the recipes developed so far are "vegetarian because the astronauts will not have dairy or meat products available. It isn't possible to preserve those products long enough to take to Mars — and bringing a cow on the mission is not an option," according to the senior research scientist at Lockheed Martin leading a team of three who are building the Martian menu.[122]

You do not need to be a rocket scientist to realize the millions of dollars being spent to taste test Martian meals that may never be served is lost in a black hole.

7) When robot squirrels attack – (CA) $325,000

In this corner with a triangular-shaped head, a rattle on its tail, with a venomous bite is the rattlesnake.

And in the other corner, whistling and chirping, covered in fur with a bushy tail, is the squirrel.

These two critters are long-time adversaries. Squirrels are frequently preyed upon by the rattlesnakes, but the snakes rarely attack squirrels who are wagging their tales. When they do, they usually miss the fast moving squirrel.

But what happens when a snake is confronted by a robot squirrel, built to look, act, and even smell like the real thing?

Researchers at San Diego State University and the University of California (Davis) spent a portion of a $325,000 National Science Foundation (NSF) grant to construct a robotic squirrel named "RoboSquirrel" to answer that question.[123]

RoboSquirrel is "a taxidermied actual squirrel that is stored with live squirrels so it smells real. The body and tail are heated with copper wiring, so the snake can see the squirrel's

Robosquirrel: More than meets the eye, a robot in disguise.

heat signature as if it were real. The tail is controlled by a linear servo motor that makes it wag back and forth."[124]

"Robosquirrel" moves on a track near a rattlesnake nesting in grass. Approaching the snake on the track, the robot squirrel can flip its tail back and forth – with or without heating it – and then retreat.[125]

The snakes observed as part of this research "appear to accept the robot as real, with one snake even biting the robot's head." Because real squirrels "possess a 'remarkable ability' to dodge a snake attack," the snake rarely strikes a real squirrel.[126]

Tail wagging, known as flagging, causes rattlesnakes to "abandon their ambush sites if a squirrel tail-flagging visit verifies that they have lost the advantage of surprise."[127] Heating the tail is also important to the squirrel's defense, they found.[128] A lack of tail wagging or heating, however, does nothing to scare the snakes.[129]

The next generation of robot squirrels may have come with some added features. Future versions will include "substrate throwing and looming" which will allow the mechanical varmint to pelt the snake with stones.[130]

Rattlesnake faces off against Robosquirrel.

While the interaction between squirrels and rattlesnakes has been understood from observations in the wild, the researchers suggest federal funding of projects like the robot squirrel will help perform public outreach, mentor students, and develop the next generation of robot animals.[131] In fact, the team is already constructing other robot mammals.[132] Coming soon are RoboSquirrel 2.0 as well as RoboKangarooRat.[133]

During these difficult fiscal times of massive deficits, paying $325,000 for a robot squirrel seems a bit squirrelly.

8) USDA's caviar dreams – (ID) $300,000

Many Americans are finding it difficult to afford to put just the basics on their family's dinner table. Yet, the U.S. Department of Agriculture (USDA) spent $300,000 this year to promote caviar.[134]

As "one of the world's most expensive delicacies, selling for as much as $400 per ounce, or $14 a gram," caviar has been considered a "luxury cuisine for thousands of years."[135][136] In fact, Aristotle "described great platters of caviar garnished with flowers, served amid trumpet fanfare" at Greek banquets.[137]

While there are "no reliable" estimates on world-wide caviar production and profits, the "insatiable appetite among the wealthy" for the delicacy keeps "demand for caviar far outpacing the supply."[138]

Fish Processors of Idaho was given a $300,000 Value-Added Producer Grant by USDA to create a website, print flyers and send the company's owner to trade shows "in places like Boston and Chicago" to "entice distributors to bring his caviar to the masses."[139]

"At $28.40 an ounce wholesale (it goes for as much as $100 retail)," the Fish Processors of Idaho has "brought in about $150,000 in revenue annually from caviar sales in the past six years. If all goes according to plan, revenue could skyrocket to $1.5 million soon."[140]

The federal government is spending $300,000 to promote caviar – costing as much as $100 an ounce – to taxpayers, many of whom are struggling just to put the essentials on their family dinner table.

Currently, Fish Processors of Idaho produces 300 pounds of caviar annually.[141] Leo Ray, the owner who was born in Oklahoma, plans "to multiply his caviar production tenfold, to as much as 3,000 pounds annually" over the next three years.[142][143] As of now, the company's caviar is only sold domestically.

Former President George H.W. Bush even "served a batch of Ray's caviar at a party a few years ago."[144]

The business Ray built stands out as a great example of how hard work can result in success – Ray calls caviar his "401(k) plan."[145]

The federal government spending $300,000 of taxpayer funds to promote caviar or any other lucrative luxury cuisine, however, is just plain fishy.

9) Bailed out tourist boat sinking private business – (AK) $3.3 million

Over $9 million in federal money was earmarked to a failing for-profit ferry verging on bankruptcy, which very few people benefitted from and a small town in Alaska did not want.[146] To make matters worse, this project is threatening the economic health of once vibrant local tour and ferry operator businesses.

Operating about one hundred miles south of Anchorage, the federally funded ferry duplicates and threatens services offered by existing private businesses and the state's own ferry service.[147] The ferry, *Kachemak Voyager* – which is managed by the Seldovia Village Tribe – runs between Seldovia and Homer, towns 16 miles apart from one another across the bay.[148]

Since 2010, the $3.3 million *Kachemak Voyager* has frustrated Seldovia's two other private tour and ferry operators who had run successful businesses for years.[149] The companies are unable to compete with the ferry's millions in taxpayer support, which lowers *Voyager's* ticket prices. "The tribe was supposed to build a ferry for moving people, cars and freight. Instead they took that money and bought a tour boat," said Tim Cashman, owner of Alaska Coastal Marine Services, one of Seldovia's two private tour operators.[150] "It has taken a 30-40 percent bite out of my business - our losses are in the hundreds of thousands. The federal government has actually borrowed money from my children to put me out of

Millions of dollars of federal subsidies have kept the *Kachemak Voyager* afloat while threatening to sink private tour boat companies.

business."[151] Cashman has 23 employees who work for his company.[152]

Another local tour operator, Jack Montgomery, who started Rainbow Tours in 1982, feels the government agencies that were supposed to be watching this project "failed us."[153]

"I have been running the Seldovia route for 28 years. But, now I can only afford to run one trip a day, and I can't afford to fight a government subsidized business. I just paid a $50,000 fuel bill in July," stated Montgomery.[154] "To have the federal government come in and destroy my business with my money is a slap in the face. If I go down - we all lose. I have 15 employees that depend on me."[155]

Other businesses and residents have raised similar concerns. With the help of federal funds, the Tribe is "doing everything in its power to put these guys out of business. It stinks," said Pete Zimmerman, long-time resident of Homer and ferry critic.[156]

"If they had to run their business like the rest of us, they would have been out of business a long time ago," continued Mako Haggerty, a water taxi owner-operator that is based out of the Homer harbor.[157] Mr. Haggerty estimates he has lost 10 percent of his business because of the ferry.[158]

Tim Cashman, owner of Alaska Coastal Marine Services, says the federal government is borrowing money from his children to put him out of business.

For its first two summers, the Kachemak ferry ran two routes which would include "wildlife viewing and sightseeing" along the coast of the bay.[159] Federal rules <u>prohibit federal funds from being used for sightseeing</u>. The Tribe notified the Federal Transit Administration it had abandoned sightseeing trips for the 2012 summer season.[160] Despite these assurances, the *Voyager* has been caught on video conducting sightseeing trips far away from the direct routes between Homer and Seldovia.[161]

The ferry is significantly different than the $44 million plan to improve roads and ferry service the Tribe originally proposed in 2003.[162] The community supported the original plan, desiring road improvements to encourage economic growth and recreational opportunity and a year-round, daily ferry to carry passengers, vehicles, and heavy freight.

After making changes that excluded these improvements, however, community and state leaders withdrew. Regardless, the ferry received $8.5 million in federal funds from 2004 to 2007 for construction and implementation.[163] Seldovia city officials noted the lawmakers and their staff did not consult them for their advice on the viability and need for the scaled-back project "until a few days before Congress passed the fiscal year 2004 appropriation for a ferry."[164]

Cashman warned the state's congressional delegation the "communities were promised services they will never receive, the city of Seldovia will suffer and long standing private businesses will be wiped out."[165] Written in 2010, the letter notified lawmakers the millions of dollars the Tribe received from the federal government for the tour boat "was never the purpose, intent or even the allowable use for these funds."[166]

In 2009, the tribe scaled back its proposal and bought the *Kachemak Voyager*, a 149-passenger, 83-foot ferry that carries mainly passengers, and in 2010, began running trips six times daily in the summer months.[167]

The changes to the project prompted many in Seldovia to object. "I totally agree this is not the project we funded," said state Representative Paul Seaton, the legislator integral to securing the state portion of the funding.[168] With the ferry no longer carrying vehicles or serving several bay-area ports, its purpose no longer justified the use of federal funding.

In an initial pitch to promote the project, Michael Beal, head of the Seldovia Native Association stated, "We don't think there's going to be a subsidy necessary to run" the ferry "after you get down the road a little bit."[169] However, during its 2012 and 2013 summer seasons, the tribe is expected to lose over $800,000, despite expecting to come close to breaking even in 2012 and making $100,000 in 2013.[170] The ferry would have to sell about 13,600 round trip tickets to make up this estimated loss.[171] However, the tribe previously overestimated the number of passengers the *Voyager* would carry. Expecting 47 passengers per trip on average in 2011, the boat carried just 14.[172]

The Government Accountability Office (GAO) was asked to review the project by Alaska officials.[173] GAO concluded the ferry is "financially unsustainable without further government subsidies."[174]

The Department of Transportation, the Bureau of Indian Affairs, and other federal entities should demand the *Voyager* be sold and the funds returned to the federal treasury. This is the best way to recoup at least some of this failed investment.

10) Phantom, unused grant accounts draw fees – (Department of Health and Human Services) $2 million

The government pays as much as $2 million annually in monthly service fees to maintain about 28,000 phantom grant accounts that are empty and have expired.[175]

Each of these accounts have a zero-dollar balance and their authority to operate has expired under law, yet because they have not been closed out, the federal government pays about $173,000 per month to maintain them.[176]

The agency that maintains an expired or fully spent grant simply needs to submit a code to close out the account. To help users, system reports indicate accounts waiting to be closed with a special symbol.[177] Until the accounts are closed, they continue to accumulate monthly service fees.

The Government Accountability Office (GAO) "found roughly 9,770—about 34 percent—of the expired grant accounts with no undisbursed balances remained open 3 or more years past the grant expiration date. If the grant has otherwise been administratively and financially closed out, then agencies paying fees for expired accounts with zero dollar balance are paying for services that are not needed instead of providing services to grant recipients."[178]

GAO also notes "the presence of expired grant accounts with no undisbursed funds remaining also raises concerns that administrative and financial closeout—the final point of accountability for these grants, which includes such important tasks as the submission of financial and performance reports—may not have been completed."[179]

Phantom government grant accounts cost real money. Taxpayers are charged as much as $2 million annually for service fees to maintain thousands of empty and expired grant accounts.

11) A penny made is two pennies wasted – (Department of the Treasury) $70 million

The famous proverb "A penny saved is a penny earned" may no longer apply to the actual American penny.

In fact, the cost to produce a penny in 2012 is more than *two times* its actual value. The Department of the Treasury announced the average cost of production this year was 2.4 cents – the highest it has been in years.[180] (Similarly expensive, nickel production now costs over 11 cents per coin.[181]) The total cost of producing over 5 billion pennies this year will run at least $120 million.[182] After selling the pennies at face value to the Federal Reserve, the Treasury Department will lose over an estimated $70 million.[183] That estimate does not include the cost to the Federal Reserve to handle and distribute pennies.

The most significant factor contributing to the increased cost is the higher international demand for the zinc and copper, metals used to make pennies.

To compensate for the price increases, Treasury secretary Timothy Geithner proposed changing the composition of the penny to use a steel alloy, an act that would require congressional approval since Congress has constitutional authority over coinage.[184]

Production reforms alone, however, would not address the general uselessness of the penny today. In the United States, the majority of new pennies vanish from circulation right after their initial distribution.[185] Perhaps the most common consumers of pennies are couch cushions and sewer grates.

A number of countries stopped production of their pennies long ago. France, Netherlands, Spain, and the United Kingdom eliminated their lowest denomination coins in the 1970s and 1980s, and Australia and New Zealand did the same around 1990.[186] Canada was the latest to join the club after it announced it would cease penny production in May 2012.[187]

Since a penny not made is a penny (or two) saved, the United States should follow suit and stop producing it.

It makes little sense to pay two cents for a penny that is worth one cent.

12) Call me for free, maybe – (Federal Communications Commission) $1.5 billion

"It's easy to get your free government cell phone service and a free mobile phone," declares a website that offers phones on behalf of six wireless providers.[188] "Fill out the form... You should receive your phone in just a few days. You'll never receive a bill and your minutes will replenish every month."[189]

Thanks to Congress and the Federal Communications Commission (FCC), some Americans are entitled to free or reduced-price cell phone service, and the program is ballooning out of control. What began as an effort in the 1930s to ensure all Americans had access to telecommunications service has morphed into a massive entitlement.[190]

Funding comes through the "universal service charge" tacked on to the phone bills of most Americans. As more people sign up for the subsidized phones, the charge increases, and for some cell phone users amounts to over $10 per year.[191] Americans are now paying $1.5 billion annually for the subsidized cell phone program, called Lifeline.[192] Just in the last year, enrollment grew 43 percent to 16.5 million participants.[193]

Only after a 2008 decision by the Federal Communications Commission to allow prepaid phones to receive Lifeline subsidies did enrollment soar.[194] Wireless subsidies now consume 70 percent of the Lifeline budget, with three pre-paid cell phone companies alone receiving 40 percent of the total budget.[195] One of the companies – TracFone – is controlled by the world's richest man, Carlos Slim, who is worth an estimated $70 billion.[196]

These companies are reimbursed by the federal government for every discounted phone and service they distribute for free.[197] According to the website of SafeLink Wireless, a Lifeline services provider, recipients can receive more free minutes by referring others for the program.[198] This, in turn, increases the

Wireless companies are collecting $1.5 billion in government subsidies-- funded with phone bill fees on most Americans-- to provide cell phones and service to millions of others absolutely free of charge.

Lifeline Funding, 1998-2011

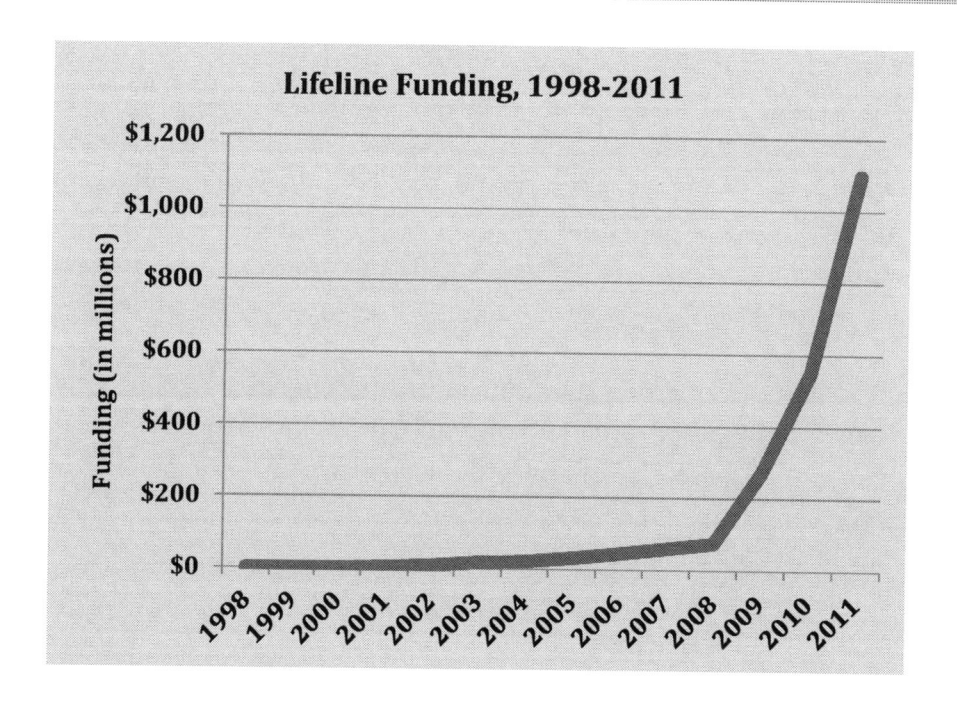

company's profits from the Lifeline program. Since 2007, the total cost of program has increased twenty-fold.[199]

To take advantage of the federal handout, prepaid wireless companies – who collect most of the subsidy – often camp out in low-income areas to get better access to those who qualify for the program. In York, Pennsylvania, for example, Budget Mobile stayed for over a month to find recipients. One "37-year-old mother grabbed a place in line and waited, determined to leave with a phone for her 16-year-old daughter, an honor-roll student who she said 'deserves a phone.'"[200] Another company, Life Wireless, set up a tent in Minneapolis. One customer received a free cell phone and then sold it for $20.[201] In St. Louis, people were spotted waiting in line for free phones, while they were talking on their cell phones.[202]

With providers incentivized to maximize the number of phones they hand out, significant fraud and abuse have plagued the program in recent years. One of the most prominent flaws in the program has been the high number of people with more than one free cell phone. An audit of 3.6 million Lifeline subscribers discovered 269,000 duplicates—seven percent of the subscribers signed up for service with more than one carrier.[203] In other instances, households had multiple people each with free phones.[204] Some customers may have both subsidized landline service and cell phone service.[205] The program is starting to crack down on these kinds of abuses.

A number of Lifeline customers are not even eligible for the service. A survey of 53,000 users found at least nine percent do not qualify for the program.[206]

Recipients are automatically eligible for the free cell phone program if they participate in any of a number of federal assistance programs, including food stamps, low-income housing, and Medicaid. They may also qualify based on income.

The government safety net exists to ensure all Americans have the essentials for living – food, shelter, and safety. Now that list apparently includes cell phones.

13) Powerful routers installed in tiny rural libraries and schools – (WV) $24 million

Government officials in West Virginia used millions of federal taxpayer dollars to purchase 1,064 high-capacity Internet routers to increase broadband access throughout the state. Each router is capable of serving a computer network with tens of thousands of users, such as the network of a large university campus, but the routers are being installed at sites with only a few users, such as government offices, schools, libraries, and other public offices.[207]

Purchased several years ago, the routers are still being installed statewide. Each router cost $22,600 for a total of $24 million, paid for with federal stimulus dollars.[208]

Seventy percent of the high-powered routers have gone to schools and libraries, even though the equipment is unnecessary for these rural institutions. Some of the libraries receiving the equipment have one computer for citizens to use, and schools receiving the equipment often have only a few computers.[209] Yet, "the routers are designed to serve a minimum of 500 users."[210]

The size of the routers presented challenges for schools and libraries unaccustomed to such technology. "Because the routers are so big," the state's library commissioner commented, "our tech guys had to build shelves for them. The libraries had no other place to put them."[211]

Some state agencies received routers even though they did not ask for them or need them. Officials sent the equipment to 10 of the state's 11 regional planning offices, but the efforts were wasted.[212] Each office generally has eight or fewer employees.[213] At least two offices sent the routers back at first. "It was something we couldn't use...This router was too big for our office, so we sent it back," said one council executive director.[214]

Another director, Lea Wolfe, stated, "We didn't need it. It's much bigger than anything we need."[215] Even after sending it back to the state, her office received another and was told it must use the router.[216] "It's now in the hallway under a table covered with papers. I have a $22,000 router that's collecting dust...We never asked for them," Wolfe said.[217]

Before the purchase, the state's technology administrator voiced concern that the routers were "grossly oversized."[218] More appropriately sized technology was available for several hundred dollars apiece.[219] His concerns were ignored.

The official in charge of the project noted the excess router capacity is important for "homeland security reasons."[220] He also wanted to ensure a school with 200 students had the "equal opportunity" as students in a school of 2,000.[221]

Before purchasing the routers, the state identified 1,064 locations to place the routers, but did not investigate which of these actually *needed* new routers. One state official made clear how such an oversight occurred: "All the engineering hadn't been submitted."[222] Over 360 of the locations already had suitable equipment.[223]

In May, 366 routers still sat unused, waiting for officials to find new locations for them.[224] That set of routers alone cost over $8 million.[225] [226]

State Homeland Security Chief Jimmy Gianato defended the purchase, claiming "I think we made the right decision...we have positioned our state to expand and move into the next generation of technology."[227] He said the state's federal application "was not based on the usage levels or number of workstations at the (community institution) today, but instead on the concept that we should be equipping our citizens to fully embrace future technology."[228]

Hundreds of routers have gone unused as state officials in West Virginia used federal funds to buy equipment so big and powerful, many public schools, libraries, and offices did not want them or have room for them.

The Inspector General of the U.S. Department of Commerce is currently investigating the state's action.

After finishing the broadband project, the state expects to have $30 million to $40 million in leftover federal funds.[229] In that situation, a consultant would probably give the state a strategy to spend the excess so the state would not have to return the money to the federal government, noted the state's commerce secretary.[230]

One regional planning director summarized the situation well: "We're fighting every day for money and grants to bring water and sewer to places, and they go out and spend $22,000 on giant routers. This is such a waste of funds."[231]

14) Relive prom week with National Science Foundation video game – (CA) $516,000

"Is Chloe dating Edward? Break them up by having Mave make a pass!"[232]

Whatever feelings high school prom may elicit, the National Science Foundation (NSF) has provided taxpayers with a chance to relive the occasion. In 2012, the agency supported the creation of "Prom Week," a video game simulating all the social interactions of the event.[233] The project used part of a $516,000 grant from NSF.[234]

Without a standard storyline, "Prom Week" players can take one of the game's characters – 18 different high school students – in many different directions.[235] As a character in the game, they may participate in "getting a date with that cute boy in algebra class" or "convincing Buzz to give Monica a second chance."[236][237]

A video trailer of the game shows one girl, Monica, described as "cold, attention hog, sex magnet, vengeful," turning down a boy like Zack (described as "arrogant, stubborn, outgoing, honest"). In another scene, Zack says to a girl, "We have so much in common. I

Taxpayers of all ages can relive prom night every day with the National Science Foundation's "Prom Week" video game.

WASTEBOOK 2012

"Prom Week" probably won't be nominated for a Nobel Prize, but the game was recently recognized at a video game festival.

mean. You like wolf spiders. I like wolf spiders. It's like we're made for each other!"[238]

Each character in the game has a mind of their own, with "detailed histories, likes, dislikes, permanent traits, and temporary statuses—all of which can be leveraged by the player to produce just the right prom night story."[239]

Prom Week is based on a set of 5,000 social rules that programmers learned by studying "interactions in movies and television shows."[240] Social rules determine how the video game's characters act and respond to one another.

The professor in charge of creating the video game sees it as "a new and powerful mode of personal expression."[241]

Hosted on Facebook, "Prom Week" has only 179 "Likes" as of October 11 since being posted in February.[242]

Researchers based the behaviors of the characters in "Prom Week" on the interactions observed in movies and television shows.

35

15) Black liquor loophole – (Taxes) $268 million

Pulp and paper companies could reap a $268 million tax windfall by asserting an industrial waste byproduct of the wood-pulping process - referred to as "black liquor" - is actually an alternative fuel.[243][244]

Since the 1930s, the black liquor byproduct has been used to generate power at paper mills.[245] Pulp and paper companies began using the fuel to claim a lucrative alternative energy tax credit several years ago.[246] The industry initially took advantage of the alternative fuel mixture credit, which was intended to stimulate mixing a hydrocarbon fuel made from biomass with small quantities of fossil fuel, including diesel fuel.[247] By slightly changing the chemical composition of black liquor, paper companies found the product qualified for the credit, opening up a billion-dollar bonanza.

However, "after Congress decided that the paper industry should not be allowed to claim" the renewable fuel credit for "its use of so-called black liquor," the Internal Revenue Service (IRS) allowed for another, even more generous tax credit to become retroactively available to pulp and paper producers – the biomass fuel assistance program (BCAP).[248][249][250] Since Congress only excluded black liquor produced after 2009 from tax credits, paper companies technically qualify to collect from BCAP for black liquor produced in 2009.[251] To claim their bounty, companies have been carrying forward the tax credit and are expected to do so until 2016. This black liquor loophole through BCAP will cost taxpayers $1.3 billion over the next four years.[252]

In 2009, about 100 paper mills were able to take advantage of one of these incentives.[253] International Paper received $1.5 billion in tax credits in 2009 alone.[254] The American Forest and Paper Association and others state "[c]ompanies have a fiduciary responsibility to their shareholders to use the credits if it is advantageous for them."[255]

Both BCAP and the alternative fuel mixture credit were intended to stimulate the development of alternative fuels for vehicles. BCAP, for example, is supposed to stimulate development of crops into cellulosic biofuels so that America can "displace imported petroleum."[256] However, Congress never intended for paper mills or anyone to reap billions from this tax credit. In fact, for just the alternative fuels incentive, total cost to taxpayers was supposed to be an estimated $100 million annually, rather than the billions received by the paper producers.[257]

This year, the U.S. Senate Finance Committee attempted to close the new "black liquor" loophole.[258] However, senators with state parochial interests were able to kill the proposal.[259]

16) California towns sell federal grants to neighbors – (CA) $206,426

Some California towns have decided to sell their annual portion of their federal Community Development Block Grant (CDBG) to get around the program's requirements.

Beverly Hills, often noted for its affluence, and the city of Santa Fe Springs will sell $206,426 of their CDBG dollars this year to other cities, in exchange for $145,662 in general revenue.[260][261] By selling the block grant for less than it is worth, states and cities free themselves of the program's requirements and collect other financial benefits.

Beverly Hills received $180,307 in CDBG funds this year.[262] To say the least, Americans generally do not consider the idealized Los Angeles suburb an impoverished town, and with good reason. With iconic landmarks such as Rodeo Drive and its celebrity population, Beverly Hills has one of the highest per capita median incomes in the nation, exceeding $66,000.[263] Yet, the city has been accumulating CDBG funds for years without spending the money and now has a balance of unspent funds near $675,000.[264]

Seeking to free up CDBG funding it did not need, the city sold $90,000 of its grant money to a neighboring town for 70 cents on the dollar.[265][266] It received $63,000 in return from the

Affluent areas of California, like Beverly Hills, are making money off a program intended for the poor and getting around federal requirements to fund projects for low-income residents by selling federal antipoverty grants to other communities.

City of Hawaiian Gardens.[267] Even after the sale, Beverly Hills had no lack of leftover CDBG funds. The balance of its grant funds decreased to about $675,000, available to fight poverty in the city and otherwise help the wealthy community develop.[268] Or, perhaps to sit in the coffers for several more years until they are sold.

Selling antipoverty grant money is not restricted to California's rich and famous. The Beverly Hills City Council has noted, "[A] number of cities in Los Angeles County have exchanged all of their CDBG funds on a yearly basis" just to report they spent a certain amount of the grant.[269]

Even Santa Fe Springs, a community outside of Los Angeles, decided this year to sell its CDBG grant for other purposes. In fact, in recent years the city has made a habit of selling its grants.[270] This year, the city received $123,667 and used $18,552 for an afterschool teen program.[271] It sold the remainder of the money to nearby La Mirada for 71 cents on the dollar.[272]

The federal government requires a recipient's CDBG dollars to fund programs that help people with low to moderate incomes.[273] Eliminating blight, providing public housing assistance, and helping the homeless are among key activities intended for the block grant.

This black market of federal grants raises the question of whether federal funds are targeted efficiently in the first place.

17) Russian weapons institutes recruiting new scientists with U.S. funds – (Department of Energy) $15.0 million

A Cold War-era program to prevent the proliferation of weapons of mass destruction has had more money than it can spend – carrying over more from year to year than Congress appropriates for its annual budget. <u>The money has helped recruit new scientists for Russian weapons institutes, contrary to the original intent of the program.</u>[274] This year, the program received almost $15 million.[275] For many years during the 2000s, it took in far more than it spent.[276]

Following the collapse of the Soviet Union, the Initiative for Proliferation Prevention program was created to ensure unemployed Soviet weapons scientists and engineers were placed in private-sector, nonmilitary employment so these experts were not hired by terrorist groups or rogue nations.[277]

A non-proliferation program may actually be recruiting Russian weapons developers.

Now, the program is recruiting young nuclear scientists, an objective far removed from its original purpose. According to the Government Accountability Office (GAO), "Officials from 10 Russian and Ukrainian weapons institutes told GAO that the IPP program helps them attract, recruit, and retain younger scientists and contributes to the continued operation of their facilities."[278] The U.S. Department of Energy (DOE) states the program created almost 2,800 private-sector jobs in Russia.[279]

Russian and Ukrainian officials, as well as U.S. companies, have raised questions about the continuing need for the program. A senior Atomic Energy Agency official in Russia told GAO, "[T]he IPP program is no longer relevant because Russia's economy is strong and its scientists no longer pose a proliferation risk."[280] GAO notes, "DOE has not developed criteria to determine when scientists, institutes, or countries should 'graduate' from the program," even when other federal programs have stopped supporting them.[281]

Critics have also questioned the need for the program given that the U.S. engages in a number of nonproliferation diplomatic activities. Even the Department of Energy has conceded this program is duplicative, as "several other U.S. Government initiatives are also aimed at preventing weapons of mass destruction proliferation."[282]

18) NASA Entertainment, Inc. – (National Aeronautics and Space Administration) $1.6 million

Over the last year, the National Aeronautics and Space Administration (NASA) has been on a mission far different from the likes of Apollo, SkyLab, and Curiosity. The agency has been working on a number of out-of-this-world apps, games, and other entertainment programs to beef up its marketing efforts. These efforts will cost taxpayers at least $1.6 million.

"World of Warcraft" NASA-style. NASA is investing $1.5 million into "Starlite," a massive multiplayer online game to simulate the journey to Mars and the life of astronauts on the planet.[283] Players will be able to explore the planet together and face a number of challenging situations, including "threats to the Earth."[284]

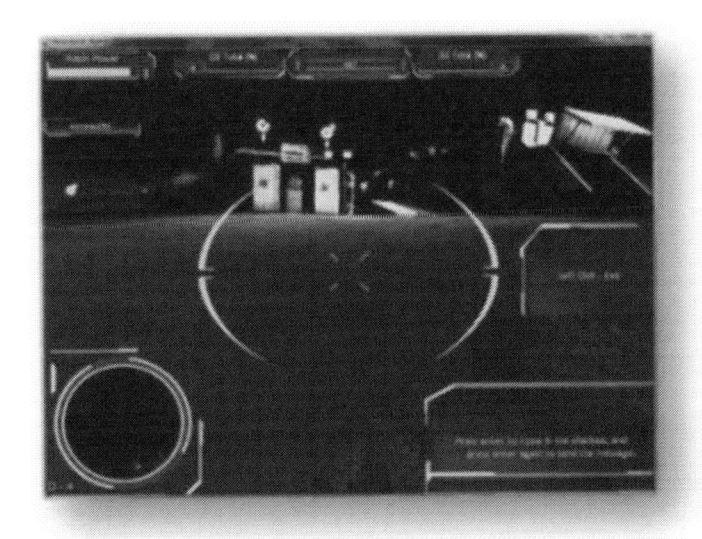

Screenshot of MoonBase Alpha, NASA's 20-minute long multiplayer game simulating astronauts at a lunar outpost.

NASA originally planned to spend almost $7 million on the project, but "budget cuts took their toll," said NASA's lead official for games and educational technology.[285] The agency partnered with a Winnipeg, Canada-based firm to develop "Starlite," which will be available on iPad, Playstation, and Xbox.[286]

"Starlite" will not be NASA's first foray into online games. In the last few years, the agency spent $300,000 to develop "MoonBase Alpha," a 20-minute-long multiplayer game set at a futuristic lunar outpost.[287]

The end of big gaming at NASA is nowhere in sight. "There are more higher-end gaming projects going on at NASA than ever before," said the agency's game director.[288]

Online rock radio station. Far from getting the next man to the moon, NASA signed a contract with a private company in Houston to develop an online rock radio station, Third Rock, targeted to 18-34-year-olds.[289]

"While NASA is synonymous with the exploration of space, technology and science education," says the station's webpage, "Third Rock, which is focused on NASA and the great things going on there every day, is all about the exploration of New Rock."[290]

NASA is no longer launching manned space craft but has launched an online rock radio station.

The station is accessible through a number of mobile phone applications, NASA.gov, and iTunes.[291] It is commercial-free, but NASA directed the developer to include a number of news breaks that feature information about NASA events, research, technology, and partners.[292] The developer is also supposed to find "high-profile, institutional-type sponsors" to support the station.[293]

Mars rover video game. This year, NASA broke new ground when it successfully landed the Curiosity rover on Mars. NASA also assisted with the development of a video game for Microsoft's Xbox where players can command a virtual Mars Rover.[294]

"Mars Rover Landing" is available for free download on the Xbox Live Store. Using the Xbox

NASA's "Mars Rover Landing" video games is "essentially a modernized version of Atari's classic arcade game 'Lunar Lander.'"

Kinect's motion-detecting system, players move their bodies to guide a virtual Curiosity rover to its landing site. One reviewer said the game is "essentially a modernized version of Atari's classic arcade game 'Lunar Lander,' but using body motions rather than a lever."[295]

NASA's part in the development process included compiling "publicly available information, imagery, and content describing the Mars exploration missions."[296] The agency also reviewed early versions of the game and recommended changes to the game.[297]

Explaining the estimated $94,000 cost to taxpayers, one NASA official said, "Because Mars exploration is fundamentally a shared human endeavor, we want everyone around the globe to have the most immersive experience possible."[298][299] Officials also hoped the game will put "the nation's space program back into the nation's living rooms."[300]

19) Smokey Bear balloons – (Department of Agriculture) $49,447

With his motto, "Only you can prevent forest fires," Smokey Bear is an American icon.

The U.S. Forest Service gave tribute by spending $31,071 in taxpayer funds to have Smokey Bear balloons at several balloon festivals throughout the American Southwest.[301] Over the last seven years, the department has spent more than $230,000 for Smokey Bear hot-air and cold-air balloon appearances.[302]

The Smokey Bear hot-air balloon – shaped as Smokey's face – made an appearance costing $4,699 at the Temecula Valley Balloon and Wine Festival in Southern California.[303] Festivalgoers who wanted a glimpse of the balloon had to pay over $20 for admission.[304] The government also paid for the balloon to be at the Panguitch Valley Balloon Rally, the Hot Air Balloon Classic, and the Salina Balloon Festival.[305] Smokey's appearances extend beyond balloon festivals. His inflatable image appeared this year at the U.S. Pro Cycling Challenge in Boulder, Colorado, at a cost of $3,047.[306] In 2010, the government paid $14,937 to have a Smokey balloon at the Boy Scouts Jamboree in Fort Lee, Virginia.[307]

Smokey takes many forms, and the federal government this year bought several other versions of the furry friend. Three Smokey statues cost taxpayers $13,938 this year alone, and a set of Smokey road signs cost another $4,438.[308] The total spent on these statues, signs, and balloon appearances was $49,447.[309][310]

While Smokey's message serves a purpose of reminding citizens of the dangers of wildfires, federally funded appearances at balloon festivals should be a government expenditure that

Only the U.S. Forest Service can prevent wasting more money on Smokey Bear hot-air balloons.

goes up in smoke. The money spent by the U.S. Forest Service could be better directed to funding more DC-10 tankers to help fight one of the more than 6,000 wildfires that plagued the United States in 2012.[311]

20) Speed reading faces – (WA) $30,000

With just a quick glance of a face, many people can accurately guess someone's sexual orientation, according to researchers at the University of Washington and Cornell University, in a study supported by the National Science Foundation (NSF).[312]

As part of the experiment, facial images of men and women who had self-identified on Facebook as gay or straight were flashed for 50 milliseconds before college students, who then guessed the sexual orientation of the faces they were shown.[313] The faces were cropped to remove hairstyles and other potential cues.[314]

"Even when viewing such bare faces so briefly, participants demonstrated an ability to identify sexual orientation: overall, gaydar judgments were about 60 percent accurate," wrote the authors, noting "the effect is statistically significant — several times above the margin of error."[315] "'Gaydar,'" the authors described, "colloquially refers to the ability to accurately glean others' sexual orientation from mere observation."[316]

In a twist, study participants were shown the same faces, except the images were flipped upside-down.[317] The researchers still "found above-chance gaydar accuracy even when the faces were presented upside down," but the "accuracy increased, however, when the faces were presented right side up."[318]

In what the researchers called a "novel finding," there was a far greater accuracy guessing the sexual orientation of the faces of women (64 percent) than men (57 percent) in both experiments.[319]

"Gaydar is indeed real and... its accuracy is driven by sensitivity to individual facial features," the researchers wrote in the *New York Times*.[320]

"In light of these findings, it is interesting to note the popular desire to learn to read faces like books," the study authors concluded.[321] "Considering how challenging it is to read a book upside-down, it seems that we read faces *better* than we read books."[322]

"To some, the idea that it's possible to perceive others' sexual orientation from observation alone seems to imply prejudice," the researcher noted, countering, "[W]e disagree."[323] Regardless, most taxpayers probably would agree that on the face of it, this study – paid for with part of a $30,000 NSF grant – was not the best investment of federal science research dollars.[324]

21) More than $1 billion overpaid annually for products and services – (Government-wide) $1 billion

Clipping coupons, comparing prices, buying in bulk, and even shopping on double coupon days, many Americans are doing everything they can to save a penny wherever they can to stretch a dollar further during these difficult economic times.

The stewards of taxpayers' dollars in Washington unfortunately are not being as thrifty. In fact, they are ignoring a policy directing them to do so, which may be needlessly be costing taxpayers as much as $50 billion a year in over payments.

Every year, the federal government spends over $537 billion on products and services.[325] With such massive purchasing power, agencies could use group orders to secure the best deals. In 2005, the Office of Management and Budget created the Federal Strategic Sourcing Initiative to leverage orders from multiple agencies to achieve such savings.

Yet, agencies rarely use this program, according to an analysis by the Government Accountability Office (GAO). As a result, agencies are missing opportunities for big savings, overpaying at least $1 billion and as much as $50 billion annually.[326]

"Agencies act more like many unrelated medium-sized businesses and often rely on hundreds of separate contracts for many commonly used items, with prices that vary widely," GAO found.[327]

Not Best Buy: The federal government overpays as much as $50 billion for goods and services every year.

Of the half-trillion dollars spent on goods and services last year, just $339 million in orders were run through the government's strategic sourcing program.[328] On those orders, the program saved 18 percent.[329]

The Department of Defense (DOD), which purchases over $300 billion in goods and services annually, used the strategic sourcing program for just six percent of orders.[330] The Department of Homeland Security, on the other hand, used the program for 20 percent of its spending and saved over $300 million, or two percent of its total budget.[331]

Most agencies GAO studied – four of the largest federal spenders – had no goals set for how much they could purchase and save through strategic sourcing.[332] These offices are "procuring many of the same types of services, such as professional services, and are missing opportunities to coordinate efforts."[333] GAO noted "a key disincentive to implementing efforts and tracking and reporting savings is a perception that program budgets may be cut as a result of producing savings."[334]

Large private-sector companies often rigorously monitor their purchases to maximize savings by bundling orders. "Private industry best practices in strategic sourcing...allowed companies to achieve savings of 10 to 20 percent of total procurement costs," GAO said.[335]

If the federal government expanded its use of the strategy, GAO concluded taxpayers could easily see savings of $1 billion every year.[336] Ten percent savings on all federal procurement – in line with private sector practices – would be over $50 billion annually.[337]

22) Book club funding goes to ghost tours, fishing lessons, and movie screenings – (National Endowment for the Arts) $1 million

In our point and click culture, book clubs are still a popular pastime. Enjoying and discussing a classic work of literature with friends requires few resources – unless, of course, the federal government gets involved.

The National Endowment for the Arts (NEA) has allocated $1 million to organizations throughout the country to "read, discuss, and celebrate one of 31 selections from U.S. and world literature."[338] Most of the classic novels sponsored by the program are already – and should continue to be – required readings in high school and college literature classes. The NEA is distributing the grants through its Big Read initiative, which is "designed to restore reading to the center of American culture."[339] Grant recipients, however, often spend the money on projects that have little to do with reading.

Perhaps offering the most unique selection of activities is the Shrewsbury Public Library, which received a $10,800 federal grant.[340] The library will host the traditional book discussions, but it will also include "a tour of the Mark Twain House and Museum in Hartford, Connecticut, a ghosts and graveyards tour for teens in Boston, a picket fence decorating contest, an old-fashioned county fair celebration for children, fishing lessons, [and] a performance by a Mark Twain historic interpreter."[341] To study the same book, another center will use its federal grant to host a "Tom Sawyer in the Park movie and costume party."[342]

Federal funds for book clubs have been used for many activities other than reading, including teaching children how to play marbles at Ohio's Massillon Museum.

Another organization – Staten Island OutLOUD – will use its grant to host "a community fence-painting session, concerts, spoken-word performances, a community symposium and film screenings in a variety of locations around Staten Island."[343]

Rutgers, the State University of New Jersey, will use its $15,000 grant to give out copies of *Bless Me, Ultima* and host discussions. Reaching beyond the written word, the organization will also host "a related stage performance; a visual arts component; and distribution of a companion book for young readers." [344]

A theater in Baltimore will use the book club money to put on "three performances to bring to life the writings of Edgar Allen Poe."[345]

Similarly, a museum in Ohio receiving federal funds to study Edgar Allen Poe has already taken eager visitors on graveyard tours and hosted a concert of "haunted acoustic instrumentation" and "dark romanticism."[346]

As fun as these types of readings and book clubs may be, they certainly do not need federal support, especially when the money goes to a plethora of activities questionably related to reading.

23) Pet shampoo company fetches more than half a million dollars – (NE) $505,000

Splish splash, pets taking a bath, long about the taxpayer's dime.

Taxpayer dollars are literally being washed down the drain to give man's best friend fresher smelling fur and breath.

Nebraska steered $505,000 of Community Development Block Grant (CDBG) funds provided by the Department of Housing and Urban Development (HUD) to Sergeant's Pet Care Products, Inc., which specializes in pet shampoo and toothpaste.[347] The company spent $500,000 for capital improvements, including machinery to manufacture the pet toothpaste and shampoo.[348] About $5,000 can be used for administrative costs.[349]

Sergeant's pet shampoos are available in tea tree oil, mild baby shampoo, brightening shampoo, and a deep cleansing herbal blend for tougher coats. The company also provides "low-sudsing, quick rinse" cat shampoo.[350] Flea and tick medications are available in clean cotton and tropical breeze scents.[351]

Coincidentally, the company even has a line of pork treats for dogs named after Uncle Sam.[352]

Sergeant's was established in 1868 and named after one of the founder's favorite dogs.[353]

Meow! Your cat can smell *purrrrrrrfect* with Sergeant's Fur So Fresh Cat Shampoo, available in Tahitian gardenia or sweet daisy fragrances.

The company is expecting to bring in $140 million in revenue this year.[354]

Another federal program – the Market Access Program – has also been helping pets look and smell better. Espree, maker of canine products such as volumizing spray, hair spray, styling gel, sparkle spray, and facial cleansers, has received federal funds from the U.S. Department of Agriculture (USDA) program to promote its pet products abroad.[355]

In addition to the half a million dollars in Community Development Block Grant funds it fetched, Sergeant's is expecting to retrieve $140 million in revenue this year from the sale of its pet products.

Taxpayers apparently need a real watchdog to protect against more wasteful spending on pet beauty products.

24) Corporate welfare for the world's largest snack food maker – (NY) $1.3 million

The U.S. Department of Agriculture (USDA) and the Department of Commerce are spending over $1.3 million to help the world's largest snack food maker build a Greek yogurt factory in New York.[356]

Last year, PepsiCo Inc. earned net revenues of $66 billion.[357] Looking to expand their earnings, the corporation is now teaming up with the German company Theo Müller Group to sell "premium yogurt products in the U.S."[358]

The money will help upgrade infrastructure at the Genesee Valley Agri-Business Park in Genesee County, New York. The park will be home to Pepsi's new Muller Quaker Greek yogurt facility, an Alpina yogurt plant, and possibly a Genesee Valley Mushroom mushroom-growing facility.[359]

The Department of Commerce's U.S. Economic Development Administration provided a $1 million grant "to construct an aquifer-direct water supply system...since municipal water is not optimal for the manufacturing process of yogurt products."[360] Meanwhile, USDA's Rural Business Enterprise Grant program is providing $199,821 to help fund a new access road into the park.[361] The USDA also provided $105,500 "to upgrade an essential pump station to increase the park's wastewater system's capacity."[362]

While PepsiCo is best known for its sodas and snacks like Cheetos and Doritos, the company is seeking to "court increasingly health-conscious consumers with 'good-for-you' foods, as opposed to what the company calls its 'fun for you' foods. Some of the new yogurt flavors, such as 'Choco Balls' and 'Chocolate Flakes,' seem to straddle that line. The yogurt will also come in standard flavors."[363]

PepsiCo, the world's largest snack food maker, is benefitting from more than $1 million in federal funds to support the multi-billion dollar company's new facility in New York.

The corporate welfare to build infrastructure to the company's facility gives it a financial edge to push into a booming market. Twenty-nine other yogurt plants are located in New York. Collectively, they "produced 530 million pounds of yogurt last year, a 43 percent increase over the year before."[364] Nationwide, yogurt sales are expected to generate $7 billion this year, "an increase of 9 percent over last year – when sales increased by 7.5 percent."[365]

With such a growing market for Greek yogurt and an abundance of dairy farmers in New York, "all of the right forces have come together to make it very attractive to build in New York state," said Bruce Krupke, executive vice president of the Northeast Dairy Foods Association.[366]

Considering the company's billions of dollars in annual profits and the plentiful demand for the Greek yogurt nationally, Pepsico clearly does not need handouts from the government to subsidize its private business.

25) Government-funded study finds golfers need to envision a bigger hole – (IN) $350,000

After a long battle from the teebox, through sand traps, ponds, and trees, nothing is more frustrating to a golfer than to miss a putt. The solution? Golfers simply need to imagine the hole is bigger, researchers found. "[P]erceived increase in target size will boost confidence in one's abilities," they wrote.[367]

Purdue University researchers used part of a $350,000 National Science Foundation grant to examine the benefit golfers might gain from using their imagination.[368] The work was also supported previously by part of a $1.1 million National Institutes of Health grant.[369] Thirty-six golfers participated in the study.[370]

A study funded by the National Science Foundation concluded golfers putt better when they imagine the hole is bigger than it actually is.

Researchers first placed the participants in front of two holes of different size, each surrounded by a set of circles projected around them from above.[371] Optical illusions made the golf holes look bigger or smaller depending on the size of the circles surrounding them. Participants were asked to use Microsoft Paint to draw what they perceived to be the size of the holes.[372]

Those who putted toward the small hole – but perceived it to be bigger than it actually was – were more successful than those who perceived it to be smaller than its actual size. Results of the research might help "an athlete get out of a slump," the investigators concluded.[373]

26) Fighting obesity with giant graffiti carrots – (ME) $13,000

Just outside of Portland, Maine, a graffiti artist who goes by the name SUBONE received $13,000 in federal money to create a 33-by-8 foot spray-paint mural at a local high school.[374] Funds came from a federal program for "evidence-based clinical and community-based prevention and wellness strategies...that deliver specific, measurable health outcomes that address chronic disease rates."[375]

What better way to do that than to create a giant psychedelic mural?

The mural is intended to promote healthy eating and sustainable living at the school. It centers on a composting bin, which is surrounded by oversized reusable water bottles, fruits and grains, skateboards to signify human-powered transportation, and other symbols of sustainability and healthy living. The entire mural springs from a riveted metal slab in the bottom-left corner.[376]

"It depicts the old metal structures that get broken by this new way of approaching life sustainably, recycling, using reuseable water bottles, that's the idea, that this wave of a change of young people breaks up these patterns," according to SUBONE.[377] "It takes its aesthetic inspiration from the form and dynamic that you often find in graffiti, but it just transfers it into contemporary art."[378]

The aerosol artwork has no doubt livened up students' walk down the hall. No word yet,

A high school in Maine received a $13,000 graffiti mural to promote healthy eating and sustainability.

though, on how authorities plan to demonstrate "specific, measurable health outcomes" from the mural.[379]

Among the stated purposes of the federal program funding the mural are to reduce obesity and decrease tobacco use.[380] These are worthy goals, but there are better ways to accomplish them than spray-painting stylized composting bins on a high school wall. For example, over 4,500 free healthy school lunches could have been provided to disadvantaged children with this funding.[381] Too bad taxpayers cannot recycle the money poured into this project.

27) Another bridge to nowhere – (OH) $520,000

More than ten percent of the bridges in Dayton, Ohio, are deficient as 13 cars drive over one of Dayton's 184 deficient bridges every second.[382] Yet, mere miles away from the city, the federal government is spending $520,000 to restore an unused bridge that is not even connected to a road or trail.[383]

Fixing Stevenson Road Covered Bridge in Greene County, Ohio, will cost $650,000.[384] The National Historic Covered Bridge Preservation (NHCBP) program is providing $520,000, and the county is paying $130,000.[385] [386]

Controversy surrounds accepting the federal money "because the bridge is not on a road, is in a fairly remote area, doesn't carry vehicles anymore, and isn't tied to any park, tourist attraction or walk/bike trail."[387] On one side of the bridge, "No Trespassing signs [warn] people away."[388]

"I don't know why they would do that, because nobody uses it," said Dorothy Pitzer, who has lived uphill from the bridge for 40 years.[389] "It sits over there by itself."[390]

Built in 1877, the covered bridge has not been used for traffic since 2003 when "a $650,000 modern concrete bridge" was built just 100 feet away.[391]

The rehabilitation of the unused bridge will cost more than Xenia Township's entire $610,000 annual roads budget.[392]

One local elected official raised concerns about the poor condition of roads in the area. "There are roads – not county roads, but local roads in nearby jurisdictions — that are so rough, you need four-wheel drive to get to people's homes," he said.[393] "You can't tell me that day-to-day travel projects aren't more important than other frivolous projects…

The amount being spent to rehabilitate this unused bridge in Xenia Township, Ohio, exceeds the township's entire annual roads budget.

[B]ecause they're somebody's pet project, [these projects] are getting priority, and it makes absolutely no sense."[394]

To justify receipt of the federal grant, the county's engineer – who approved submitting the grant application – stated, "This is money set aside in a transportation bill by senators and congressmen, and if I didn't get it, someone else would."[395]

28) Paying for veterans' health care twice – (Medicare; Veterans Administration) $1 billion

Since the creation of managed healthcare plans in Medicare in 1982 – now known as Medicare Advantage (MA) – the federal government has been paying for healthcare services twice for many older veterans. The total bill for duplicate healthcare amounts to over $3 billion, at least one-third of which could likely be saved without affecting the medical care of a single veteran.[396] [397]

Veterans of the military are generally eligible for life for healthcare services from the Department of Veterans Affairs (VA). Many veterans over age 65 also enroll in MA plans, which receive a lump sum from the federal government to provide comprehensive care to their patients. MA plans are responsible for paying almost all health costs for any necessary treatment. Regardless of how much a patient uses services under the plan, the federal government has already paid its share on behalf of the enrollee.

In recent years, almost one million older veterans have enrolled in Medicare Advantage plans.[398] Many of these patients did not limit their medical use to what the government has already purchased for them through Medicare. Half of these "dual enrollees" used both the VA and MA for health services.[399] Ten percent used only the VA, even though they were enrolled in a Medicare plan.[400] For the latter group, MA plans provided no services but still received a lump sum for each of these patients from the federal government. The VA spends 10 percent of its medical care budget on veterans who are already covered under MA plans.[401] All of these services could have been provided through these patients' MA plans, for which the government already paid.

Alternatively, the VA could seek reimbursement from MA plans for any care provided to their enrollees. Existing federal law, however, prevents the VA from doing so. The result is that even though MA plans have already been paid to provide healthcare to patients, the VA still has to pay for its obligation to veterans. In a sense, the federal government is paying twice for these services.

Due to offsetting market forces, forcing Medicare to reimburse the VA would not likely save taxpayers the full $3.2 billion it pays annually for dually enrolled veterans.[402] However, it is reasonable to expect with better coordination and efficiency, taxpayers should be able to save at least $1 billion by eliminating this duplicative spending with no negative impact on the medical care of veterans.[403]

29) Free bus rides for Super Bowl attendees – (IN) $142,419

Super Bowl XLVI took place in Indianapolis in February. At any given moment, 111 million Americans on average were watching the game, in which the New York Giants beat the New England Patriots by 21-17. Little did the rest of the country know that thousands of their taxpayer dollars were spent shuttling fans around the city for the event.

Indianapolis received a $142,419 grant from the U.S. Department of Transportation to offer free rides on several bus routes for four days surrounding the event, including game day.[404] Full fare for the service typically costs $1.75 per ride.[405] A number of other transportation options were also available to fans: hotel shuttles, other community buses, and carpooling.[406] Cabs were also an option, though city officials opted not to allow a temporary increase in the number of cabs available for fear the new cabbies might "speed on the city's roads and landmarks."[407]

While Superbowl attendees paid thousands of dollars per ticket, Indianapolis used federal funds to shuttle them around the city for free.

If they were not busy at the game, the referees may have thrown their yellow flags on this low-priority use of taxpayer money. Prices for Super Bowl tickets easily average $3,000.[408] Fans could have probably afforded the fare out of their own pockets.

30) Movie theater field trip to see *Red Tails* – (TX) $57,000

Museums, nature centers, and zoos all contribute to memorable educational moments for many students. Rarely do trips to the movie theater fall on that list, let alone those funded by federal taxpayers.

The Dallas Independent School District spent $57,000 in federal funds to send about 4,400 fifth-grade boys from 132 schools to watch *Red Tails*, a film portraying the Tuskegee airmen of World War II.[409] The girls in each class were left to watch a movie about a spelling bee, a decision that may have violated antidiscrimination laws.[410] The trip was paid for with federal Title I funds, which are "earmarked for educating disadvantaged children."[411]

While administrators saw the film as educational, one local watchdog said the students were "not concentrating on history, they [were] concentrating on watching planes blow up."[412] Because *Red Tails* depicts World War II action, some local principals opined young boys should not see the movie. "I don't think it is 5th grade appropriate," said one principal. "It is more towards 7th grade and up."[413] Another recommended renting a Tuskegee airmen documentary instead.[414]

A district spokesman tried to justify the expense, saying teachers used lesson plans both before and after the movie to maximize the impact of the experience.[415]

Once the story of the field trip broke, the district cancelled a trip for another school. The official overseeing the outing said she was concerned about the "hulabalu in the press."[416]

The district was under investigation by state and federal agencies for violating Title IX rules, which "prohibit the exclusion of participation in any program based on sex that receives federal financial assistance."[417] The U.S. Department of Education ended its investigation in April when, according to the *Dallas Morning News*, the district "promised to never exclude students based on gender again." The district has "already conducted mandatory Title IX training for principals and administrators."[418]

To the ire of local citizens, several months after the movie field trip, the administrator who authorized it was promoted to assistant superintendent.[419]

31) Self-reflection video game based on Henry David Thoreau's 1845 writings – (CA) $40,000

The National Endowment for the Arts awarded a $40,000 grant to the University of Southern California (USC) to support production costs of a video game based on the writings of Henry David Thoreau at Walden Pond in Concord, Massachusetts.[420] There, he famously spent several years, reflecting on natural beauty and learning self-reliance.

Creators of the game explained players will "walk

A Henry David Thoreau video game created with taxpayer dollars was called "the most boring idea" by one entertainment critic.

in his virtual footsteps, attend to the tasks of living a self-reliant existence, discover in the beauty of a virtual landscape the ideas and writings of this unique philosopher, and cultivate through the gameplay their own thoughts and responses to the concepts discovered there."[421] Game developers spent two years programming the Walden woods and hope to instigate a new category of video games focusing on player "reflection and insight."[422]

Game designer and USC Associate Professor Tracy Fullerton stated, "Having this support will allow the time we need to really bring the world of Walden to life ... We anticipate a rich simulation of the woods, filled with the kind of detail that Thoreau so carefully noted in his writings."[423] Her inspiration for making the game was to introduce Thoreau to young people who may not have read his work yet.[424]

The lack of excitement surrounding the Thoreau game led one entertainment critic to quip, "We might have just discovered the most boring idea for a video game ever."[425]

32) Flushing down taxpayer dollars – (MI) $10,000

In an effort to prevent drunk driving, the Michigan State Police used $10,000 in federal funds to purchase 400 talking urinal cakes.[426] [427]

Urinal cakes are typically used only to freshen receptacles. Cleverly named Wizmark, a Maryland-based company invented the Interactive Urinal Communicator, which has a motion-detector. As men approach the urinal, the device plays a recording.

Nearly 200 bars and restaurants received the cakes from the state transportation department in hopes the device would "generate a conversation" among male bar-goers and their friends.[428]

For the male Michiganders relieving themselves, one of the messages read by a female voice says:

"Listen up. That's right! I'm talking to you. Had a few drinks? Maybe a few too many? Then do yourself and everyone else a favor. Call a sober friend or a cab. Oh, and don't forget. Wash your hands."[429]

The top of the urinal cake features text that

says "Call a Ride. Get Home."[430]

In response to hearing a demo of the urinal accessory, one male said, "Wow! That is disgusting."[431]

"It's a waste of money, because it'll be a joke," said another local.[432]

Purchasing professional breathalyzers for local bars would have been a more effective way for the state to curb drunk driving. Professional U.S. Department of Transportation-tested devices are available on Amazon.com for under $100 each.

33) No laughing matter, cartoon school receives real taxpayer money – (VT) $255,000

Cartoons aren't just for Saturday mornings anymore. In fact, they never were.

Cartooning is serious business. From politics to entertainment, comics have long been part of nearly every aspect of American popular culture. This year, three of the biggest blockbuster movies in the theater are based upon comic books— "The Dark Knight Rises," "The Amazing Spider-Man," and "The Avengers," which is now the third highest-grossing movie of all time.[433]

The demand for comic books and graphic novels is also on the rise. "According to Diamond Comic Distributors, the largest distribution company to comic book retailers, orders for comic books and graphic novels in April increased 16.1 percent in North America compared with the same time last year. Nearly 24 million unit sales of comic books and graphic novels have been made this year, up 15 percent from last year."[434]

Although the cartooning business is clearly doing fine on its own, federal authorities decided it was a national priority to support cartoonists and comic book artists. The state of Vermont has committed $255,000 of its federal Community Development Block Grant to support a program for graduates of the Center for Cartoon Studies (CCS).[435] The CCS provides one- and two-year certificate programs for creating "visual narratives" for "comic and non-comic geeks alike."[436]

The federal funds will be spent to build the Inky Solomon Center, a program to assist CCS alumni and produce "comics, graphic novels, and other visual narratives for print and digital industries."[437] The center will also support public lectures and events and assist "low and moderate income graduates of CCS."[438][439] A major goal of the grant is to lease

The debt monster cannot be defeated with more red ink.

and renovate an historic building to house the center and to "create workspaces for low and moderate income graduates of CCS."[440]

Aspiring cartoonists and comic book artists and writers are eligible to receive federal financial aid to attend art schools across the country. So it may be no laughing matter to taxpayers that the unaccredited cartoon school with fewer than a hundred students would receive hundreds of thousands of dollars from the U.S. Department of Housing and Urban Development (HUD).[441]

While the school may receive other federal grants, it cannot participate in the federal program that offers subsidized loans and grants to students.[442] But "the absence of federal financial aid does not hinder the ability of CCS to meet its annual admissions goals," according to a review by the Vermont Higher Education Council, which also notes the school assists students in finding financial aid and housing.[443]

"The Center is satisfied with current enrollment level and is not driven by pressure to grow. Enrollment of 40 is considered ideal, in order to provide students the rich educational experience where one-on-one critique is so critical to pedagogy. The Center accepts 24 applicants per year."[444]

With the maximum amount of financial assistance any student can receive from the federal Pell grant program is $5,550, nearly every student attending CCS could have been awarded the maximum Pell grant to attend the accredited school of their choice—with the federal assistance going towards supporting their education rather than office renovations.[445]

34) U.S. Iraqi police training program burns through hundreds of millions of dollars, crashes in flames – (Department of State) $400.2 million[446]

Potentially a "bottomless pit" is how the Special Inspector General for Iraq (SIGIR) described a key State Department's security program.[447] After receiving authority over the program from the U.S. military, the Department of State (DOS) has bungled planning and implementation of the program.[448] [449] Because of the high security costs of working in Iraq, most of the program's support costs are spent on security, not on the provision of police training. Only six percent of the program's budget goes to police training services.[450] And, what training the State Department has provided so far has largely failed to meet the Iraqis' needs.[451]

From its start, the State Department's Police Development Program (PDP) was plagued with problems and poor management. The agency did not assess the needs of the Iraqi police force or develop a comprehensive plan. Even though it had been planning the PDP for two years, DOS did not develop clear goals, cost estimates, and metrics with which to guide the program.[452] The IG called the program "largely unstructured and undefined."[453]

With poorly defined objectives, PDP done little to benefit the Iraqi police. Iraqi officials noted "training was not beneficial" and "police advisory services are 'subpar'."[454] Training material covered administration, finance, technology, and planning – all issues with which Iraqi police said they did not need assistance.[455] At first, material covered in the classes was not even relevant in the Iraqi context. One former deputy inspector general recalled one class in which an American police-training officer taught how a terrorist could be identified by alcohol consumption.[456] Terrorists in the region, however, may be unlikely to consume alcohol due to religious reasons. Some of the only positively reviewed classes were provided by the Federal Bureau of Investigation in Quantico, Virginia.[457]

One of the biggest flaws in PDP's implementation was the lack of buy-in from the Iraqi government. DOS has never obtained a written agreement from the government of Iraq about participation in the program, nor a financial contribution. Without an agreement, the program has languished, and the State Department has downsized the program dramatically.[458]

Most of the money allocated to the PDP was not even directed toward police training, and the State Department wasted hundreds of millions of dollars on construction. At the end of this year, for example, the department will turn over the recently constructed Baghdad Police College to the Iraqi government. The complex was meant to house hundreds of U.S. police advisors for the program and serve as one of its hubs. "It appears that about $108 million in construction costs that will be expended is at risk of being wasted because the investment will not be meaningfully used for the purpose of the appropriation," wrote the IG of the construction project.[459]

The State Department also built another police complex in Basra, at the cost of $98 million, which it then shut down this year.[460] Questionably, DOS continued construction in each area even when it had not obtained a formal agreement with the Iraqi government about the implementation of the program.[461]

A high-ranking Iraqi official in charge of its police forces may have summarized the solution best: "[T]ake the program money and the overhead money and use it for something that can benefit the people of the United States."[462] We agree.

35) Science research dollars go to musical about biodiversity and climate change – (NY) $697,177

The Civilians, a New York City-based theatre company, received $697,177 from the National Science Foundation to create a musical about climate change and biodiversity.[463] The musical opened this year at the Kansas City Repertory Theatre.

"The Great Immensity" is the story of a woman searching for her lost sister, who disappeared from a Panamanian jungle research station.[464] The disappearance has something to do with an upcoming international climate change conference set to take place in Auckland, New Zealand.[465]

Unfortunately, taxpayer dollars did not go very far in advancing any sort of scientific dialogue. One reviewer – who was eager to see the play – quickly dismissed the musical as a waste of money.[466]

Characters in the first act stand around awkwardly in a train station, and sometimes head into the "jungle," complete with flying monkey poop.[467] Throughout the musical, character dialogue is "heavy-handedly laced with facts that easily could've been cribbed from the Wikipedia entry on [climate change]...In fact, many of the songs (I'm not kidding about this) sounded like a Wikipedia entry set to music."[468]

"The audience...spent an evening visibly fighting off sleep," wrote the reviewer.[469]

"But like Kyoto and subsequent agreements, though ultimately disappointing, there's hope that it's a work in progress," wrote another.[470]

36) The streetcar named No Desire – (MO) $35.6 million

Clang, clang, clang goes the money for the trolley.

St. Louis is receiving more than $35 million in federal funds for "an old-fashioned style-trolley system" that will run on a 2.2-mile line from the Missouri History Museum to the University City Library.[471] The federal funds for the project include a $25 million Federal Transit Administration Urban Circulator grant, a $3.5 million New Markets Tax Credit, and $7.1 million in other federal transportation grants.[472][473] The federal amount will pay more than half of the project's $44 million construction cost.[474]

The president of the Loop Trolley Co., also the president of the History Museum, said the trolley service "will be both a pleasure and a portent for future development."[475] And a local developer predicts the trolley will be "a source of pride for the metropolitan area."[476]

However, not everyone in the community is on board.

Some residents say the trolley is a poor use of federal money and others question its financial viability.[477]

Others note the library and museum – to be connected by the trolley – already have nearby MetroLink light-rail stops and bus service. "It's duplicating public transit," said Tom Sullivan, who lives in University City and opposes the project.[478] "I can't see what type of benefit that would bring."[479]

St. Louis is spending more than $35 million in federal funds to construct a 2.2 mile trolley system duplicating existing public transportation destinations and opposed by some residents who refer to it as "The Streetcar Named No Desire."

Elsie Glickert, a resident and former City Council member, calls the Trolley project the "Folly Trolley" and "The Streetcar Named No Desire to Nowhere."[480]

The project's supporters are "vague about what happens if the trolleys don't make enough money" to cover the administration budget, but have suggested "the difference could be made up by increasing revenues from the sales tax."[481]

37) Congress splits new line of ships between two completely different designs, increasing costs and undermining Navy's capabilities – (Department of Defense) $148 million

In the coming decades, the U.S. Navy plans to spend over $37 billion to build 55 littoral combat ships (LCS), a new line of light, fast ships that are able to operate in littoral (near-shore) waters.[482] They will be a major investment for the country in the coming century. Yet, a decision by the Navy to ask two different companies to build the LCS will cost taxpayers hundreds of millions dollars over the lifetime of the program.[483] From the four ships being constructed this year, the waste may amount to at least $148 million.[484]

The LCS is designed to navigate near-shore waters inaccessible to other Navy vessels. The ships can be adapted with mission packages for tasks such as anti-submarine warfare, mine countermeasures, combat against small boats, intelligence gathering, maritime interception, and special-operations.

The Navy has argued its dual-award strategy will speed up ship construction slightly and will cost less than picking a single winner.[485] The Congressional Budget Office (CBO), however, estimated the plan will increase costs by $740 million over just six years for 20 ships.[486] Over the life of the program, there is substantial risk the cost of maintaining two completely different types of LCS will greatly increase.

LCS program costs have already risen dramatically. The cost for each ship has almost doubled from $340 million apiece to almost $600 million.[487] The large cost jump was partly due to the Navy's decision to allow ship construction to begin when designs were less than 20 percent complete.[488] Later construction changes drove the budget higher.

More spending increases may be on the horizon, says the Pentagon's lead official in charge of cost evaluation.[489] The Navy recently decided to increase the total capacity of the ships by 20 sailors, which will increase personnel costs.[490] In addition, the full cost for the 64 planned mission packages has not yet been estimated or included in the current program costs.[491] GAO noted the packages "require a total of 24 critical technologies...none of which, at full capacity, have been tested on board LCS in a realistic environment."[492]

Lockheed LCS Design (Top) and General Dynamics LCS Design (Bottom)

In 2010, Congress hastily approved the Navy's request to split its line of Littoral Combat Ships between two manufactures, a move that CBO estimates will cost taxpayers hundreds of millions of dollars more than if the Navy used just one manufacturer.

Cost concerns aside, having two separate lines will likely undermine the Navy's strategic flexibility. Each company's version of LCS will have unique weapons systems and internal components and will require separate crew training, construction oversight, parts, and maintenance infrastructure throughout the life of the ships. Crew members trained to serve on one version will not be qualified to serve on the other.[493] Naval tacticians could be constrained when developing mission strategies by the need to accommodate differing capabilities and needs.

In light of these readily identifiable challenges, the LCS program would likely be better off fiscally and strategically with one design.

38) Anti-trash poster contest for college students – (NY) $67,926

Syracuse University received a $67,926 grant from the Environmental Protection Agency (EPA) to run "Students Against Trash," a poster contest targeting students in New Jersey, New York, and Puerto Rico.[494] Organizers hoped to involve at least 25 other universities in their efforts to "use design to defeat trash and get people excited to reuse, recycle, and stop littering."[495] [496]

Students are to "compete to create the most fresh and engaging poster campaign which will engage many stakeholders in a cost-effective way."[497] Ironically, contest administrators must watch how many posters are printed, lest they be found in the rubbish bin. Social media will be used to help reduce waste.[498]

A poster submitted to the anti-trash poster contest for college students funded by the EPA.

Voting for the contest took place online using Facebook. Contestants received one point for every "like" received, 2 points for every "share," and 3 points for every pledge to "take action against trash" left in a comment attached to their poster.[499] Three winners will receive trips to New York City.[500]

Contests finalists certainly found creative ways to advertise the anti-trash message. One poster shows some trash on the ground with plastic GI-JOEs attacking it. "Declare war on trash," says its caption.[501] Another poster shows a Styrofoam cup filled with celebrities, next to a caption stating, "Some things really do last forever," drawing a contrast between the decomposition of a cup and the short-lived existence of some celebrity marriages.[502]

39) Bus stops or small houses? City spends nearly $78,000 each on bus shelters – (OR) $388,000

The city of Grants Pass, Oregon, will spend $388,000 in federal money, $77,600 apiece, for five bus shelters along its small, four-route bus system.[503]

When the bus stop project was started in 2007 under a different mayor and city council, the goal "was to create shelters that were better than the basic Plexiglas cubes that you see in other cities. The deal was to draw attention to those shelters with public art and make them an interesting and attractive place—something that was truly unique to the City of Grants Pass," according to the city's grant specialist who took over the project.[504]

In 2009, the city planned to spend $322,000 for between six and ten shelters.[505] By 2012, however, the price estimate rose to more than $530,000 for only five shelters.[506] That would have put the cost at $106,000 each.

"Around here, that's enough to build a three-bedroom house," commented Grants Pass Councilman Dan de Young, "What we should do is build a house at each station, and if you miss your last bus, you can stay there overnight."[507]

City officials hope to reduce the project's cost to the $388,000 available from federal grants. Even that sum could buy two houses in Grants Pass.[508]

Federal restrictions were one of the reasons for the sharp cost increase. According to the specialist, "Those involved with the project at the time [local and federal authorities] underestimated the complexities of a seemingly simple project."[509] For example, due to federal rules, the city found it was not eligible to directly administer federal highway funds, which prevented it from doing in-house design work, bidding, purchasing, and construction. This restriction added costs for private consulting fees.[510]

In 2012, the city council faced citizen backlash over the cost of the bus stops and considered modifying or cancelling the project. If it cancelled the project, however, the city would need to reimburse the federal government $81,000 for the portion of the grant the city had already spent on the project's consulting engineers.[511] Faced with this choice, the council ultimately decided to push ahead with the project, voting to scale back on the project's art installations. This reduced the total cost of the shelters, ensuring a minimum amount of local money was lost to the project.

Using federal funds, the city of Grants Pass, Oregon, will build bus stops costing as much as some homes in the area.

As of May 2012, the total projected cost for the five bus stops was $413,544, although the city was still pursuing more options to bring the cost within the $388,000 available from the federal government.[512] One Grants Pass councilor made it clear he thought the project was ridiculous, but voted to complete it anyway to minimize the amount of local money going to what he called "this federal boondoggle."[513]

40) YouTube video contest on fruits and veggies – (Department of Health and Human Services) $106,000

"An apple a day keeps the doctor away," says the old adage. Although there are endless ways to find ideas for healthy eating, the federal government decided to add one more – a YouTube video contest.

A search for "veggie ideas" on YouTube turns up over 1,000 privately created videos offering creative advice on using vegetables. Yet, the Department of Health and Human Services spent $97,000 to design and hold the "MyPlate Fruits and Veggies Video Challenge," a contest in which people could submit 30-second videos to "share positive messages about the benefits of consuming fruits and vegetables with their peers."[514] A prize pool of $9,000 was promised for the winners, bringing the total cost of the video contest to $106,000.[515]

Winning videos were judged on a number of criteria, such as inclusion of the message "make half your plate fruits and vegetables," encouragement to visit ChooseMyPlate.gov, and advice to leave out fried foods.

"The Fruit and Veggie Pokey!" was one of the winners of a federally funded YouTube video contest.

Despite its cost and prize pool, the contest only lured in 142 video submissions.[516] One of the most popular videos features a group of schoolgirls doing the hokey pokey with the lyrics, "You put your fruit in, you take your junk food out."[517]

As adorable or fun as some of the videos may be, such words are falling on ears that have heard messages about fruits and veggies for years. A description of the video contest itself states "efforts have been underway nationally for nearly 20 years to promote fruits and vegetables."[518] Its videos are unlikely to compete with millions of others that command people's attention, and federal programs already exist promoting healthy eating.

This project proved to be nothing but an unhealthy use of taxpayer dollars.

41) Faulty FEMA calculations lead to building replacement instead of repair – (IA) $75.4 million

The Federal Emergency Management Agency (FEMA) asserted this year two buildings on the University of Iowa (UI) campus should be replaced after damage from the 2008 flood of the Iowa River. However, an investigation by the agency's Office of Inspector General (IG) concluded the agency made a faulty decision and could save taxpayers $75.4 million by taking back some of the money it gave toward the buildings' replacement and instead focusing efforts on rehabilitating the existing buildings.[519]

In June 2008, the Iowa River breached its levees throughout southeastern Iowa. Water filled the basements of two university buildings next to the river – a music building with an auditorium and recital hall, and an art building. The ground floor of the music building and some of the ground floor of the art building were covered with over 12 inches of water. Each building experienced damage to its interior design, floors, and mechanical and electrical equipment. Yet, according to the Inspector General, "site inspections identified no structural damage."[520]

To make decisions on whether to fund replacement or repair of a building, FEMA uses a "50 percent rule." If estimated repair cost exceeds half the cost of replacement, FEMA will provide funding to replace the building. In this case, regional FEMA officials repeatedly made faulty cost estimates that led to their decision to replace the buildings.

FEMA's first estimates – which significantly underestimated the true cost of replacement – were incorrect because the staff rushed to finalize them. In November 2008, staff learned on a Friday they needed final estimates by the following Monday.[521] Given one weekend to finalize the data, officials only used square footage data and aerial photos, rather than site visits and available detailed descriptions of damage.

Weeks later, the assessment team revised its estimates using a computer program intended only for small projects. Numbers from the program stated the buildings could be replaced at $142 per square foot.[522] Actual local construction costs are 3-4 times higher.[523]

Over the next several years, regional FEMA officials performed a more detailed analysis of the repair and replacement costs, and their replacement estimates grew over 300 percent from their original numbers.[524][525]

Wastebook 2012

Not only did officials inaccurately estimate the cost of replacement, the cost of repair was inflated by including projects that agency guidelines excludes from estimates. For example, upgrades to meet newer building codes do not qualify as repairs.

The IG concluded FEMA should reverse its decision to replace the two buildings and instead award funds to repair them. This action would save taxpayers $75.4 million.[526]

42) "Game Time!" toy exhibit – (NY) $150,000

The Institute of Museum and Library Services may be playing around with taxpayer money. This year, the federal agency awarded $150,000 to the Strong National Museum of Play in New York to create an exhibit featuring board games, toys, and puzzles from the country's past.[527] "Game Time!" – the new exhibit – will be the second component of the museum's larger "America at Play" exhibit.

A diverse range of America's games and puzzles will be on display in the new 4,200-square-foot wing built with taxpayer funds. "[G]uests will become pieces of a giant game board as they move through the exhibit to learn about the history of board games, card games,

Playing around: The Strong Museum of Play received federal funding to develop an exhibit of games and puzzles.

puzzles, and more public amusements such as electromechanical coin-operated games, pinball machines, and products for home or public game rooms such as foosball and hockey," according to the museum.[528]

Other aspects of the "America at Play" exhibit will be "electronic games ... dolls and doll houses, construction toys and miniature worlds" from the country's past. "eGameRevolution" is the museum's display of the nation's video games, from Atari's Pong to the Guitar Hero on an Xbox 360.[529] A number of artifacts decorate the exhibit, including "rare and unique artifacts like *Computer Space* and a Nintendo NES gray cartridge."[530] Visitors will be able to view notes and drawings from legendary game inventors."[531]

Museum officials do not want to just play with taxpayers' hard-earned dollars. They hope the exhibit will "tell the story of the evolution of play and how it has affected both children and adults." Admission to the toy museum is $13 for adults, $11 for children.[532]

The museum itself boasts "more than 7,500 examples of board, card, role-playing, and other games"[533] It has over 850 unique card decks that may find their way into the new exhibit.[534] Others items that could go on display are some of museum's 450 Milton Bradley games, such as The Game of Life.[535]

43) Sidewalks to nowhere anger local citizens – (FL; MI) $1.1 million

Florida. Some locals call it the "sidewalk to nowhere" – a 20-block-long sidewalk intended to help kids walk to school.[536] The sidewalk was funded with $1.1 million from the Safe Routes to School program, but the highway along which it was built is not considered safe by many in the community.[537]

County officials targeted the area for a sidewalk believing the new path would alleviate the safety concerns and eliminate the need to bus the students.[538] Neither goal is likely to pan out, making the project "questionable from the beginning."[539] [540]

The sidewalk winds through a desolate area with "railroad tracks and woods... a boat yard, storage units, warehouses, and other light-industrial businesses."[541]

"I wouldn't let a child walk down that street by himself. It's isolated. It's out of sight," said one resident.[542]

The local school district's transportation director noted he does not expect the sidewalk to affect bus service. The sidewalk's effect on students at one local school is unclear, said the district official.[543] Because of the lack of safety in the area, the school district already

A look at the sidewalk's route with Google Streetview

busses kids to school, even if they live within 2 miles of the school (normally the district's cutoff for bus service).[544]

Most people still live "a half mile or more" from the new path, since officials could not find a way to build segments of the sidewalk to one of the district's residential areas.[545] Officials began to recognize problems with their plans for the sidewalk last year, but needed to move forward to spend the federal grant before it expired. They had to cut a seven-block section of the sidewalk that went through a key residential area. "That sidewalk they have now doesn't do Gifford any good," said an angry citizen.[546]

Some residents question the value of the sidewalk in an industrial area at all. This project deserves the simple description given by one resident: "ridiculous."[547]

Michigan. At a large intersection of a highway and local four-lane road, three newly constructed ramps not connected to sidewalks caught the eye of Gabe Hudson, a Kent County, Michigan, local.[548] Hudson photographed one of the ramps, which dead-ends at a utility pole a few feet from the street.[549] Neither of the streets at the intersection have sidewalks, and the only "pedestrians" he has seen using the intersection were "a dead skunk and two dead raccoons."[550]

County officials built the three ramps this summer at the intersection to comply with federal regulations associated with using federal funds to resurface the road.[551] The

Before and after photos of a ramp built at a Michigan intersection that has sidewalks and hardly any pedestrians. Local officials had to build the ramps, to comply with rules to use federal funds they used for road resurfacing.

regulations did not take into account the lack of sidewalks in the area, only the presence of a traffic light with a pedestrian signal at the intersection. Construction of the ramps cost about $10,000.[552] The project of which the ramps were a part was paid for mostly with federal funds.[553]

As Hudson put it, the ramps "could cost $500 and it'd still be a waste."[554]

44) NASA keeps paying for unused, outdated database– (National Aeronautics and Space Administration) $771,000

The National Aeronautics and Space Administration (NASA) is fond of touting technological advancements the agency has helped develop over the years, such as Velcro, reflective coatings for lenses, and new methods in computing. Despite this progress, NASA continues to operate an outdated and poorly utilized "Lessons Learned" database costing taxpayers over $771,000 every year.[555]

The Lessons Learned Information System (LLIS) is a database that allows NASA managers to document best practices and other information gained from completed projects. NASA managers rarely contribute to or access the database, according to a review by the agency's Inspector General (IG).[556]

Employees found the database to be "outdated, not user friendly, and generally unhelpful."[557] Instead, they opt to use other forms of knowledge-sharing that NASA maintains, including an engineering network, a training academy, seminars, and a magazine.[558] The NASA official in charge of the database has acknowledged the agency has no plan for how LLIS will be utilized in the future.[559]

A number of NASA guidelines state the agency's 10 centers should have lessons-learned committees to contribute to LLIS.[560] Yet, at the time of the audit, eight of the 10 centers were not fully complying with agency guidelines.[561] Four of the centers did not even have lessons-learned committees to oversee the process.[562]

The IG questioned "whether the three quarters of a million dollars NASA spends annually on LLIS activities constitutes a prudent investment."[563]

45) Alaska's sightseeing trains for cruise ship tourists – (AK) $38.8 million

The Alaska Railroad will receive $38.8 million this year and $33 million next year through a federal mass transit program, even after the Senate tried to end the railroad's funding this year.[564] The train serves mostly to benefit tourists and freight – far from what most think

The Alaska Railroad receives federal funds to carry tourists to scenic destinations.

of as "mass transit" – but has received federal transit funds for over a decade.[565]

Over two-thirds of the railroad's 412,200 passengers were cruise ship customers last year.[566] Alaska Railroad operates a special line, the *Grandview Cruise Train*, to ferry cruise ship passengers from Whittier or Seward, where they dock, to Anchorage. The train's schedule is timed to meet the arrival of the ships.

Other customers rode one of the three other prominent train lines – *Denali Star*, *Coastal Classic*, and *Glacier Discovery*. Each primarily serves to transport passengers to national parks and scenic locations.

The *Coastal Classic*, for example, takes adventurers to Alaska's Resurrection Bay for "whale watching, sea kayaking, tidewater glacier viewing, fishing, and dog sled rides."[567] Similarly, passengers on the *Glacier Discovery* leave Anchorage for the coast outside the city, destined for "glacier cruises…canoe tours, rafting, and hiking."[568]

More important to the railroad than passengers is freight. Over half of the railroad's total revenue, including the federal grant, comes from cargo (over half of which is oil and coal).[569]

Yet, federal subsidies for the Alaska Railroad come from a mass transit program. Funding per railroad passenger – about $87 in future years – significantly outweighs what most public transportation systems receive.[570] The average subsidy per passenger across the country is $3 to $4.[571] The transit system of Lincoln, Nebraska – whose population of over 250,000 is about the same size as that of Anchorage – receives $1 to $2 in federal money for every passenger.[572][573]

The company first qualified for federal mass transit funding in 2000, when the Federal Transit Administration ruled the railroad eligible for public transportation dollars.[574] Only ten percent of the railroad's 500 miles qualified for the subsidy, however.[575] In 2006, over sixty percent of the line became eligible after Alaska's at-large representative inserted language into legislation making the change specifically for the railroad.[576][577]

Recognizing the railroad's federal funding as a low-priority earmark, some have called the project a "railroad to nowhere."[578]

During the debate on the multi-year transportation bill passed this year, the Senate initially voted to reject the mass transit funding for the railroad altogether. Nevertheless, clever politics and legislative linguistics ensured the railroad continued to receive taxpayer dollars when the final version of the bill passed.[579]

Ensuring federal funds are going to essential projects is the first stop on the track to fiscal stability. This earmark benefitting cruise ship passengers and lucrative energy producers needs to end.

46) Vineyards' cups overfloweth – (Department of Agriculture) $1.5 million

In 2012, vineyards and wineries received at least $1.5 million in federal taxpayer funds to assist with their grape-growing endeavors.[580]

One such recipient, the Belle Joli' Winery, operated by Jackson Vineyards in Belle Fourche, South Dakota, received $300,000 to expand its product line.[581] According to the owners, Belle Joli' reflects the rich aesthetics of the Black Hills, located near the winery.[582]

Another recipient, Olde Chautauqua Vineyards of Portland, New York, received $299,999 to assist with its production and marketing.[583] The vineyard used the funds to launch its new winery, 21 Brix Winery.[584]

The Vineyards at Dodon, in Davidsonville, Maryland, used $299,974 to start a winery to be run on the owner's nine-generation-old farm.[585] [586] Likewise, Maryland-based Boordy Vineyards, a 30-year-old company, received $239,200 in federal grants to assist their business.[587] In Chatham, Virginia, a grant totaling $208,571 was awarded to The Homeplace Vineyards, and in Kennedyville, Maryland, the Crow Vineyard & Winery received $48,600 in federal grant funds.[588]

Drunk in debt: A handful of vineyards received over $1 million from the federal government this year

47) Tax cheat? Medicaid says no problem – (Medicaid; Internal Revenue Service) At least $330 million

One of the largest federally funded programs – Medicaid – provides billions of dollars in payments to tax cheats who owe millions in unpaid taxes. Almost 7,000 Medicaid providers in just three states owed $791 million in unpaid federal taxes but received $6.6 billion in Medicaid reimbursements in just one year, found a Government Accountability Office (GAO) investigation.[589]

Some examples of tax-cheating doctors, dentists, and other providers will make taxpayers sick.

For example, one nursing business owes over $3 million in unpaid taxes and has collected $200,000 from the Medicaid program.[590] The business's owners – a married couple – "purchased a new home while their business was accumulating debt."[591] The Internal Revenue Service (IRS) had to refer the case to the Department of Justice.

Another nursing business has received over $2 million in federal Medicaid funds yet owes over $200,000 in unpaid taxes dating from the late 2000s.[592] The IRS has taken corrective actions against the organization a number of times.

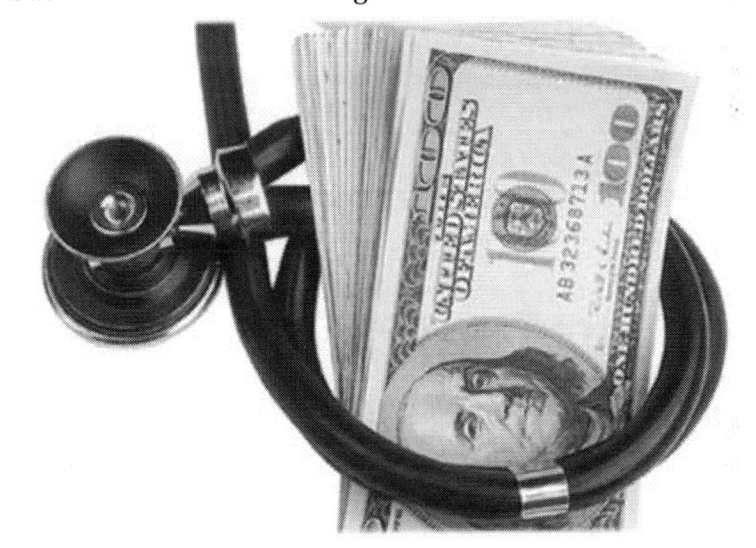

A social services company owes over $1 million in unpaid federal taxes, though it has received over $4 million in Medicaid payments.[593] The business has tried to settle its debt with the IRS, but its offer was rejected as insufficient. Its owner also has a "history of outstanding personal tax debt for unpaid individual income taxes."[594]

A fix to the problem seems simple: the IRS should garnish a portion of each provider's future Medicaid payments. Yet, because of a loophole in federal law, the IRS cannot hold a continuous levy (a process similar to garnishment of wages) against Medicaid payments from states to providers. The agency is allowed to send onetime levies to state Medicaid agencies, but these have not been effective.

GAO estimated in Florida, New York, and Texas alone, the IRS could collect anywhere from $22 million to $330 million annually in unpaid taxes if it could better levy Medicaid payments.[595]

48) Courthouse design, construction takes a decade and is no longer a priority – (CA) $322 million

The federal government continues to move forward with a plan to construct a 600,000-square-foot federal courthouse in downtown Los Angeles, despite objections from both Democrat and Republican lawmakers and government watchdogs that the project is unneeded.

A January 2012 notice announcing the courthouse construction explained the project needs to be a "Federal landmark in the heart of Los Angeles that represents the dignity of the U.S. Government" and the new structure should "express solemnity, integrity, rigor and fairness."[596] The new building – expected to cost $322 million – would replace the current federal courthouse, which is said to have security and asbestos problems.[597] [598]

An artist's rendering of a proposed federal courthouse in Los Angeles, of which GAO has remained critical for years.

The project has a long and troubled history of wasteful spending. Between fiscal years 2001 and 2005, Congress appropriated $400 million for the project.[599] By 2008, the new courthouse's estimated costs had ballooned to $1.1 billion, and the project at one point was slated to feature 54 courtrooms.[600] In that same year, a Government Accountability Office (GAO) report found the design of the courthouse featured 13 more courtrooms than authorized by Congress.[601] This news, coupled with increased overhead costs and lack of competitive bids, caused the project to be delayed.[602]

In autumn 2011, the government came forth with another plan to get the project moving again, reducing its size and budget. Despite the revisions, the criticism continued. Chairman Jeff Denham (R-CA) and Ranking Member Eleanor Holmes Norton (D-DC) of the House Transportation and Infrastructure Subcommittee on Economic Development, Public Building, and Emergency Management, questioned the courthouse project in a joint statement, arguing it was an unneeded expense imposed on taxpayers during a time of tight budgets.[603] Likewise, GAO stood by its critique of the project, saying the plan still exceeded the congressionally authorized size, overestimated the quantity of future judges, and had not even considered courtroom sharing among judges.[604]

Nevertheless, federal officials sprinted to spend their appropriated funds, issuing the new construction notice in January.[605]

GAO remains critical of the newest proposal. "The current plan to build a new 24-courtroom courthouse would provide more courtrooms than are needed and will not solve the problem of a split court posed by two separate buildings – one of the key justifications of this project," the watchdog said in a 2012 review of the project.[606]

49) Pentagon raids weapons program to buy jerky – (Department of Defense) $700,000[607]

Beef jerky so good it will shock and awe your taste buds.

That is the goal of an ongoing Pentagon project, which is attempting to develop its own brand of jerky treats that are the bomb! Only, the money is coming from a program specially created to equip soldiers with the weapons they need.

The Foreign Comparative Testing (FCT) program has spent more than $1.5 million to develop the savory snacks.[608] This is a highly unusual initiative since the purpose of the FCT is "to improve the U.S. warfighter's capabilities" by testing "items and technologies of our foreign allies that have a high Technology Readiness Level (TRL)" that could satisfy "mission area shortcomings."[609] One of the program's stated objectives is "eliminating unnecessary duplication."[610]

"In the last 12 years, enhanced body armor from Germany; a mine-clearing system from Denmark; and a bunker-busting, multi-purpose rocket warhead from Norway were a few of the 105 items tested and deployed by U.S. forces that originated in the FCT program. Other examples include advances in lightweight body armor and lighter, longer-lasting rechargeable batteries," according to the U.S. Army website.[611]

Meat Roll-Ups: Defense research dollars are being spent to create a new form of beef jerky that comes in thin flat pieces like a Fruit Roll-Up. This is first time the Pentagon's Foreign Comparative Testing program has ever funded a project not related to weaponry or combat systems.

Now beef jerky will be added to this list.

"I was told this is the first time FCT has funded a project that wasn't related to weaponry or combat systems. Mine was the first one related to food. FCT was happy to fund this novel technology," said Tom Yang, a South Carolina-based senior food scientist on the Food Processing, Engineering and Technology team at the Combat Feeding Directorate.[612]

The U.S. Army Natick Soldier Research, Development and Engineering Center, Department of Defense Combat Feeding Directorate is "partnering" with the food processing company FPL Food to develop the new meat snacks.[613]

The DOD meat treats will differ from traditional jerky, since they will be developed using osmotic dehydration, a process developed in France. As part of that process, "the meat is extruded into a thin sheet on a sheet of parchment paper on a conveyor system."[614] According to the Pentagon, the result is "a meat roll-up that can be consumed as a savory snack or used as a filling for a shelf stable sandwich."[615] "The finished product resembles a Fruit Roll-up" rather than a traditional meat stick such as the popular Slim Jim.[616]

A variety of flavors and varieties are being developed, including salami, chipotle, turkey, pork, and smoked ham. There is also a product made from fish, but "the recipe needs to be tweaked to make it less fishy," according to Yang.[617]

Several flavors are already available from a number of commercial producers. In fact, the jerky market is flourishing. "Sales of jerky increased by 13.6% to $760.2 million for the

Wastebook 2012

year ended [August] 12, according to SymphonyIRI Group, a Chicago market research firm. That follows several years of growth, including a 13.4% sales jump in 2011."[618]

And while our men and women in uniform certainly would welcome new menu options, these dollars could be better spent at this time when sequestration imposed by the Budget Control Act is set to cut billions of dollars from our national defense budget.

While this may be the first time the Pentagon's FCT program has spent research dollars on developing meat treats, a number of federal programs are also involved in the jerky industry.

This year, the Department of Housing and Urban Development's Community Development Block Grant program provided $356,000 to pay for infrastructure improvements to help the expansion of Link Snacks Inc., which boasts being "the fastest-growing meat snack manufacturer in the world, and [selling] more than 100 different meat snack products."[619] [620] [621]

The Department of Agriculture (USDA) has also been providing jerky grants for years. This year, the Sunburst Trout Farms, which produces trout jerky as well as smoked trout dip and trout caviar, received a $283,884 USDA Value-Added Producer Grant to help expand the market for its products.[622]

50) Grant for struggling schools wasted on "tinkering" and finger-pointing – (WA) $7.3 million

In the last three years, schools across the nation received $1.6 billion dollars in School Improvement Grants (SIG) from the U.S. Department of Education to improve student performance.[623] An evaluation of the program in the state of Washington has revealed the program resulted in little to no improvement. Washington public schools will use $7.3 million from the program in 2012 and have gathered over $60 million in the past three years.[624] [625]

A report by the Center on Reinventing Public Education found most Washington schools receiving SIGs made only marginal changes.[626] Not one of the schools outpaced the state average in reading and math standardized tests.[627] "[T]he majority of schools studied show little evidence of the type of bold and transformative changes the SIGs were intended to produce," the report states.[628] One district SIG director interviewed about the program asked the researchers "how to successfully turn around a failing school…He went on to explain that he was at a loss as to how to do this."[629]

The district and its schools tried to implement change, but failed at many stages. Communication between the district and schools was cited as "confusing and incomplete."[630] District officials did not establish clear policies to assist schools with policy questions.[631] Similarly, individual schools did not receive enough autonomy from the district to enact the most effective changes.[632]

In many cases, changes implemented with the grant were questionable from the start. For example, three schools used a combined $5.8 million in grant money to slightly extend the school day and add administrative staff.[633] Other schools paid for extra gym and art teachers, consultants, and intramural sports classes.[634]

Washington state principals called into question the need for the grant to implement the changes. "The principals were glad to have the money," the SIG researchers wrote, "but said that the work could be done without it."[635] Successful schools noted the administrative flexibility provided by the grant, not the funding, was the most important part of the program.[636] Of course, giving more flexibility to local schools should cost less – not more.

51) Identity thieves bilking the IRS out of billions – (Internal Revenue Service) $3.9 billion

This year, identity thieves will collect an estimated $3.9 billion in tax refunds on fraudulent returns they will file using stolen Social Security numbers (SSN).[637] The Treasury Inspector General for Tax Administration (TIGTA) released an investigation this year outlining what the Internal Revenue Service (IRS) needs to do more to prevent rampant tax fraud. Over five years, taxpayers could lose more than $20 billion to crooks. These losses are largely preventable with better anti-fraud measures.[638]

Identity thieves submit false returns to collect handsome refunds, often through direct deposit or in debit cards sent by the IRS. To file false tax returns, many thieves used another person's name and SSN. For example, investigators in Tampa, Florida, found most successful scams involved identities stolen from the deceased or from people on government assistance.[639] Most identities used are from individuals with incomes low enough they would not even have to file tax returns. Of the 1,492,215 potentially fraudulent tax returns filed for 2010, over 950,000 utilized the identities of low-income people, accounting for $3.3 billion erroneous in tax refunds issued.[640] The second most common type of fake returns filed – 288,252 – used the identities of students, and nearly 105,000 claimed the identities of deceased people.[641]

The TIGTA found thieves filed 4,864 potentially fraudulent tax returns using only five addresses to generate $8.1 million in refunds in 2010.[642] One address in Lansing, Michigan, accounted for 2,137 returns.[643] Another tactic was to send the direct deposits from the refunds to the same bank account. The IRS will send refunds to an account even if its holder is not the same as the name on the tax return. In one case, a single bank account received 590 direct deposits in 2010 totaling $909,267.[644]

The IRS has made some effort to stop identity thieves in the last year. But, according to the Treasury IG, the agency is not maximizing all the tools at its disposal. "The review identified that the IRS uses little of the data from identity theft cases...to identify commonalities, trends, etc., that could be used to detect and prevent future tax refund fraud," the IG wrote.[645]

Though the agency has developed a number of fraud filters, they need to be tightened, recommended the IG report. A test of the filters allowed most potentially fraudulent returns through the system.[646] The IRS has worked to prevent use of the SSNs of deceased individuals. Congress could also allow the IRS greater access to the federal database that tracks employment and wages to help the agency detect false documents and returns.

With the explosion of identity fraud in the last few years, the IRS needs to move as fast as possible to end such widespread looting of honest taxpayers.

52) Return of the Jedi – (MA) $365

Not so long ago in a library not so far, far away...

The struggle against the evil galactic empire and the dark side of the Force has come to Earth. Accompanied by Stormtroopers, Darth Vader was among the special guests at a federally funded Star Wars fan event that included a history of Star Wars, trivia, and "name that character" games.[647] [648] Those attending were encouraged to bring "their Star Wars toys and collectibles for show and tell as

Fans attending the federally funded Star Wars Day were encouraged to dress up as their favorite characters

well as to dress as their favorite character."[649] On the library's social networking website, it noted after the trivia contest, "the group played with action figures, did puzzles and took photo ops with their favorite characters."[650]

The Star Wars Day event, held at the Abington Public Library in Massachusetts, was paid for with $365 in federal funds, part of an $11,700 grant provided by the federal Institute of Museum and Library Services.[651][652][653]

The Star Wars franchise has grossed over $4.5 billion over the past 35 years,[654] so taxpayers may wonder why the government is subsidizing fan events for one of the most popular and successful movie series in the universe.[655]

53) NASA spends millions on visitor center to replace old one just miles away – (MS) $12.4 million

The National Aeronautics and Space Administration (NASA) has a knack for completing projects with delays and out-of-this-world budgets. Adding to a list of questionable decisions, the agency funded a state-of-the-art visitor center to replace an existing one five miles down the road. The old structure is located on the grounds of the Stennis Space Center facility in Mississippi, NASA's main engine testing facility. The need for a new facility was certainly not driven by an overwhelming number of visitors. The previous visitor center, which closed this year, received fewer than 40,000 visitors a year on average since 2007 – or roughly 100 people a day.[656]

NASA opened the original visitor center in conjunction with the 1984 World's Fair in New Orleans.[657] Visitors could learn about NASA's space program and the Stennis Space Center itself. The center is also home to an office of the National Oceanic and Atmospheric Administration (NOAA). In 2000, a remodeling doubled the visitor center's size, and it was officially dubbed the StenniSphere.[658][659] With the renovation, "NASA entered the tourism market with a full-fledged visitor center with hopes of becoming a major regional attraction," according to one observer at the time.[660] NASA again made improvements to the original visitor center in 2003 at the cost of $453,000.[661]

Only, the vision to attract tourists never paid off and over time, NASA's desire to maintain the center appeared to wane. Yet, as early as 1999, NASA examined the possibility of moving the visitor center offsite.[662] Additionally, the agency raised security concerns about the onsite facility after the terrorist attacks of September 11, 2001.[663]

NASA spent millions to move its visitor center at the Stennis Space Center just miles down the road. The previous visitor center averaged under 40,000 patrons per year.

Instead of addressing these issues in a cost-effective manner, NASA decided in 2001 to contribute a significant amount of money to a new visitor center off-site. The agency worked with state officials to build a $31 million, 72,000-square-foot science center that opened this year just over five miles away from the original facility.[664] [665]

NASA contributed $10 million to the project, while NOAA added $1.9 million and the federal Department of Interior kicked in $500,000 in environmental conservation funds.[666] Private organizations and the Mississippi state government contributed $18.8 million in funding for the new science center, which charges $8 per adult for admission.[667] [668]

Over five times the size of the old facility, the new Infinity Science Center houses displays from the old visitor center and many other exhibits as well.[669] According to the center's website, "studies estimate that the INFINITY Science Center will attract over 300,000 visitors each year," or more than seven times the annual attendance of the old center.[670]

54) Circus classes – (MO) $20,000

The circus is a traditional American pastime long associated with elephants, clowns, impossible-to-win games, and acrobatics that make heads spin. Older circuses featured freak shows filled with strange sights. Lately, an even more peculiar sight has come to the circus – taxpayer funding.

Over the last three years, the National Endowment for the Arts has awarded $84,000 – including $20,000 in 2012 – to the Circus Day Foundation to host a theatrical circus arts program for students.[671][672] The program lasts one year and students "work with professional circus educators, choreographers, costume designers, and musicians to learn theatrical circus skills [through] sequential, skills-based classes and perform for the public."[673]

The Circus Day Foundation – which has renamed itself Circus Harmony, boasting the slogan "Peace Through Pyramids" – offers classes to teach students "real circus skills" such as "juggling," "magic levels," and "hula hoops."[674]

The organization also has a youth troupe, "The St. Louis Arches," that can be rented starting at $1,000 for the first hour.[675]

55) Tune in to reruns and feel better – (NY) $666,905

Watching television reruns gives people an energizing chance to reconnect with pseudo-friends, according to a National Institutes of Health (NIH) study published this year.[676] Researchers used part of $666,905 in NIH grants to look at the phenomenon.[677][678]

"There is something special and comfortable about a 'relationship' in which you already know what the other person is going to say and do," says the study's lead investigator.[679] As people enjoy laughs from well-known characters such as *Seinfeld's* George Costanza, they are benefiting from "[their] interaction with the TV show's character, and this activity restores [their] energy."[680]

Old television shows are not the only activity that can boost one's mood, according to the study. Researchers found favorite books and movies (described as "familiar fictional worlds") also help to restore self-control, while writing about a well-liked television show can also restore energy levels.[681]

Even though watching the tube may be beneficial for mood in the short-run, the study's author is careful to note the irony of the results: "Seeking sedentary activities to restore self-control, rather than physical exertion, could have deleterious effects on long-term health."[682] Watching television may also leave people with "fewer social resources over time," the study notes.[683]

The NIH grants that funded this study were targeted for alcohol abuse treatment and intimate partner violence.[684] [685]

56) Old-fashioned x-rays for prisoners – (Department of Justice) $1.3 million

In an era when x-rays have become almost entirely digitized, the Bureau of Prisons still spends about $1.3 million every year to create hard copies of prisoner x-rays.[686] The bureau also spends taxpayer dollars to mail the copies to different institutions when prisoners are transferred.[687]

The bureau could cut back on waste by using digital x-rays instead, which are available for almost instantaneous analysis. Since they would be stored as computer files, the x-rays also could easily be transferred to other doctors and prisons.

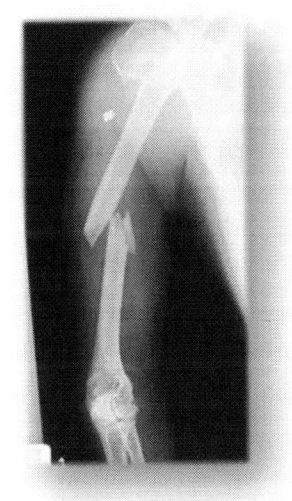

57) Online lawyer training gets science funding – (PA) $500,000

Law schools are "too far removed from practice," say some critics of the institutions.[688] To give lawyers a leg up, the National Science Foundation (NSF) has awarded a $500,000 for LawMeets, an online training program for rookie attorneys.[689]

Giving students a chance to act like business lawyers, LawMeets presents them with a real-world legal problem, such as how to manage executive pay.[690] Students record three-minute videos of themselves responding to the situation, and they vote on their colleagues' videos.[691] The highest-rated answers get expert legal reviews and advice.[692]

"You get to actually see what you look like. It really gives you a great way to make sure that what you think you're saying is what you're actually saying," one student said of his experience with LawMeets.[693]

To date, the company that started LawMeets – ApprenNet – has received $680,000 from NSF.[694] It plans to expand its online platform into K-12 education and the restaurant industry.[695]

While practice as a lawyer may be valuable in the law community, a product that is valuable to rising attorneys should be funded privately and science dollars saved for advancing higher-priority research endeavors.

58) Missile defense agency begins building interceptors before research is complete, costs skyrocket – (Department of Defense) At least $1 billion

Missile defense may be a necessary component to our national security, but a high-risk, unrealistic acquisition strategy has increased the cost of one system by more than $1 billion.

In 2002, the Missile Defense Agency (MDA) was created to rapidly field and update numerous missile defense systems. In its first decade, the MDA spent over $80 billion developing the Ballistic Missile Defense System.[696] [697]

In order to meet an unfeasible development schedule, however, the agency used a risky, haphazard "concurrent" acquisition strategy. Under the strategy, production of new weapons systems begins before design and testing are complete.[698]

For the missile defense system, the strategy has led to "performance shortfalls, unexpected cost increases, schedule delays, and test problems," according to a Government Accountability Office (GAO) review.[699]

Development of the missile defense system's ground-based midcourse defense (GMD) component illustrates the pitfalls of the concurrent strategy as the program's costs have exploded, and completion has been greatly delayed.[700]

In the early 2000s, MDA began producing a first-generation GMD before the agency had finished research and development on the weapons. As a result, MDA put interceptors into silos "although it had little of the [testing] data, such as interceptor reliability, that it would normally have had fielding a system."[701] The interceptors failed a number of flight tests, and MDA "could not determine the root causes of the failure," according to a GAO review.[702] "GMD was unable to assess the [interceptor] against countermeasures."[703] To make the already-produced interceptors effective, MDA has begun retrofitting them at the cost of at least $14 million each.[704] Currently, there are 30 GMD interceptors fielded in Alaska and California.[705]

MDA failed to learn from its experience with the first-generation interceptors, unfortunately. Before completing the development of the first-generation interceptors, MDA ordered a second generation of interceptors – once again beginning production before research and testing was finished.[706] MDA "prematurely committed to production before the results of [GMD] testing were available," GAO said.[707]

The newer generation has also failed in a number of key tests, even though 12 new interceptors have already been produced at the cost of $421 each.[708] MDA has not yet corrected the issue. After the agency discovers what is wrong with the interceptors, it will have to spend at least $18 million per weapon to make them functional.[709] Unfortunately, future

Launch of the ground-based midcourse defense interceptor

flight tests will continue to increase costs. GAO also found the cost of "flight testing has increased from $236 million to about $1 billion dollars due to the flight test failures."[710]

Due to the concurrent acquisition strategy, the Ground-based Midcourse Defense's newer interceptors alone have cost the taxpayers well over $1 billion more than originally planned.[711] MDA will continue to use the risky development method, accepting the risk that new issues "may require costly design changes and retrofit programs to resolve."[712]

After GAO has repeatedly highlighted the programs of the concurrent strategy, DOD's action plan does "not appear to consistently address the implications for concurrency in the future."[713]

59) Arcade-style floormats for gym class – (CA) $90,750

Some California students will soon be lighting up during their gym classes. The Gateway Unified School District in Northern California plans to spend $90,750 in federal funds to purchase high-tech exercise gaming equipment that seems more at home in an arcade than a school.[714]

Three 10' x 10' LED "Lightspace Play" floormats will comprise the bulk of the purchase.[715] Each device costs $22,500.[716] The floormats have clear tiles that are sensitive to the motion of children (and fun-loving adults), and they have a number of preprogrammed games. In one game, players walk around trying to stomp on certain colored dots, which move about the floor until they are tromped on. Another game forces players to avoid touching unlit tiles.

The district will also purchase three $7,750 "3 Kick" games, a device composed of three towers that light up in various places.[717] Players kick and hit the lights to gain points.

The goal is to "get the kids moving…Our [goal] is to get their heart rates up," said the director of the district's gym program.[718]

Meanwhile, the district's superintendent noted some local parents may object to such an extravagant purchase. The federal grant had to go to this specific purpose, he said, so none of the funding was at his disposal.[719]

After the editorial editor of the local paper realized the federal application required the district to spend the money on the flashy equipment, he wrote, "[It's] a great place to start cutting the federal budget."[720]

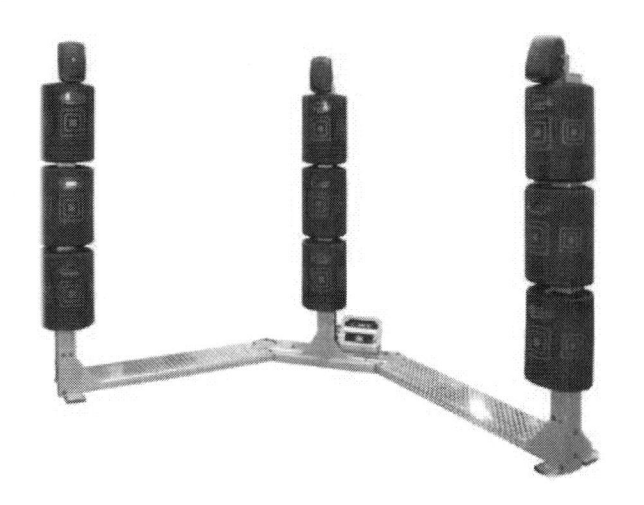

60) Department of Energy offered cash reward to create app that already exists – (Department of Energy) $100,000

The Department of Energy (DOE) launched a contest offering $100,000 in prizes for development of mobile phone apps allowing users to track their home energy usage.[721] Yet, the agency was looking for an app that already exists.

The government contest – Apps for Energy – rewarded developers for apps that use consumer data from utility companies and other sources to show users how much energy they are using. Apps are also supposed to track goals users set, according to the agency's rules for the contest.[722]

Private application developers have long sought to develop the next big app that targets the needs of consumers. Energy tracking is no exception. Using data from utility companies, one program – Opower – already allows consumers to tap into their energy usage data and to create an energy plan.[723] Users can compare their usage with that of their peers on Facebook.[724] Other apps are able to track energy consumed by specific light switches and outlets and even turn them off.[725] "EnergySaver," "Energy Tracker," "U-Tracker," and "SD Energy" all provide consumers with energy-tracking options.[726]

Instead of investing taxpayer dollars in this project, the department should let the marketplace determine the best apps for consumers. Maybe Uncle Sam needs to develop an app to track duplicative government apps.

61) How not to flip a house: renovate with federal funds and sell far below market value – (NY) $18,410

The City of Ogdensburg, New York, renovated two area houses using money from the federal Neighborhood Stabilization Program (NSP), but then sold them at an enormous loss.

This year, the city spent $18,410 for these and other renovations as part of a $250,000 federal grant used for both improvements to and demolitions of blighted structures.[727][728]

Renovations of one of the program's five houses cost $80,000 in total.[729] Yet, the city was only able to sell the house for $51,000.[730] Despite the high amounts spent on renovation, city councilors criticized the contractor for shoddy work. "I thought the paint job was terrible," said one.[731] "I can't imagine who was paying for it. I know the person interested in buying the house is complaining to me that he has 15 to 16 floor jacks in the cellar, so many he can barely walk down there. The cellar is useless to him now."[732]

Another small house cost $105,000 in federal and state funds to renovate, but was sold for only $42,000.[733] The firm responsible for the city's housing program neglected to survey the property before renovation, and as a result could not add a driveway, even though the house is located on a steep hill.[734]

Unfortunately, the city council's troubles with the properties did not end with the careless work.

NSP required at least 25 percent of the grant to be spent on renovation projects that met extremely specific requirements. According to one of the city councilors, however, none of these requirements were explained to the council when they signed up the program.[735] "[T]he

This house cost $105,000 to renovate, but was sold for only $42,000. The city neglected to survey the property prior to the renovation and a result a driveway could not be added because the house is located on a steep hill.

program was extremely rushed and under the gun, and unfortunately things fell through the cracks," he said.[736]

For example, eligible properties had to be owned by the city, and after renovation, had to be sold at their appraised value. For some properties, the family that benefitted from the project had to be an appropriate size for the structure and have an income below the area's median income. The city was also required to provide some funds for the purchase of the homes.[737]

Though Ogdensburg is a city of over 11,000 people, due to the highly restrictive program rules, city officials found only one interested buyer eligible for each property.[738] Anxious to be done with the debacle, the city council quickly approved the sales.[739] In the case of one the sold homes, the family paid only $198 per month, and the city covered the remainder of the cost.[740]

"This is a nightmare," said the city's deputy mayor. "We weren't told that we would have to give the property away."[741]

The city is still not free from this "nightmare" federal program. Contrary to the city council's desire, the money from the sales cannot go to the city's general fund. Instead, it must remain in the city's Neighborhood Stabilization Program, where it must be spent in compliance with program rules.[742]

The official in charge of the program has noted that "the best thing the city can do is to get out of this program and be done."[743]

62) A gateway arch on an Oregon Main Street – (OR) $15,000

The United States Department of Agriculture (USDA) awarded $15,000 in federal funds for the construction of a gateway arch at the entry point of the Cottage Grove Historic District in Oregon.[744]

Made possible by the USDA's Rural Business Enterprise Grant, the project was pursued by community leaders for years, who hoped to attract new patrons to local businesses.[745] They seek to revitalize the city's downtown area, and putting an arch to mark its entrance was among the best ideas of the community, which has a population of about 10,000.[746]

The gateway arch, however, ironically illustrates the gateway to wasteful federal grants. While intentions for the project were noble, the use of federal funds for a vanity project clearly is not.

63) Largest Job Corps contractor pays the highest bidder – (Department of Labor) $4.6 million

Government investigators have identified the U.S. Department of Labor's largest Job Corps contractor, Management and Training Corporation (MTC), as a prime case of waste, fraud, and abuse. MTC has been improperly awarding subcontracts to the highest bidders. Investigators scrutinized as much as $4.6 million of questionable costs.[747][748]

MTC is the nation's largest Job Corps contractor, managing and operating 19 job centers in 16 states.[749] Among its contracts, MTC operates the Paul Simon and Clearing Job Corps Centers in Chicago and Clearfield, Utah, respectively. Both centers improperly awarded about 80 percent of sub-contractor awards reviewed.[750][751]

Several of the questioned sub-contracts involved overpaying for medical services.[752][753] In multiple cases, after soliciting bids for physician and mental services, the centers selected the highest bids. The centers had lower-priced options to choose from and did not obtain required documentation to support choosing the higher-cost option.[754][755]

In another example, the city of Chicago contracted MTC Paul Simon for academic training provided to Job Corps students by a Chicago Public Schools System charter school program. For seven expenditures related to the training, the city of Chicago denied MTC Paul Simon's claims.[756] Although it had been denied by Chicago, MTC Paul Simon then improperly claimed the costs on reimbursement reports submitted to Job Corps.[757]

Unfortunately, every taxpayer dollar wasted by MTC is one that could be helping people train for gainful employment in the private sector.

WASTEBOOK 2012

64) Athletes' overseas vacations – (Department of State) $5.5 million

SportsUnited is touted by the Department of State as being the premier sports exchange program for what the department calls "sports diplomacy." Through this initiative, the Bureau of Educational and Cultural Affairs sends American professional athletes and coaches all around the world to "conduct drills, lead teambuilding sessions, and engage youth in a dialogue on the importance of education, health, and respect for diversity."[758] Taxpayers will spend $5.5 million on SportsUnited this year.[759] [760]

Since 2005, the United States has sent over 220 athletes to more than 50 countries.[761] Taxpayers have sent Major League Soccer player Tony Sanneh to Ethiopia, NBA players like Dikembe Mutumbo and George Gervin to Sudan and India, and a former WNBA star to China.[762] [763]

SportsUnited also brings athletes from other countries to the United States as part of their Sport Visitors program. The program has brought nearly 1,000 international visitors since 2003.[764] For example, the government paid for Tunisian swimmers' trip to the U.S. Olympic Swimming Trials this summer.[765] Taxpayer dollars also paid for track and field athletes to travel from the Caribbean to Oregon and beach volleyball players from Russia to southern California.[766] [767] [768] [769]

In our current fiscal climate, investing scarce resources in overseas trips for high-paid, jet-setting professional athletes should not be a high priority for the federal government.

65) Video game controller design – (UT) $1.5 million

A new video game controller being designed with taxpayer dollars might help players catch virtual fish, say researchers at the University of Utah. The new device, which has joysticks that move in response to actions in games, was designed with part of nearly $1.5 million awarded by the National Science Foundation.[770] [771]

Catching a virtual fish, for example, might cause the joysticks to jerk back and forth, mimicking the feel of a fish on a real-life fishing pole. Other possible movements include "recoil from a gun, the feeling of being pushed by ocean waves or crawling prone in a first-person shooter game."[772] As a quarterback in a football game, a player might sense he is about to get tackled.[773] The joysticks might also move to the beat of musical notes in games similar to Rock Band and Guitar Hero.[774]

Inspiration for the "multimillion dollar idea" came when the lead researcher on the project was playing video games to relax.[775]

With big aspirations, the developers are now seeking to coax the makers of video game systems like the Xbox and Playstation to purchase their taxpayer-funded product.[776] One of the team's researchers traveled to the Game Developers Conference to promote the new device to those who could potentially license the technology.[777]

66) Crime pays! Prisoners receive college tax credits – (Internal Revenue Service) $3.2 billion

A tax credit that is supposed to help Americans pay for college has been abused by millions of taxpayers not attending school, including at least 250 prisoners, according to the Inspector General (IG) in charge of monitoring tax collection.[778] This year, the scam may cost the country $3.2 billion.[779]

The American Opportunity Tax Credit was established in the 2009 stimulus package as a way to help people pay for undergraduate education.[780] Eligible taxpayers are able to receive a tax credit of up to $2,500.

The IG's analysis of 2.1 million claims for the credit found 1.7 million filers have received the credit for students even though they provided "no supporting documentation that they attended an educational institution."[781] Among those improperly receiving the credit were

At least 250 prisoners took advantage of a $2,500 education tax credit even though they had no documentation to show they were in college.

over 63,000 students double-counted as dependents or spouses, 250 prisoners, and 84,754 students who did not have valid Social Security numbers (SSN).[782] The Inspector General said to receive federal education aid, students generally must have valid SSNs, but for this tax credit, they did not.[783] Unfortunately, the IRS has no effective process in place to identify false claims.[784]

These 1.7 million claims are not a small portion of those seeking the credit. Rather, the IRS' own audit showed that by July 2011, over 72 percent of claims for the credit were erroneous.[785] What is more, IRS management has said "they expect the percentage found to be erroneous to further increase [in fiscal year 2012]."[786] Over half of the wrongful claims were submitted by professional tax preparers.[787]

The tax credit is available through 2012.[788] In a startling indictment of the waste in this credit, the Inspector General stated: "Over 4 years, erroneous claims for education credits could potentially reach $12.8 billion."[789]

67) "Make Chai, Not War": State Department sends American comedy tour to India – (Department of State) $100,000

The Department of State paid for an American comedy group to make a seven-city tour across India called "Make Chai, Not War." The full cost to taxpayers was $100,000.[790]

Made up of three Indian-Americans, the tour sought to promote U.S. culture abroad, as part of the department's educational and cultural exchange program, which has an annual operating budget of $637 million.[791]

"The reason we decided to support this tour is because, among the things that they ["Make Chai, Not War"] are known for is their talk about religious tolerance, about the importance of breaking down prejudices, and about the positive experiences they had growing up as Indian Americans in the United States," the State Department spokesperson said.[792]

No joke: The State Department paid $100,000 to send an American comedy group on a seven-city tour of India.

Comedian Azhar Usman "got the crowd warmed up for the evening with his loud, boisterous, often risqué cracks on terrorism, desi aunties and —'at the risk of deportation'— on the U.S. government itself," according to one local news review of the show.[793]

Looks like this joke is on you, taxpayers.

68) Medicaid audit program costs more than it brings in – (Medicaid) $30 million

An audit program designed to identify overpayments in the Medicaid system costs more than it saves. As it looks for fraud and waste, the federal government is creating even more, producing a "negative return on investment" for taxpayers.[794]

Since 2005, the National Medicaid Audit Program (NMAP) has cost taxpayers at least $102 million and has only identified $20 million in overpayments.[795] Without significant changes, NMAP will waste over $30 million annually to perform audits.[796]

From 2009 to February 2012, 1,077 of the audits – 69 percent – that the program performed were unproductive.[797] The audits that were successful identified only a small number of overpayments, not enough to recoup the cost to run the program.[798]

The program's poor performance rests in the federal government's decision to use an incomplete set of payment data for audits, a Government Accountability Office (GAO) review found.[799] NMAP only uses a limited set of data taken from state sources, which undermines the program's ability to detect improper payments. GAO attributed NMAP's failure to detect more overpayments to this key decision.[800] In its review, GAO noted, "[O]fficials said that they were aware that the MSIS data had limitations for auditing and could produce many false leads."[801] NMAP directors assumed states would not want to provide their full data sets, though 13 out of 16 states surveyed by GAO were willing to provide them.[802]

Contractors hired to perform the audits also alerted officials running NMAP that they needed better data. In annual reports, contractors said the incomplete data was "not timely or accurate…Nevertheless, the [federal officials] continued to assign MSIS-based audits to contractors," according to GAO.[803]

Furthermore, NMAP's original audit methodology duplicated and hindered state efforts to detect overpayment.[804] The audits "were not well coordinated with states, and duplicated and diverted resources from states' program integrity activities," said GAO.[805] Though states often communicated certain federal audits were duplicative of state work, the federal program's contractor usually made no response.[806]

Medicaid auditors are redesigning the program, but have not "articulated how its redesign will address flaws in NMAP."[807]

69) County courthouse cameras violate constitutional rights – (AL) $500,000

Officials in one Alabama county used federal taxpayer dollars to purchase a surveillance system so advanced they cannot even utilize its full capabilities without violating constitutional rights.

Alabama officials finished the installation of 196 cameras in three county courthouses using $500,000 from the Department of Justice.[808] Each piece of equipment is capable of recording both video and audio in courthouse hallways, which is beyond the scope of a regular camera. Each camera is "capable of high-resolution images and could be manipulated to zoom in on text messages or computer screens as well as conversations between attorneys and their clients."[809] Because of the system's potential for eavesdropping, federal officials launched an investigation into its potential for trampling on citizens' right to privacy.[810]

The multi-month investigation concluded county officials had no intent to obtain illegal audio recordings when they purchased the equipment.[811] However, to avoid pesky constitutionality issues, the courthouse security team has decided to turn off the audio recording features of the system. A cheaper system without audio recording technology would have undoubtedly been a smarter investment and would not have infringed upon the privacy rights of courthouse patrons – or more importantly, our nation's right to fiscal responsibility.

70) Fruit fly beauty is fleeting – (MI; TX) $939,771

Male fruit flies are attracted to young females more than to older ones, according to academics funded by the National Institutes of Health (NIH).[812] Their research, published this year, found pheromones – one of the hormones produced in many species, including humans, that causes sexual attractiveness – wane in female fruit flies over time. As they age, they produce fewer pheromones, and as a result males try to mate with younger flies instead.

"Video of the encounter," researchers wrote, "showed that the male was much more attracted to the young fly."[813] Scientists "introduced a male fly into a chamber that contained two females – a young fly and an old fly."[814] Flies were even introduced to one another in the dark, so that males could not see which females they were approaching. Even still, younger females attracted the males more than the old ones did.

Researchers are attracted to more than studying the phenomenon in just fruit flies. "We want to examine the exciting possibility that the mechanisms underlying attractiveness are also conserved across species," one of the researchers stated.[815]

They have received more than $900,000 from the NIH over the last year, and several million over the last several years, in part for this project.[816][817][818] A $120,000 National Science Foundation grant also contributed to the project in years past.[819]

71) Gone with the wind: Loans to Rhode Island businesses – (RI) $3.4 million

In Rhode Island's capital city, taxpayer dollars have met anything but a providential fate. The city of Providence has been using part of its federal Community Development Block Grant (CDBG) to issue millions of dollars in risky loans. Now 25 percent of the program's loans, collectively worth $3.4 million, and are delinquent the city is actively trying to collect $1,365,660 from 11 businesses.[820]

The Providence Economic Development Partnership (PEDP) makes a point to fund businesses whose loan applications have been rejected repeatedly in the marketplace. It serves as a lender of last resort, which is certainly a questionable use of federal dollars that could be directly benefiting the poor. "[E]veryone who gets a loan from us has either been rejected by two banks or has been offered a loan that is not sufficient to do the

The Providence Economic Development Partnership used millions of dollars to issue risky loans to area businesses. Now 25 percent of the loans are delinquent.

project...our loans are very risky," the organization's executive director said of its operations.[821] Seemingly unfazed by his employer's reckless use of federal taxpayer money, PEDP's lawyer claimed when it comes to economic development, "It's no guts, no glory."[822]

One of Providence's city council members noted private financial institutions in the area might otherwise be more willing to make loans for local businesses, but currently they are "hampered by excessive regulatory policies."[823]

The city has targeted a number of businesses for loan repayment, including "Fatty McGee's Restaurant," "KO Shoe Company," and "Invictus Arc," all of which have since gone out of business.[824]

Not only has the program made several faulty loans, PEDP is under federal investigation for spending up to $1.5 million in federal funds on catering, limos, and marketing – expenses that are disallowed under federal rules – in the last few years.[825] For example, a marketing company developed an orange "P" for the city's branding using federal funds.[826] At the time, former Mayor David Cicilline, who now represents Rhode Island's 1st congressional district, oversaw the program.[827] On the hook for the money, Providence may have to repay taxpayers if the expenses are ruled ineligible.

CDBG funds are generally to be used for programs to benefit low- to moderate-income people, such as low-income housing and anti-poverty measures.

72) Electric vehicle tax credit increases the deficit without decreasing emissions – (Taxes) $74 million

Going green has taxpayers seeing red.

A federal income tax credit created to encourage the purchases of electric vehicles will have "little or no impact on the total gasoline use and greenhouse gas emissions of the nation's vehicle fleet" in coming years, according to an analysis by the nonpartisan Congressional Budget Office (CBO).[828] Through 2019, the credit may cost taxpayers $2 billion, including $74 million this year.[829] So while the new tax credit will increase the deficit, it will most likely do little if anything to decrease emissions. CBO projects there may be benefits but is unsure how cost-effective they would be.[830]

Created by the 2009 stimulus bill, the nonrefundable federal tax credits of $2,500 to $7,000 are available to those who purchase new electrics vehicles.[831] The first 200,000 electric

WASTEBOOK 2012

A federal tax credit for electric cars will cost the government billions in coming years, though it will not decrease nationwide gasoline consumption or emissions, an independent analysis by the nonpartisan Congressional Budget Office concluded.

cars sold by any automaker qualify for the credit, which has "no expiration date" and "no limit on the number of eligible vehicle manufacturers."[832] Even with the tax benefit, electric cars still have higher lifetime costs than traditional hybrid or conventional vehicles.[833]

Because of other federal regulations intended to increase our nation's overall fuel efficiency, the impact of the tax credit is limited. As car manufacturers sell more electric cars, "the more low-fuel-economy vehicles that automakers can sell and still meet" federal fuel standards.[834] The federal government sets corporate average fuel economy (CAFE) standards that automakers must meet based on which types of cars they sell in a given year.[835]

CBO also found the credit has a limited impact on electric car sales. "CBO estimates that about 30 percent of current and future sales will be attributable to the tax credits, and 70 percent would have occurred even without the credits."[836]

Beyond this complication, CBO noted the incentive may "effectively subsidize the release of additional greenhouse gas emissions" in some situations.[837] For example, a person may buy an electric car instead of a traditional hybrid and live in an area where electricity is generated by coal-fired power plants. In that case, "more emissions are released per mile traveled on electric power than per mile traveled on gasoline."[838] Coal-fired power plants generate half of the country's electricity.[839]

Another concern about the low cost-effectiveness of the credit is some cars will not be driven often, CBO found. "Because [all-electric vehicles] are unlikely to be driven as extensively as other vehicles, they produce smaller reductions in emissions, and consequently, the government's cost for those reductions is higher."[840]

Changing the value of the tax credit would not improve the efficacy of the tax credit in the short-run, according to CBO's analysis.[841] Furthermore, while changes to the incentive may have some long-term benefits, other federal policies could meet the same objectives "at a lower cost to the federal government than the tax credits for electric vehicles could," CBO concluded.[842]

73) Smuttynose brewery gulps down taxpayer dollars for sewage connections – (NH) $750,970

A New Hampshire brewery, Smuttynose, will use $750,970 in federal funds to construct a new brewery and restaurant on farmland outside of Portsmouth.[843][844] The taxpayer money will help the brewery purchase three brew tanks and install sewer connections to its 42,000-square-foot facility.[845][846]

Smuttynose crafts a variety of beers, including Shoals Pale Ale, Old Brown Dog Ale, Finestkind IPA, and Robust Porter. The brewery's success has been astounding. Annual revenues are well over $5 million, and one popular beer-ranking website has even listed the maker on a top 100 list.[847][848]

Part of the brewery's federal funding comes from the Community Development Block Grant, among whose primary purposes is to help alleviate economic hardship for low- to moderate-income people, especially through housing and anti-poverty programs.

Construction on the new facility, which will cost $16 million, will finish in late 2012.[849] As the federal safety net is in danger and our country faces a fiscal crisis, taxpayers do not need to be contributing to

Part of Smuttynose's new brewery, which is financed by over $750,000 from the federal government.

an already-successful brewing business.

74) So you think you can dance? Dancing robot serves as an iPhone DJ – (GA) $547,430

Robot servants may no longer only belong to the Jetsons. Using taxpayer dollars, an academic team developed a dancing robot named Shimi to serve as a disc jockey for smartphones.

Shimi "is designed to change the way that people enjoy and think about their music," said its creator.[850] When a smartphone is connected, Shimi "gains the sensing and musical generation capabilities of the user's mobile device."[851] More than the average robot, Shimi can also "[dance] to the rhythm" of the music. Shaped like a small pet, Shimi shakes its speakers and moves a mechanical foot to groove. The robot's camera will sense a person's movement and turn its speakers to face the listener.

In a commercial for the device, one of the robot's developers said, "[Shimi] doesn't just play your music, it actually listens to it and enjoys it as much as you do."[852]

Shimi can also select songs from a phone's music library based on a person's clapping or tapping. Shimi can recommend songs based on user choices, a feature already available in applications such as Apple's iTunes.[853]

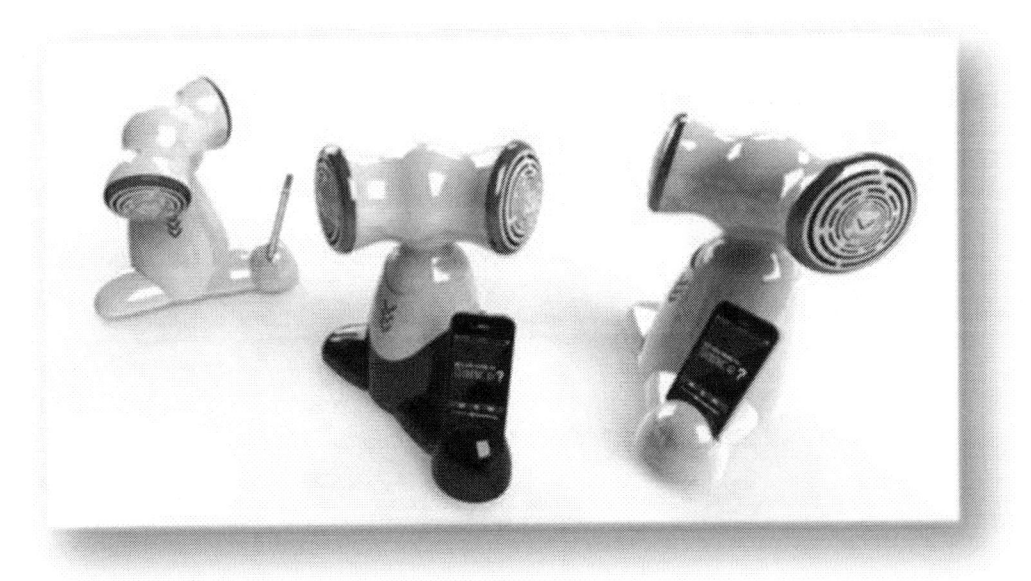

Created with taxpayer funds, "Shimi" will dance and DJ using an iPhone's song library.

Developers expect Shimi to work with apps for gaming, telepresence, and education in the future.[854]

This "musical buddy" was developed using part of a $547,430 grant from the National Science Foundation.[855] The research team is looking for more funding and attempted to raise private support on a crowdsourcing site.[856] They plan to sell Shimi for $199.[857]

75) Healthy Food Financing Initiative pursues ineffective strategy – (Department of the Treasury; Department of Health and Human Services) $32 million

Tens of millions of federal dollars are being spent to increase access to healthy foods in low-income communities. Motivating the initiative is the idea that access to healthy food leads to healthier eating. Unfortunately, a number of recent studies and investigations yielded no evidence that the strategy actually works. A review by the *Washington Post* found: "Multiple studies have scoured local, state and national data looking for a causal relationship between weight and access to healthy food. None has found it."[858]

Multiple government agencies will provide over $32 million in 2012 for the Healthy Food Financing Initiative (HFFI) – a program intended to expand access to healthy foods and fresh produce in some low-income communities.[859] Officials hope to lure grocery stores and farmers markets into the areas with federal loans, tax credits, and grants.[860] They are also handing out money to corner stores to purchase refrigerators for fruits and vegetables.[861]

Yet, at least two recent academic studies found no relationship between diet and proximity to grocery stores.[862] Policies promoting healthy food access have been tried before and shown to produce few results. A

15-year study of the relationship between food access and obesity rates came to similar conclusions.[863] "By promoting greater access to supermarkets, several U.S. policies aim to improve diets through provision of affordable healthy foods, particularly fresh produce in underserved areas. Our findings do not support this initiative in young to middle-aged adults. Rather, they suggest that adding neighborhood supermarkets may have little benefit to diet quality across the income spectrum."[864]

The U.S. Department of Agriculture (USDA) itself has questioned the value of such programs to promote access to health foods: "Increasing access to specific foods like fruits and vegetables, whole grains, and low-fat milk alone may not make a dent in the obesity problem…Without also changing the dietary behaviors of consumers, interventions aimed at increasing access to healthy foods may not be successful in addressing obesity."[865]

While there are many studies underway to determine the effectiveness of HFFI and other programs that target food deserts, it would seem prudent during a time of unprecedented budget deficits to ensure such programs are effective before implementing them on a large scale.

"My concern would be that we're investing in a strategy that may not be very promising," said one key researcher.[866] "If you're investing government money, you should carefully be evaluating how much you've invested and how much you're getting out of that."[867]

76) Exploring the nature of happiness with a philosophy booth – (NM) $24,995

New Mexico State University, Las Cruces received a $24,995 grant to develop a course titled, "Should we want to be happy?"[868] [869] The curriculum will focus on "the nature, value and means to obtain happiness."[870]

According to the project's leader, the course will question the happiness of the characters in Aldous Huxley's dystopian *Brave New World*, examine Plato's cave

Students at New Mexico State University will put up a "philosophy booth" using federal funds.

allegory in the *Republic*, and determine if the foundation for happiness is rooted in knowledge and virtue by covering Aristotle's *Nicomachean Ethics*.[871] The class will also watch and study the first "Matrix" film.[872] Students will set up a "philosophy booth" that will be used to question other students about the nature of happiness.[873]

The course was funded by the National Endowment for the Humanities' "Enduring Questions" grant program, which awards funds to applicants to use for a "question-driven course" that encourages people "to grapple with a fundamental concern of human life addressed by the humanities, and to join together in a deep and sustained program of reading in order to encounter influential thinkers over the centuries and into the present day."[874]

77) Antarctica science dollars go to anything but research – (Antarctica) $20.5 million[875]

For every day researchers spent in one of the U.S. Antarctic research centers, government contractors spent nine days working just to support the science studies.[876] Only one in five taxpayer dollars spent on the centers goes directly toward science projects.[877]

A high-level federal review of the $300 million U.S. Antarctic Program (USAP) found the program needed dramatic reforms to improve the use of taxpayer dollars on the world's coldest continent.[878] The recommendations drew on each of the panel members' experience at the Antarctic science centers.

Among their proposals is a reduction of contractor labor by 20 percent, which would save approximately $7.5 million annually.[879] The logistical support contract for the USAP is managed by Lockheed Martin and worth up to $2 billion.[880]

Additional savings could come through increasing researcher

National Science Foundation's McMurdo Station in Antarctica. The research program could save millions by reducing unused labor, veteran researchers say.

awareness of the true price of goods. Use of goods in the remote location is much more expensive than using them elsewhere in the world. "Considering all that is involved," the commission wrote in its report, "the true value of a gallon of fuel at the South Pole is, on average, nearly *eight* times its original purchase price" (emphasis original).[881] Consolidating flights to and around the continent could produce major fuel savings. One way to reduce fuel and personnel expenses would be to cut the number of flights across the continent and instead utilize ground-based vehicles that are partly automated. Making this switch alone would save over $13 million.[882]

The United States could draw on the experience of France, which realized "significant savings" by funding only the highest-priority projects, according to the commission.[883]

As some of the Antarctic research stations and equipment will soon need repair or replacement, reducing unnecessary costs will ensure essential operations can continue and remain uncompromised.

78) Potato chip pork – (NY) $49,990

What do Whoopi Goldberg and the U.S. Department of Agriculture (USDA) have in common? Both are big fans of taxpayer-subsidized potato chips.

The USDA awarded a nearly $50,000 Value Added Producer Grant (VAPG) to help New York's Martin Sidor Farms "revamp their marketing strategy to raise brand awareness and increase sales of their North Fork Potato Chips."[884] The grant will be used to update the company's website and brochures, and to engage the services of Slightly Mad Communications, a marketing firm, to boost sales.[885]

The "thick-cut, hearty kettle-cooked morsels" – cooked in sunflower oil, come in six varieties: regular, sweet potato, barbeque, sour cream and onion, cheddar and onion, and cheddar.[886] The chips have received rave reviews from several celebrities.[887] Online sales of the chips took off when they were named the "official snack of the day" on The Rachel Ray Show. Whoopi Goldberg has also heaped praises on them, buying out one local retailer's supply of the North Fork chips in Manhattan's West Village, according to the company's website.[888]

Despite the popularity of the chips, the federal government apparently thought they needed taxpayer support.

Sidor Farms is one of 298 recipients receiving a total of $40.2 million in assistance through the VAPG grants.[889][890]

79) Duplicate magazine preservation – (OK; RI) $270,000

In 2012, the Modernist Journals Project, a joint venture administered by Brown University and the University of Tulsa, was awarded $270,000 in federal funds from the National Endowment for the Humanities (NEH).[891] The award was for the creation of "a digital archive of a group of important early 20th-century American periodicals."[892]

The once-popular *McClure's* magazine will be among the magazines digitized, though much of it is already available for free online at Google Books. Researchers will also archive *The Masses*, *The Smart Set*, *Camera Work*, and *The Seven Arts*.[893] Need for federal funds to undertake the work is questionable, however. Thanks to the work of libraries and hobbyists, the magazines are also available on the Internet at repositories such as Archive.org, Google Books, and Project Gutenberg.

A total of $972,208 has been awarded to this project over the last nine years.[894] Between

2003 and 2010, the universities were given three grants totaling $615,373 to digitize early twentieth-century magazines.[895] Additionally, in 2009, a separate grant for $86,835 was awarded to the University of Tulsa and used for a four-week "seminar for sixteen participants to explore the 'golden age of magazines.'"[896]

Preservation of periodicals for educational enrichment is certainly a noble cause, but many of these are already digitally available. Is it truly a priority for federal taxpayers in a time of mounting deficits and debt?

80) Flat tire: Agriculture Department awards grant to billion-dollar tire company – (OH) $6.9 million

The U.S. Department of Agriculture (USDA) awarded the Cooper Tire and Rubber Company nearly $7 million for the development of natural rubber tires using guayule.[897]

Guayale is a plant native to the American Southwest and Mexico, with a long history as a natural rubber alternative.[898] Cooper Tire will work with academic and government researchers and the Yulex Corporation, a developer of natural rubber products including condoms, latex free gloves, and other medical supplies.[899] [900]

Research, development and commercialization of guayule-derived natural rubbers has gone on for more than a century, including during World War II and again during the 1970s oil crises, a history making the grant particularly questionable.[901]

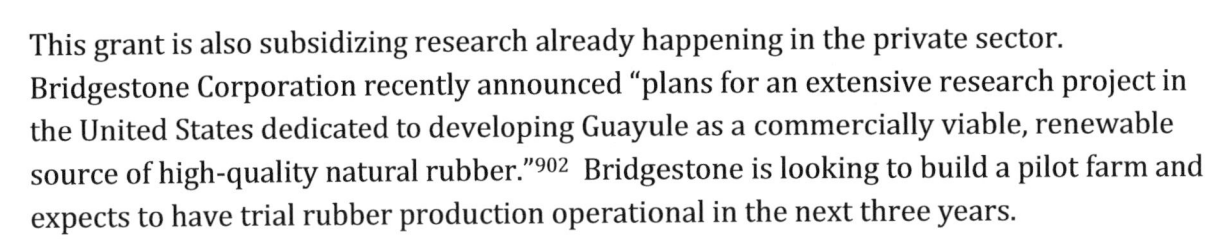

This grant is also subsidizing research already happening in the private sector. Bridgestone Corporation recently announced "plans for an extensive research project in the United States dedicated to developing Guayule as a commercially viable, renewable source of high-quality natural rubber."[902] Bridgestone is looking to build a pilot farm and expects to have trial rubber production operational in the next three years.

81) Highways funds go to bronze sculptures rather than rusty bridges – (IA) $145,000

There are 78 structurally deficient bridges in Iowa, yet the state is spending thousands of dollars of federal transportation funds to pave the way for a sculpture garden rather than fixing the state's bridges.[903]

The sculpture garden will be located in the town of Waterloo, Iowa, and will be dedicated to former resident Lou Henry Hoover, the wife of 31st U.S. President Herbert Hoover.

The town recently added a statue of Mrs. Hoover "on the corner of West Fourth and Washington, the former site of Hoovers' home," which will be relocated within the park.[904] This existing bronze statue completed in 2004, shows "Hoover as a child with her dog back-to-back with her adult image."[905] A new bronze statue of Mrs. Hoover will be added.[906]

The garden will feature the various sculptures of the first lady as well as landscaping and sidewalk enhancements, paid for in part with $145,000 of federal transportation enhancement funds.[907] In addition, "three 7-foot-tall, three-sided limestone pillars, or kiosks, would be located along the sidewalks and would have bronze plaques with information about Hoover."[908]

Of the total, $75,000 was allocated to pay for the artwork itself including "all artist fees, fabrication, shipping/transportation, travel to Waterloo, and installation costs."[909] The city expressed a hope that the "artwork and it[s] environs will serve as an outdoor interpretive

Federal transportation dollars are being spent to construct a sculpture garden in Iowa while Pennsylvania Avenue, our nation's "main street," has fallen into such disrepair it has been named an "endangered landscape."

visual reflection on the life and accomplishments Lou Henry Hoover…the first modern first lady."[910]

All work on the project was originally expected to be completed by September 30, 2011.[911] Initially there was no interest in the project when it was open to construction bids, but a contract was finally awarded in August.[912][913]

While taxpayers certainly respect and honor America's First Ladies, federal funds for roads, highways and bridges could be better spent ensuring the safety of roads and bridges.

Iowa is also home to the Herbert Hoover Presidential Library and Museum, which features a permanent gallery tracing the life and accomplishments of Lou Henry Hoover.[914]

Coincidentally, a sculpture garden dedicated to the former First Lady already exists. Lou Henry Hoover Park is located at the corner of Beverly and Norwalk Boulevards in Whittier, California. This park features a large sculpture that includes a young girl the city says "can either represent the young Lou Henry Hoover or a modern child gaining inspiration from the many accomplishments of the women of Whittier."[915]

82) Games for Change festival – (NY) $50,000

Can video games change the world for the better?

The National Endowment for the Arts gave $50,000 to fund the 9th Annual Games for Change Festival, a conference focused on "the creation and distribution of social impact games that serve as critical tools in humanitarian and educational efforts."[916][917] One featured game, Zombie Yoga, "uses Yoga and visualization to empower the player emotionally."[918] Another game puts players through life situations that would increase someone's risk for HIV.[919]

Workshops, networking, and speakers discussed how to design video games for the common good. One workshop, "Yourturn!: Designing a music game for social impact," focused on using "social interaction and identity construction among youth minority groups in Vienna, Austria."[920] "Game-o-matic: A tool for generating journalistic games on the fly" helped journalists think about news "as systems rather than as stories."[921] Another workshop featured Deepak Chopra, a popular public speaker on spirituality who discussed his Nintendo Wii video game designed to connect people to "their own internal power to be happy."[922]

Wastebook 2012

"Zombie Yoga" – a game to help people learn yoga to empower them emotionally – was advertised by taxpayer-funded Games for Change Festival.

This year's festival was billed to be "bigger than ever," and acquired significant private support from companies and foundations, including Microsoft and the Entertainment Software Foundation.[923][924] General admission for the event, which was held in New York City, cost $330-$550.[925] Though its goals are laudable, the federal funding directed to this festival would have been better spent providing direct help to the poor, such as antiretroviral drugs for many HIV patients on waiting lists for drugs from the Ryan White program.[926]

83) Mobile app industry gets a free download – (UT) $1 million

The U.S. Department of Commerce provided $1 million to Ogden City, Utah, to create a "Mobile App Lab."[927] The "lab" will include a "code shop operated by the Weber State University Research Foundation, a training center, and office space from high-tech start-ups."[928] Some hope the lab will "inspire entrepreneurs to get creative in their application development."[929]

With the spread of iPhones, tablets, and other portable devices, developers are rushing into the wireless sector in hopes of creating the next big app. Since the start of 2008, more than 30

114

billion mobile phone apps have been downloaded onto iPhones.[930] At a time of trillion dollar deficits, it makes little sense to spend money in an economically thriving industry and force future generations to fund the next Instagram or Angry Birds.

84) Los Angeles Harbor touring yacht gets new engines – (CA) $489,000

The Port of Los Angeles will be spending nearly half a million dollars in energy efficiency funds to upgrade its tour yacht's engines.

The Port uses the 73-foot *Angelena II* to provide tours, lasting 60 to 90 minutes, of the Port of Los Angeles facilities for up to forty guests. The yacht provides several hundred tours a year "to highlight the capabilities of the Port facilities to customers, constituents, public leaders, foreign dignitaries, media and stakeholders."[931]

The mayor of Los Angeles insisted, "It's not a yacht. It's a boat," but several boat insurance providers state boats are generally considered to be 26' or smaller, and yachts are considered to be 27' or larger.[932] [933]

Two 350-horsepower diesel engines that had powered the yacht no longer met strict California emissions standards. To meet the requirements, the Port used the federal funds

The Port of Los Angeles' 73-foot yacht, used at times for VIP cruises and business prospects, received two new engines this year paid for with federal funds.

to retrofit the tour boat with "a hybrid propulsion system that will reduce emissions and fuel usage by more than 95 percent."[934]

The Port will use a total of $489,000 from the Department of Energy to pay for the retrofit.[935] [936]

Officials argue the boat is mostly used for business and official purposes, but two years of the ship's log show guests included screenwriters from Universal Studios, members of the exclusive Jonathan Club, and dozens of the mayor's interns.[937]

Nevertheless, the Port maintains the yacht is an important tool to attract business, stating it is used to educate current and future customers. "The *Angelena II* has also been used to assist Port tenants in their business development efforts, helping showcase their cargo terminals to customers that bring additional revenues to the Port."[938]

If the yacht actually attracts business, however, it would seem more logical for the Port and the tenants financially benefiting from the vessel to pay for it. The Port contributed only $200,000 of its own money to pay for the retrofit.[939]

85) A novel idea taxpayers will not want to read about – (CA) $35,000

Many readers are increasingly going high tech, switching from paperbacks and hard cover books to e-books that can be read on Kindles and Nooks. The Fullerton Public Library in California, however, is going a different direction, spending thousands of dollars to install a vending-style book machine at a train station just blocks from the library.

The book machine is intended to provide more convenient access to books for commuters. The Fullerton Public Library used "a $35,000 federal grant to install the machine, which will include a drop box for returns and a selection of about 500 books for checking out."[940] [941] The vending machine "is believed to be the first of its kind in Orange County," and the library director says the project is "kind of an experiment for us."[942]

Fullerton Public Library is spending a lot of money these days on gadgets and other projects rather than books. It recently underwent a $10 million renovation and expansion that added thousands of square feet of space. The library also installed a solar power system, which "was funded through an Energy Efficiency and Conservation Block Grant from the U.S. Department of Energy, which is part of the American Recovery and Reinvestment Act."[943]

The newly renovated library is a short walk from the SOCO West Parking Structure, where the new book vending machine is located. It only takes about nine minutes to stroll the four blocks between the two locations.[944]

"On any given workday, an average of 3,000 commuters travel through the Fullerton Transportation Center," according to the city.[945] With Nooks selling from $90 each and Kindles from $70, up to 500 Orange County commuters could have been provided these reading devices.[946] The paperback editions of many of the great literary classics—such as *Hamlet*, *Great Expectations*, *Black Beauty*, and *The Great Gatsby*—are selling for less than $10 on Amazon, meaning that for the cost of the book machine, every commuter could have been given a gift card to purchase the book of their choice.

The 3,000 daily commuters who travel through the Fullerton Transportation Center could have been provided with a paperback edition of the literary classic of their choice with the $35,000 spent for this book vending machine.

Encouraging reading by providing easier access to books is a noble goal, but spending tens of thousands of dollars on a costly vending machine is probably not what taxpayers want to read about.

86) The 2012 Alabama Watermelon Queen Tour – (AL) $25,000

The Alabama Watermelon Queen went on a tour this year with some financial assistance from the U.S. Department of Agriculture (USDA).[947][948] The state allocated $25,000 in federal funds to the Alabama Watermelon Association "to promote the consumption of

Alabama's watermelon through appearances of the Alabama Watermelon Queen at various events and locations."[949][950]

The queen serves as the association's spokesperson and educates those she encounters "about the many benefits of watermelon and all the interesting facts including how to pick the perfect melon!"[951] The queen is "a paid public relations representative" and is selected annually as part of a competition.[952]

The 2012 queen was crowned at the association's annual conference held earlier this year at the Beau Rivage Resort & Casino. Four beautiful contestants participated in evening gown and seed-spitting competitions to win the crown.[953]

Throughout the year, the Watermelon Queen made "appearances at Welcome Centers, Supermarkets, Parades, Festivals, Schools, TV Interviews, as well as many other functions" to promote the watermelon industry.[954] The queen may "turn up anywhere" during her "12-month reign — trade shows, fairs, schools, corporate events, in grocery stores doing watermelon promotions and even on Capitol Hill helping industry lobbyists carry their concerns to member of Congress."[955] The 2012 queen attended the Florida Watermelon Convention in Tampa, Florida, and a "queen-training weekend" in Naples, Florida, with other watermelon queens representing nine states.[956][957]

In addition to the funds for the Alabama Watermelon Queen promotional tour, USDA also provided taxpayer funds to "various events, billboards, workshops, and radio/television

The Alabama Watermelon Queen's promotional tour was paid for in part with $25,000 from the U.S. Department of Agriculture.

promotions" to "increase the sales, price, and consumption of Indiana Grown watermelon" and "to educate consumers and trade members about North Carolina watermelon by sending" a representative of the North Carolina Watermelon Association "to in-state and out-of-state industry events."958

Americans love fresh watermelon, with "the value of watermelons for the fresh market" reaching $492 million in 2010.959 "Exceptionally warm weather throughout all of 2012 has brought watermelons to the market early, and growers in every region are ahead of schedule with abundant yields and a high-quality crop."960

87) Should grandparents play *World of Warcraft?* – (NC) $1.2 million

Soon, grandma may have to skip dinner to join her *World of Warcraft* guild in a dungeon raid. Researchers believe they have found another means to help our memories as we age: the "World of Warcraft," a fantasy video game featuring characters like orcs, trolls, and warlocks. The team of academics used part of $1.2 million in grants from the National Science Foundation to continue a video game study this year.961 962

Wow! Taxpayer-funded researchers study whether grandma and grandpa should play *World of Warcraft* – a game of warlocks, dungeons, and spirit healers – to exercise their cognitive skills.

The study asked 39 adults ages 60 to 77 to play "World of Warcraft" for two hours a day over two weeks.963 In the game, players choose a character and rove around the virtual world participating in guild (group) missions, casting spells, and defeating evil creatures. Millions of people around the world play, with the average player spending almost 11 hours per week playing.964

At the end of the two-week study period, researchers found no cognitive improvement in older people who already scored well on cognitive tests.965 People who started out with lower initial results, however, experienced some improvements.966

The group is also studying the Boom Blox, a puzzle and action video game for the Nintendo Wii. It is designed in part by Steven Spielberg and described as "blending the simplicity of the wildly popular block game *Jenga* and the crazy complexity of a Rube Goldberg machine."[967]

88) Abandoned New Orleans homes still on federal rolls seven years after Katrina – (LA) $21.6 million

As recently as October 2012, a federally funded program to help facilitate the sale of nearly 9,000 homes abandoned after Hurricane Katrina was still holding over 3,000 homes.[968] Over $21.6 million was spent in the last year to maintain the homes and administer the program, with $5.8 million remaining.[969] Since the program's creation, the federal cost has been over $200 million, much of it coming through the Department of Housing and Urban Development.[970]

The Louisiana Land Trust (LLT) was created in 2006 to help New Orleans and surrounding parishes manage thousands of derelict properties, many of which were destroyed or left in disrepair from the aftermath of Hurricane Katrina.[971] City and parish governments were

An empty lot held by the federally funded Louisiana Land Trust. Taxpayers have funded lots like this one for years.

supposed to find buyers in the neighborhoods and through auctions. LLT has almost run out of federal funds, yet it still maintains an inventory of over 3,000 homes.[972] New Orleans and other parishes will have to take ownership of unsold homes.

Since its inception, LLT has used at least $86 million to perform basic maintenance for "abandoned parcels" of land, which includes lawn-cutting, trash cleaning, and pest control.[973] Costs per lot total up to $100 per month.[974] In many cases, LLT is only maintaining an open space after demolishing existing homes that were beyond repair.[975]

Local officials have said they are not working to sell the homes because they do not want to hurt current housing prices.[976] Yet, some developers have noted officials have not been acting quickly enough. "How many years does it take them to do something?" asked Donald Vallee, a New Orleans developer and board member of LLT.[977]

Inaction has allowed blight to persist. One New Orleans local said several stolen or abandoned cars have been set on fire in these properties over the previous year. "Right now, it's an eyesore. It's not serving any purpose."[978]

Built on a poor foundation, this $200 million investment in real estate has left taxpayers with nothing but empty homes and open lots.

89) Healthy food: Celebrity chefs and high-tech vending machines – (FL) $612,808

In the name of increasing access to healthy food, healthy food vending machines costing $11,000 each are being installed in schools throughout Miami-Dade County.[979]

The machines are stocked with healthy lunch options such as wraps, salads, and fruit and yogurt parfaits. While the machines may be cool, there are more cost-effective ways to provide these healthy options to students, such as serving them from the regular cafeteria counters.

So why use the vending machines at all? "Students are very tech-savvy and love to text, punch in numbers and get things quickly," one school official explained.[980]

Many of the recipes were designed by local celebrity chefs such as Food Network's Michelle Bernstein.[981] Chef Bernstein described one of her gourmet recipes to a local television station: "It's a vegetable wrap and inside is cabbage and carrot sautéed with a little bit of curry sauce, and the wrap is actually brushed with a little mango chutney. And then we add a little grilled chicken and jasmine rice."[982]

The meals are made and packaged beforehand and loaded into the machines once during each lunch period.[983] Since the machines are cashless, students access them by punching in their student number and birth date, and "parents must set up an account beforehand."[984] A meal from the machine costs $2.50.[985]

Using federal funds, Miami-Dade County Public Schools purchased 56 vending machines at $10,943 each, for a total of $612,808.[986]

The rest of the $3 million federal grant used to pay for the machines will be spent implementing a wellness program and instituting a "farms at schools" program throughout the entire district. The program provides fresh farm foods for all of the district's school cafeterias, albeit without high-tech vending machines.[987]

Miami-Dade County Public School's grant came from a larger $14.7 million grant provided to the County Health Department through the Communities Putting Prevention to Work program at the Centers for Disease Control and Prevention, a creation of the 2009 stimulus bill.[988] Other expenses funded by the grant included bicycle racks, signage, shelters, and $1.9 million in payments to three marketing firms for television commercials, public service announcements, social marketing, and on-site event marketing.[989]

90) Vodka, bourbon, brandy for taxpayers – (NY) $99,000

Last year, Americans bought almost $20 billion of liquor, an increase of four percent from 2010.[990] Top-of-the-line vodkas and whiskeys saw the greatest sales increases at over 10 percent.[991]

In spite of the robust demand for alcoholic beverages, the U.S. Department of Agriculture awarded a $99,000 grant to the new Clayton Distillery Company – a New York distillery – in 2012.[992] The distillery hopes to get off the ground and start producing beverages by the end of the year. Using taxpayer money, owners plan to buy a copper still and stainless steel vodka column.[993] The distillery believes the grant will cover two-thirds of the equipment cost.[994]

Included in the distillery's line-up will be "vodka, gin, white whiskey, bourbon, fruit-flavored brandies, and maple liquors."[995] With its maple beverage in particular, the company hopes to appeal to Canadian tourists from across the border.[996]

The government grant gave the company an unfair advantage over its competitors. Roger Reifensnyder, owner of another new area distillery – Dark Island Spirits – said his business might never get started because of the grant to his future competitor.[997] He stated, "I think (the Clayton distillery) should pay a fair market value for the equipment they obtain so that we aren't at a competitive disadvantage."[998]

Making his opposition to the grant clear, he said, "I don't believe in public funding. We're doing it all ourselves."[999]

Taxpayer funds should not be used to advantage one company over another, nor should they be used to subsidize an industry that already enjoys wide market appeal.

91) How to build a farm in a galaxy far, far away – (TX) $300,000

The Department of Defense is literally shooting for the stars with federal funds, but it is not likely to reach them anytime soon.

With $21,000 from the Pentagon, the 100-Year Starship organization hosted a September symposium for interstellar discussion.[1000] The focus of the gathering was to discuss how to

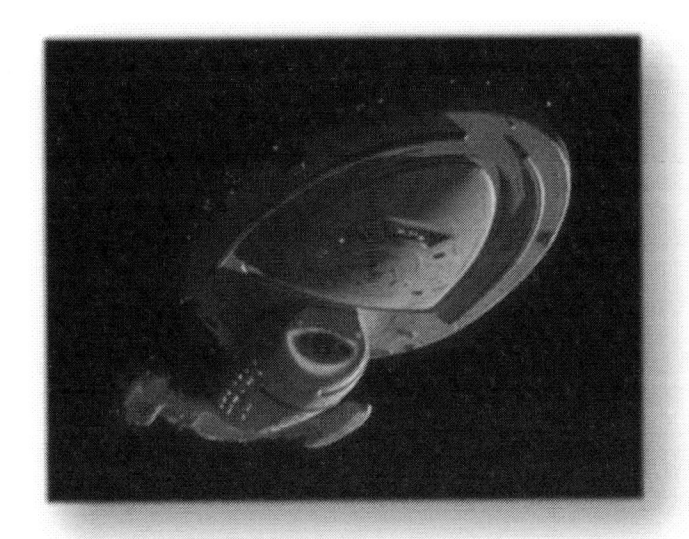

The 100-Year Starship organization used federal funds this year to run a conference on how to establish a civilization trillions of miles away in another solar system.

get a manned spaceship to a planet in another solar system within the next century – a goal described as "most grandiose ... at a time when only two nations – neither of them the United States, at least currently – can send humans into space."[1001]

Most of the sessions were out-of-this-world. Participants discussed very long-distance traveling that would take thousands of years, proposing either we need to create much faster spaceships or to manipulate space-time to accommodate our human needs.[1002] The ship would likely be propelled by a "warp bubble," but a scientist with the National Aeronautics and Space Administration (NASA) researching such a possibility cautioned "nobody should get excited at this point."[1003] He further noted the type of energy needed would costs tens of billions of dollars a gram to produce.[1004]

The conference examined a number of "issues that might otherwise be overlooked, like this simple but important one: what will interstellar explorers wear?"[1005]

A University of Rhode Island professor asked, "[C]an you really ask someone to dress in polos and khakis for 30 years?"[1006] He then suggested, "[W]e may need to rethink the idea of clothing altogether ... we might have to really reevaluate what constitutes being dressed or undressed."[1007]

Another topic, "Destinations and Habitats,"[1008] explored what it will mean to "design and construct residences, schools, offices, and farms that are more than 6 trillion miles from the nearest pine forest...feed, entertain, care for and govern the humans."[1009]

Still others discussed what was described as the "necessary political, economic, social and cultural shifts that will enable our transition from a 'near Earth' society into an interstellar civilization."[1010] One session questioned "what role, if any, religion should play on a multigenerational starship to identifying potential destinations for such missions."[1011]

"We might have to really reevaluate what constitutes being dressed or undressed" when it comes to interstellar travel, one presenter concluded, after pondering whether you can "really ask someone to dress in polos and khakis for 30 years."

"Many of the conference attendees might be best classified as enthusiasts: people interested in the concept of developing a starship, but have, at most, only ideas for research topics."[1012] As a result, it might be easy to confuse the symposium for a Star Trek Convention. In fact, former Trekkies Levar Burton and Nichelle Nichols made special appearances.[1013] The latter headlined an "intergalactic gala celebration."[1014] Attendees needed to wear "starship cocktail attire."[1015]

Overall, the gathering, which was held in a hotel in Houston, attracted 250 attendees, a sharp decline from the 700 who attended a similar conference held a year earlier.[1016]

This year, the 100 Year Starship Initiative will spend $300,000 of its $500,000 grant provided by the Defense Advanced Research Project Agency.[1017] To date, the Pentagon has spent over $1 million on the project.[1018]

Is this project a priority while we have over a $16 trillion debt?

92) Thirty-thousand Legos to build an 18-foot long model street – (WV) $3,700

Thirty-thousand Lego pieces, paid for with a $3,700 National Scenic Byways grant, are being assembled to build a miniature replica of a historic downtown street in Martinsburg, West Virginia.[1019] The 18-foot-long display will depict Queen Street as it likely appeared in the 1920s and '30s.[1020] It is expected to be a permanent exhibit at the "for the kids, by George" Children's Museum, which will showcase George Washington's "adventures in the Eastern Panhandle" of West Virginia.[1021] [1022] The museum is primarily funded with a $290,000 National Scenic Byways grant awarded by the Federal Highway Administration.[1023]

Thirty-thousand Lego pieces paid for with a $3,700 National Scenic Byways grant are being assembled to build an 18-foot-long display of Martinsburg, West Virginia.

With 2,593 structurally deficient or functionally obsolete bridges in West Virginia, federal transportation dollars would probably be better spent on real rather than toy roads.[1024]

93) Contracts for trophies and typewriters – (General Services Administration) $24 million

For years, the General Services Administration (GSA) has been awarding contracts to thousands of companies for outdated products like typewriters, trophies, photographic equipment, and commemorative items, even though most of the contracts produce little or no sales.[1025] The agency has not previously taken the time to determine which contracts it no longer should maintain.

GSA is now planning to eliminate contracts for unused products and hopes "directing scarce acquisition resources away from the more than 8,000 obsolete contracts – which each cost at least $3,000 per year to administer – will streamline the schedule process and save more than $24 million a year."[1026]

94) Summers studies of concubinage, *M*A*S*H*, and Mother Goose – (National Endowment for the Humanities) $498,000

The National Endowment for the Humanities (NEH) is funding over half a million dollars in summer stipends for scholars and teachers to examine a variety of projects, a large number of which range from the irrelevant to the bizarre.[1027]

Kalamazoo College received $6,000 in summer stipends to study "Priests and Concubines in England, 1375-1559."[1028] It will "examine both cultural perceptions of clerical concubinage and the lived experiences of priests, concubines, and their children in late medieval England."[1029] At Ohio University, a professor used $6,000 for her scholastic inquest into romantic literature and suicide in Britain.[1030]

And the list rolls on: $6,000 for a University of Illinois at Urbana-Champaign professor to lead a project titled "Music in the Films of Robert Altman: From *M*A*S*H* to *A Prairie Home Companion*" and another $6,000 was awarded to the University of Utah to lead a project titled "The Mother Goose Translation Project."[1031]

Though not a summer study, a grant to Franklin and Marshall College in Lancaster, Pennsylvania, may ironically provide the best example of misguided spending at NEH. Titled "Defining Moral Communities: Respect, Dignity, and the Reactive Attitudes," the $50,400 project addresses our nation's most pressing problem: the moral obligation to rein in the mounting debt and deficits by respecting the founding principles of a limited federal government.[1032]

95) Heavy drinking in thirties linked with immaturity – (MO) $548,731

For some, college partying never stops with age, and heavy drinking extends into post-graduate life. With part of $548,731 in grants from the National Institutes of Health (NIH), one group of researchers discovered adults in their thirties who drink heavily also feel immature.[1033]

A National Institutes of Health-funded study found people who drink heavily at age 29 view themselves as Peter Pans of partying.

At age 25, people are not likely to feel immature even when they drink significantly, the federally funded research found.[1034] They "are out at the bars with their friends and drinking is a bonding experience," one researcher said.[1035] "They also view blacking out, vomiting, and drunk driving as more acceptable because peers are behaving similarly."[1036] Only a few years need to pass before an age group's view of alcohol changes. "[B]y 29, when many of their peers have settled down, individuals who still drink heavily may start to view themselves as 'Peter Pans' of partying, who never fully matured."[1037]

Looking to explain the relevance of what seem to be obvious results, one of the study's co-authors stated, "When a heavy drinking 30-year-old comes in for therapy and says he doesn't feel like an adult, we can present this study and suggest that cutting back on alcohol could help him feel more mature."[1038]

96) Guns ablazin': USDA studies Idaho firearm industry – (ID) $24,877

A firearms business group in Idaho spent nearly all of a $25,000 grant from the U.S. Department of Agriculture (USDA) this year.[1039] The Idaho Firearms and Accessories Manufacturers Association (IFAMA) received the taxpayer funds to study the economic success of the Idaho gun

USDA awarded a $25,000 grant to an Idaho firearms association to study the success of the state's gun industry, where over half of households own a gun.

industry. The group said it also spent part of taxpayers' money on what amounted to a gun show.[1040]

IFAMA's report intends to boost the perception of the industry by giving information on how many jobs it creates in the state. Yet, in Idaho the firearms and accessories industry already supports thousands of jobs.[1041] Over half of the states households own a firearm, well above the national average.[1042] Gun sales nationwide have increased in recent years.[1043] The industry produces over $4 billion in revenue annually.[1044]

In September 2011, a two-day "conference" in Boise featured over 30 gun and accessory exhibitors "to show you their new services and products."[1045] The conference also had a number of sessions, including some in which companies were able to present their new firearm products and learn how to receive other government grants and loans.[1046]

The right to bear arms is guaranteed by the Constitution but government funding for the firearms industry is not.

97) Crazy for cupcakes! – (Small Business Administration) $2.0 million

Red Velvet, snickerdoodle, and cinnamon buttercream are cupcake flavors that are attractive not only to the paying consumer, but also to Uncle Sam.

The Small Business Administration in 2012 arranged over $2.0 million in loan guarantees for ten cupcake shops across the country.[1047] Taxpayers are on the hook for the loans if the businesses fail.[1048] To set up and finance the loans, taxpayers have already paid out $19,935.[1049]

Under the loan program, small businesses not "otherwise [able to] obtain financing under reasonable terms and conditions" are eligible to receive help from the government.[1050] These cupcake shops were no exception; they were "unable to obtain financing in the private credit marketplace," perhaps

Taxpayers are liable for almost $2 million in loans made to specialty cupcake shops this year.

surprising to many given the growing popularity of cupcakes.[1051]

"Smoky Mountain Cupcakes," "Heavenly Cupcake," and "Cupcake Station" all received thousands of dollars of taxpayer-backed loans.[1052] They offer customers products like "Brown-Sugar Pound Cupcakes," "Twisted Love," and Peanut Butter. [1053] [1054]

98) Over one billion served: federally funded smartphone research – (NY) $1.3 million

By 2016, over one billion people worldwide will own a smartphone.[1055] Even with a strong private sector incentive to make products as excellent as possible, the National Science Foundation (NSF) awarded $1.3 million for a study to test "the user experience, WiFi, 3G, and 4G performance, and even the performance of the operating system."[1056] [1057]

Using taxpayer dollars, researchers will give 200 students new Samsung Nexus S phones running Google's Android.[1058] The phones will come with one year of free, unlimited service from Sprint, who is donating the service to the study.[1059] After the one-year period ends, the students will pay a discounted rate of $44 per month.[1060]

A National Science Foundation-funded study will hand out hundreds of free smartphones to study how to make Google's Android operating system perform better. Google generated over $40 billion in the last year.

Students are supposed to use the free devices as their primary phones, and they will participate in a few hours of cell phone experiments monthly.[1061] Some of the experiments will be interactive, such as downloading apps and using them during the experiment.[1062]

While advancing cell phone technology and development may be helpful to consumers, research is better funded by private industry, which will be the primary beneficiary from future successes.

99) Construction of an agricultural and motorsports museum featuring a tribute to dirt track racing and a large toy train display – (IA) $300,000

A motorsports museum showcasing the "rich agricultural and motorsports history" in Kossuth County, Iowa, "through the display of key pieces of farm equipment, farm tools, and racing displays" was approved for a U.S. Department of Agriculture (USDA) grant in June. [1063] [1064]

A large toy train display will be among the features of the Kossuth County Agricultural & Motorsports Museum being constructed with the assistance of a $300,000 grant from USDA.

The Kossuth County Agricultural & Motorsports Museum will be built at the county fairgrounds. "When completed, the museum will contain tributes to agricultural history in Kossuth County, a tribute to the history of dirt track racing in the area, and also a large toy train display."[1065]

The $300,000 USDA grant will "help finance the construction" of the museum.[1066] Do our children have this money to spare?

100) D'oh! Postal Service overprints Simpsons and other commemorative stamps – (Postal Service) $2 million

The U.S. Postal Service (USPS) wastes $2 million in printing and manufacturing costs annually producing commemorative stamps that must later be destroyed.[1067] Several stamps series have been printed so excessively that had every person in the nation sent a piece of mail using them, there still would have been leftovers.

In 2009, the USPS printed one billion stamps commemorating one of television's most well-known families, the Simpsons.[1068] Homer, Marge, Bart, Lisa, and Maggie each received their own portrait.[1069] Sales were far below USPS' expectations, leaving managers to perhaps say "D'Oh!"[1070] In their first two years, only 318 million Simpsons stamps sold.[1071] This move alone wasted $1.2 million.[1072] "Nearly twice as many Simpsons stamps were printed

Wastebook 2012

In 2009, the U.S. Postal Service printed 1 billion Simpsons commemorative stamps, 700 million more than were needed.

than the most popular commemorative ever issued," according to the IG.[1073] An Elvis stamp issued in 1993 was the agency's most popular at 517 million sold.[1074]

Similarly, USPS overprinted one series of its "Flags of our Nation" collection in 2010, by 317 percent, producing 500 million and selling only 120 million in two years.[1075]

Other excessively printed stamps include the 2009 Lunar New Year (Year of the Ox), an angel playing a lute, Supreme Court Justices, and Zion National Park.[1076]

USPS picks several commemorative stamps series to produce each year. Among the 2012 series are "Wedding Cake," "Weather Vanes," "Bonsai," and "Aloha Shirts."

The IG concluded the USPS has no "objective forecasting methodology and review process" to determine demand for special stamps.[1077] In the past, one manager has used historical information and "personal professional expertise" to come up with a production figure.[1078] Of the 50 different stamps that USPS released in 2009 and 2010, it overprinted stock for 37 by an average of 34 percent.[1079]

Wedding Cake stamps are one of this year's commemorative series. Excess printing of commemorative stamps costs the agency $2 million annually.

The Postal IG recommends USPS limit the number of stamps initially produced for each series and increase promotion. By more accurately printing commemorative stamps, the agency would save $2 million in printing costs.[1080] Considering taxpayers are on the verge of spending billions to bail out the U.S. Postal Service again, any savings the agency can find are relevant.

APPENDIX

The House Appropriations Committee held 135 hearings in 2012, more than any other committee. With only two hearings this year, the Senate Rules and Administration had the fewest.[1081] By a wide margin, House committees have been far more active with hearings. The Senate Appropriations Committee conducted 49 hearings, more than any other committee in the upper chamber. However, almost half of the House committees held 60 or more hearings. Nine of the 10 committees with the fewest hearings in 2012 are Senate committees.

Congressional Committees Holding the Fewest Hearings in 2012[1082]

Rank	Committee	Hearings Held
1	Senate Rules and Administration	2
2	House Administration	3
3	Senate Small Business and Entrepreneurship	4
4*	Senate Aging	9
4*	Senate Agriculture, Nutrition, and Forestry	9
6	Senate Budget	12
7	Senate Indian Affairs	14
8	Senate Veterans Affairs	16
9*	Senate Environment and Public Works	19
9*	Senate Health, Education, Labor and Pensions	19

*tie

Congressional Committees Reporting Out and Discharging the Least Amount of Legislation in 2012[1083]

Rank	Committee	Bills and Resolutions Reported and Discharged
1*	Senate Small Business and Entrepreneurship	3
1*	House Small Business	3
3	Senate Intelligence	6
4	Senate Agriculture, Nutrition, and Forestry	7
5*	House Foreign Affairs	8
5*	House Intelligence	8
5*	House Science, Space, and Technology	8
8	Senate Indian Affairs	10
9*	House Education and Workforce	11
9*	Senate Finance	11

*tie

[1] Rugaber, Christopher. "US economy adds 96K jobs, rate falls to 8.1 pct.," *Associated Press*, September 7, 2012. Available at http://finance.yahoo.com/news/us-economy-adds-96k-jobs-123111662.html, accessed September 17, 2012.

[2] "Deficient Bridges by State and Highway System As of December 2011," Department of Transportation Federal Highway Administration website, http://www.fhwa.dot.gov/bridge/nbi/defbr11.cfm, accessed September 12, 2012.

[3] This sum is 10 percent of the budget formember, leadership, and committee offices.

[4] Davis, Susan. "This Congress could be least productive since 1947," *USA Today*, August 15, 2012. Available at http://www.usatoday.com/news/washington/story/2012-08-14/unproductive-congress-not-passing-bills/57060096/1, accessed September 14, 2012.

[5] Strong, Jonathan, and Humberto Sanchez. "Congress On Pace to Be Least Productive," *Roll Call*, September 13, 2012, http://www.rollcall.com/features/Guide-to-Congress_2012/guide/Congress-On-Pace-to-Be-Least-Productive-217538-1.html, accessed September 14, 2012.

[6] Newport, Frank. "Congress Approval Ties All-Time Low at 10%," Gallup, August 14, 2012, http://www.gallup.com/poll/156662/congress-approval-ties-time-low.aspx, accessed September 14, 2012.

[7] Newport, Frank. "Congress Approval Ties All-Time Low at 10%," Gallup, August 14, 2012, http://www.gallup.com/poll/156662/congress-approval-ties-time-low.aspx, accessed September 14, 2012.

[8] "Roll Call Tables," U.S. Senate website, http://www.senate.gov/pagelayout/legislative/a_three_sections_with_teasers/votes.htm, accessed August 30, 2012.

[9] As of September 1, 2012, the Senate has cast 189 roll call votes in 2012 and the House of Representatives has cast 556 recorded votes.

[10] "U.S. House of Representatives Roll Call Votes," U.S. House of Representatives website, accessed August 30, 2012; http://clerk.house.gov/evs/2012/index.asp.

[11] This statistics were derived by reviewing the list of legislation sponsored by senators listed under "Browse Bills by Sponsor" on the Library of Congress Thomas website. The status of each amendment submitted was reviewed. No action on each amendment could result from a variety of reasons including the sponsor not calling it up or being blocked from offering it.

"Legislation in Current Congress," Library of Congress THOMAS website, http://thomas.loc.gov/home/thomas.php, accessed September 20, 2012.

[12] *Congressional Record*, September 19, 2012, page S6420.

[13] Halper, Daniel. "'1,200 Days and $5 Trillion in New Debt Since Senate Dems Passed a Budget,'" *The Weekly Standard*, August 10, 2012. Available at http://www.weeklystandard.com/blogs/1200-days-and-5-trillion-new-debt-senate-dems-passed-budget_649673.html, accessed September 14, 2012.

[14] Halper, Daniel. "'1,200 Days and $5 Trillion in New Debt Since Senate Dems Passed a Budget,'" *The Weekly Standard*, August 10, 2012. Available at http://www.weeklystandard.com/blogs/1200-days-and-5-trillion-new-debt-senate-dems-passed-budget_649673.html, accessed September 14, 2012.

[15] See appendix. Hearings held by congressional committees in 2012, as of August 20, 2012, provided by the Congressional Research Service and compiled by the ProQuest Congressional database.

[16] By comparison, the House Budget Committee did produce a budget that was approved in that chamber and then voted down in the Senate, and held 20 hearings in 2012.

See appendix. Hearings held by congressional committees in 2012, as of August 20, 2012, provided by the Congressional Research Service and compiled by the ProQuest Congressional database.

[17] See appendix. "Browse Committees & Subcommittees with Legislative Action; The 112th Congress," Congress.gov website, http://www.congress.gov/billsumm/vwList.php?&lid=1#notes, accessed August 22, 2012.

[18] See appendix. Hearings held by congressional committees in 2012, as of August 20, 2012, provided by the Congressional Research Service and compiled by the ProQuest Congressional database.

[19] See appendix. "Browse Committees & Subcommittees with Legislative Action; The 112th Congress," Congress.gov website, http://www.congress.gov/billsumm/vwList.php?&lid=1#notes, accessed August 22, 2012.

[20] See appendix. Hearings held by congressional committees in 2012, as of August 20, 2012, provided by the Congressional Research Service and compiled by the ProQuest Congressional database.

[21] See appendix. "Browse Committees & Subcommittees with Legislative Action; The 112th Congress," Congress.gov website, http://www.congress.gov/billsumm/vwList.php?&lid=1#notes, accessed August 22, 2012.

[22] See appendix. Hearings held by congressional committees in 2012, as of August 20, 2012, provided by the Congressional Research Service and compiled by the ProQuest Congressional database.

[23] See appendix. "Browse Committees & Subcommittees with Legislative Action; The 112th Congress," Congress.gov website, http://www.congress.gov/billsumm/vwList.php?&lid=1#notes, accessed August 22, 2012.

[24] See appendix. Hearings held by congressional committees in 2012, as of August 20, 2012, provided by the Congressional Research Service and compiled by the ProQuest Congressional database.

[25] The Senate Special Committee on Aging was established in 1961 as a temporary committee and granted permanent status in 1977. While special committees have no legislative authority, they can study issues, conduct oversight of programs, and investigate reports of fraud and waste.
Senate Special Committee on Aging website, http://aging.senate.gov/about/index.cfm, accessed August 30, 2012.

[26] See appendix. "Browse Committees & Subcommittees with Legislative Action; The 112th Congress," Congress.gov website, http://www.congress.gov/billsumm/vwList.php?&lid=1#notes, accessed August 22, 2012.

[27] See appendix. Hearings held by congressional committees in 2012, as of August 20, 2012, provided by the Congressional Research Service and compiled by the ProQuest Congressional database.

[28] The NFL and NHL received about $260 million in membership dues from their teams in 2010, the last year for which information is available. Applying the 35 percent corporate tax rate to these earnings would generate about $91 million in tax revenue. Any amount of league revenue spent on lobbying is already taxed. It is unclear how other league revenue streams would be affected, including the PGA's $300-million-plus television earnings. Full financial information about each league is unavailable, making estimates difficult.

[29] 2010 IRS Form 990 filed by the National Football League.

[30] 2010 IRS Form 990 filed by the National Football League.

[31] Daly, Dan. "Another Way to Look at the NFL's $9 Billion In Revenue," *Washington Times* Daly OT Blog, February 24, 2011, http://www.washingtontimes.com/blog/daly-ot/2011/feb/24/another-way-look-nfls-9-billion-revenue/, accessed August 6, 2012.

[32] Badenhausen, Kurt. "The World's 50 Most Valuable Sports Teams," Forbes.com, July 16, 2012, http://www.forbes.com/sites/kurtbadenhausen/2012/07/16/manchester-united-tops-the-worlds-50-most-valuable-sports-teams/, accessed September 10, 2012.

[33] 2010 IRS Form 990 filed by PGA Tour, Inc.

[34] 2009 IRS Form 990 filed by the National Hockey League.

[35] 2010 IRS Form 990 filed by the National Football League.

[36] Florio, Mike. "Goodell will get nearly $20 million per year by end of decade," NBC Sports Pro Football Talk Blog, February 13, 2012, http://profootballtalk.nbcsports.com/2012/02/13/goodell-will-get-nearly-20-million-per-year-by-end-of-decade/, accessed August, 6, 2012.

[37] 2010 IRS Form 990 filed by the National Football League.

[38] Yousuf, Hibah. "These nonprofit CEOS are getting raises," CNNMoney.com, September 29, 2009, http://money.cnn.com/2009/09/29/news/companies/nonprofit_salary/index.htm, accessed September 24, 2012.

[39] 2009 IRS Form 990 filed by the National Hockey League.

[40] Yousuf, Hibah. "These nonprofit CEOS are getting raises," CNNMoney.com, September 29, 2009, http://money.cnn.com/2009/09/29/news/companies/nonprofit_salary/index.htm, accessed September 24, 2012.

[41] 2010 IRS Form 990 filed by PGA Tour, Inc.

[42] 2009 IRS Form 990 filed by the National Hockey League.

[43] Sherlock, Molly, and Jane Gravelle. "An Overview of the Nonprofit and Charitable Sector," Congressional Research Service, R40919, November 17, 2009.

[44] 2010 IRS Form 990 filed by the National Football League.

[45] 2009 IRS Form 990 filed by the National Hockey League.

[46] Delaney, Andrew. "Tacking a Sack: The NFL and its Undeserved Tax-Exempt Status," *Social Sciences Research Network*, May 11, 2010. Available at http://papers.ssrn.com/sol3/papers.cfm?abstract_id=1605281, accessed October 15, 2012.

[47] Delaney, Andrew, "Tacking a Sack: The NFL and its Undeserved Tax-Exempt Status," *Social Sciences Research Network*, May 11, 2010. Available at http://papers.ssrn.com/sol3/papers.cfm?abstract_id=1605281, accessed October 15, 2012.

[48] "Business Leagues," Internal Revenue Service, http://www.irs.gov/Charities-&-Non-Profits/Other-Non-Profits/Business-Leagues, accessed October 11, 2012.

[49] Wilson, Duff. "N.F.L. Executives Hope to Keep Salaries Secret," *New York Times*, August 11, 2008. Available at http://www.nytimes.com/2008/08/12/sports/football/12nfltax.html, accessed August 6, 2012.

[50] Olson, Scott. "CIB expects to lose money during Super Bowl," *Indianapolis Business Journal*, January 16, 2012. Available at http://www.ibj.com/cib-expects-to-lose-money-during-super-bowl/PARAMS/article/31969, accessed August 6, 2012.

[51] The NFL and NHL received about $260 million in membership dues from their teams in 2010, the last year for which information is available. Applying the 35 percent corporate tax rate to these earnings would generate about $91 million in tax revenue. Any amount of league revenue spent on lobbying is already taxed. It is unclear how other league revenue streams would be affected, including the PGA's $300-million-plus television earnings. Full financial information about each league is unavailable, making estimates difficult.

[52] Note: In July, all three states discontinued the bonus food stamp benefit for pot users at the direction of the USDA.

[53] Luke Rosiak, "Top secret: $80B a year for food stamps, but feds won't reveal what's purchased," The Washington Times, June 24, 2012; http://www.washingtontimes.com/news/2012/jun/24/top-secret-what-food-stamps-buy/?page=all .

[54] "SUPPLEMENTAL NUTRITION ASSISTANCE PROGRAM: NUMBER OF PERSONS PARTICIPATING," U.S. Department of Agriculture website, data as of June 29, 2012, http://www.fns.usda.gov/pd/29snapcurrpp.htm, accessed September 24, 2012.

[55] "Agency Snapshot: Department of Agriculture," Performance.gov website, http://finance.performance.gov/initiative/improper-payment/agency/USDA, accessed July 18, 2012.

[56] "Supplemental Nutrition Assistance Program: Eligible Food Items," US Department of Agriculture website, modified February 16, 2012, http://www.fns.usda.gov/snap/retailers/eligible.htm, accessed July 25, 2012.

[57] "Supplemental Nutrition Assistance Program: Eligible Food Items," US Department of Agriculture website, modified February 16, 2012, http://www.fns.usda.gov/snap/retailers/eligible.htm, accessed July 25, 2012.

[58] "Federal food program pays billions for sugar-sweetened beverages," Yale University website, September 17, 2012, http://news.yale.edu/2012/09/17/federal-food-program-pays-billions-sugar-sweetened-beverages, accessed September 25, 2012.

[59] "Where Can I Use CalFresh (Food Stamps)?" City and County of San Francisco website, http://www.sfhsa.org/156.htm, accessed October 15, 2012.

[60] Lopez, Ricardo. "State seeks to educate food-stamp recipients about fast food," *Los Angeles Times*, August 2, 2011. Available at http://articles.latimes.com/2011/aug/02/local/la-me-food-stamps-20110802, accessed September 24, 2012.

[61] Lopez, Ricardo. "State seeks to educate food-stamp recipients about fast food," *Los Angeles Times*, August 2, 2011. Available at http://articles.latimes.com/2011/aug/02/local/la-me-food-stamps-20110802, accessed September 24, 2012.

[62] Brand, Natalie. "FOX 12 Investigators: Food stamps used for Frappuccinos," KPTV-Fox12, November 30, 2011. Available at http://www.kptv.com/story/16160615/fox-12-investigators-find-food-stamps-used-for, accessed September 24, 2012.

[63] Brand, Natalie. "FOX 12 Investigators: Food stamps used for Frappuccinos," KPTV-Fox12, November 30, 2011. Available at http://www.kptv.com/story/16160615/fox-12-investigators-find-food-stamps-used-for, accessed September 24, 2012.

[64] "How does marijuana use affect your brain and body?," National Institute on Drug Abuse, http://m.drugabuse.gov/publications/research-reports/marijuana-abuse/how-does-marijuana-use-affect-your-brain-body, accessed September 24, 2012.

[65] Note: In July, all three states discontinued the bonus food stamp benefit for pot users at the direction of the USDA.

[66] "How does marijuana use affect your brain and body?," National Institute on Drug Abuse, http://m.drugabuse.gov/publications/research-reports/marijuana-abuse/how-does-marijuana-use-affect-your-brain-body, accessed September 24, 2012.

[67] Wing, Nick. "Medical Marijuana Costs Can Be Deducted From Income For Food Stamp Eligibility in Oregon," *Huffington Post*, July 5, 2012. Available at http://www.huffingtonpost.com/2012/07/05/medical-marijuana-food-stamp-oregon_n_1651920.html, accessed October 15, 2012.

[68] Crombie, Noelle. "Marijuana's medicinal value boosted by Oregon's food stamp deduction," *The Oregonian*, July 3, 2012. Available at http://www.oregonlive.com/health/index.ssf/2012/07/marijuanas_medicinal_value_gai.html, accessed August 16, 2012.

[69] Leary, Mal. "Maine ends medical marijuana deduction for food stamps," *Lewiston Sun Journal*, July 17, 2012, http://www.sunjournal.com/news/maine/2012/07/18/maine-ends-medical-marijuana-deduction-food-stamps/1224675, accessed September 24, 2012.

[70] Scurlock, Stephanie. "Store Stops Taking EBT Cards After We Catch Them Breaking Rules," WREG-3, July 16, 2012, http://wreg.com/2012/07/15/food-land-retailer-stops-food-stamps-after-news-3-investigation/, accessed September 24, 2012.

[71] Buduson, Sarah. "Ohio food stamp recipients waste millions of U.S. tax dollars buying guns, drugs, beer," WEWS-5, February 20, 2012, http://www.newsnet5.com/dpp/news/local_news/investigations/ohio-food-stamp-recipients-waste-millions-of-us-tax-dollars-buying-buy-guns-drugs-beer#ixzz21fvXoo1p, accessed September 24, 2012.

[72] McMahon, Paula. "Brenda Charlestain: Food stamp fraud convict had plastic surgery and souped-up car, prosecutors say," WPTV-5, September 14, 2012, http://www.wptv.com/dpp/news/region_c_palm_beach_county/greenacres/brenda-charlestain-food-stamp-fraud-convict-had-plastic-surgery-and-souped-up-car-prosecutors-say#ixzz27VTkvLux, accessed September 25, 2012.

[73] McMahon, Paula. "Brenda Charlestain: Food stamp fraud convict had plastic surgery and souped-up car, prosecutors say," WPTV-5, September 14, 2012, http://www.wptv.com/dpp/news/region_c_palm_beach_county/greenacres/brenda-charlestain-food-stamp-fraud-convict-had-plastic-surgery-and-souped-up-car-prosecutors-say#ixzz27VTkvLux, accessed September 25, 2012.

[74] McMahon, Paula. "Brenda Charlestain: Food stamp fraud convict had plastic surgery and souped-up car, prosecutors say," WPTV-5, September 14, 2012, http://www.wptv.com/dpp/news/region_c_palm_beach_county/greenacres/brenda-charlestain-food-stamp-fraud-convict-had-plastic-surgery-and-souped-up-car-prosecutors-say#ixzz27VTkvLux, accessed September 25, 2012.

[75] May, Caroline. "USDA suggests food stamp parties, games to increase participation," *The Daily Caller*, June 27, 2012, http://dailycaller.com/2012/06/27/usda-suggests-food-stamp-parties-games-to-increase-participation/, accessed August 16, 2012.

[76] "Tips & Tools: Resources for Outreach," US Department of Agriculture, http://www.fns.usda.gov/snap/outreach/pdfs/toolkit/2011/State/Tips-Tools/resources.pdf, accessed August 16, 2012.

[77] May, Caroline. "USDA uses Spanish soap operas to push food stamps among non-citizens, citizens [AUDIO]," *The Daily Caller*, July 12, 2012, http://dailycaller.com/2012/07/12/usda-uses-spanish-soap-operas-to-push-food-stamp-participation-among-non-citizens-citizens/, accessed August 16, 2012.

[78] May, Caroline. "USDA uses Spanish soap operas to push food stamps among non-citizens, citizens [AUDIO]," *The Daily Caller*, July 12, 2012, http://dailycaller.com/2012/07/12/usda-uses-spanish-soap-operas-to-push-food-stamp-participation-among-non-citizens-citizens/, accessed August 16, 2012.

[79] In July, the novelas were removed from the USDA website and the department's Under Secretary for Food, Nutrition and Consumer Services announced production of SNAP advertisements would be ceased.
May, Caroline. "USDA suggests food stamp parties, games to increase participation," *The Daily Caller*, June 27, 2012, http://dailycaller.com/2012/06/27/usda-suggests-food-stamp-parties-games-to-increase-participation/, accessed August 16, 2012.

[80] Luhby, Tami. "Government wants more people on food stamps," CNNMoney.com, June 25, 2012, http://money.cnn.com/2012/06/25/news/economy/food-stamps-ads/index.htm, accessed August 16, 2012.

[81] "Analysis of Massachusetts' Supplemental Nutrition Assistance Program (SNAP) Eligibility Data," USDA Office of Inspector General, Audit Report 27002-0008-13, April 2012, p. 11, http://www.usda.gov/oig/webdocs/27002-0008-13.pdf, accessed September 24, 2012.

[82] "Analysis of New York's Supplemental Nutrition Assistance Program (SNAP) Eligibility Data," USDA Office of Inspector General, Audit Report 27002-00010-13, June 2012, p. 12, http://www.usda.gov/oig/webdocs/27002-0010-13.pdf, accessed September 24, 2012.

[83] "Analysis of Massachusetts' Supplemental Nutrition Assistance Program (SNAP) Eligibility Data," USDA Office of Inspector General, Audit Report 27002-0008-13, April 2012, p. 11, http://www.usda.gov/oig/webdocs/27002-0008-13.pdf, accessed September 24, 2012.

[84] "Analysis of New York's Supplemental Nutrition Assistance Program (SNAP) Eligibility Data," USDA Office of Inspector General, Audit Report 27002-00010-13, June 2012, p. 12, http://www.usda.gov/oig/webdocs/27002-0010-13.pdf, accessed September 24, 2012.

[85] "Analysis of Massachusetts' Supplemental Nutrition Assistance Program (SNAP) Eligibility Data," USDA Office of Inspector General, Audit Report 27002-0008-13, April 2012, p. 11, http://www.usda.gov/oig/webdocs/27002-0008-13.pdf, accessed September 24, 2012.

[86] "Analysis of New York's Supplemental Nutrition Assistance Program (SNAP) Eligibility Data," USDA Office of Inspector General, Audit Report 27002-00010-13, June 2012, p. 12, http://www.usda.gov/oig/webdocs/27002-0010-13.pdf, accessed September 24, 2012.

[87] Palmer, Jennifer. "Oklahoma Aeronautics Commission votes against closing Lake Murray State Park Airport," *The Oklahoman*, July 20, 2012. Available at http://newsok.com/oklahoma-aeronautics-commission-votes-against-closing-lake-murray-state-park-airport/article/3693943/?page=1, accessed August 22, 2012.

[88] Palmer, Jennifer. "Oklahoma Aeronautics Commission votes against closing Lake Murray State Park Airport," *The Oklahoman*, July 20, 2012. Available at http://newsok.com/oklahoma-aeronautics-commission-votes-against-closing-lake-murray-state-park-airport/article/3693943/?page=1, accessed August 22, 2012.

[89] Information provided by the Oklahoma Aeronautics Commission to the Congressional Research Service, August 20, 2012.

[90] Information provided by the Oklahoma Aeronautics Commission to the Congressional Research Service, August 20, 2012.

[91] Information provided by the Oklahoma Aeronautics Commission to the Office of Senator Tom Coburn, August 22, 2012.

[92] Information provided by the Oklahoma Aeronautics Commission to the Office of Senator Tom Coburn, August 22, 2012.

[93] Palmer, Jennifer. "Oklahoma Aeronautics Commission votes against closing Lake Murray State Park Airport," *The Oklahoman*, July 20, 2012. Available at http://newsok.com/oklahoma-aeronautics-commission-votes-against-closing-lake-murray-state-park-airport/article/3693943/?page=1, accessed August 22, 2012.

[94] Palmer, Jennifer. "Oklahoma Aeronautics Commission votes against closing Lake Murray State Park Airport," *The Oklahoman*, July 20, 2012. Available at http://newsok.com/oklahoma-aeronautics-commission-votes-against-closing-lake-murray-state-park-airport/article/3693943/?page=1, accessed August 22, 2012.

[95] Palmer, Jennifer. "Oklahoma Aeronautics Commission votes against closing Lake Murray State Park Airport," *The Oklahoman*, July 20, 2012. Available at http://newsok.com/oklahoma-aeronautics-commission-votes-against-closing-lake-murray-state-park-airport/article/3693943/?page=1, accessed August 22, 2012.

[96] Federal Aviation Administration, "Airport Improvement Program Grant Histories," Fiscal Years 2002, 2004, 2006, 2007, http://www.faa.gov/airports/aip/grant_histories/, accessed September 24, 2012.

[97] Palmer, Jennifer. "Oklahoma Aeronautics Commission votes against closing Lake Murray State Park Airport," *The Oklahoman*, July 20, 2012. Available at http://newsok.com/oklahoma-aeronautics-commission-votes-against-closing-lake-murray-state-park-airport/article/3693943/?page=1, accessed August 22, 2012.

[98] "Audit of USAID/Morocco's Economic Competitiveness Project," USAID Office of the Inspector General, Audit Report No. 7-608-12-002-P, December 15, 2011, p. 1. Available at http://transition.usaid.gov/oig/public/fy12rpts/7-608-12-002-p.pdf, accessed June 7, 2012.

[99] "Audit of USAID/Morocco's Economic Competitiveness Project," USAID Office of the Inspector General, Audit Report No. 7-608-12-002-P, December 15, 2011, p. 6. Available at http://transition.usaid.gov/oig/public/fy12rpts/7-608-12-002-p.pdf, accessed June 7, 2012.

[100] "Audit of USAID/Morocco's Economic Competitiveness Project," USAID Office of the Inspector General, Audit Report No. 7-608-12-002-P, December 15, 2011, p. 6. Available at http://transition.usaid.gov/oig/public/fy12rpts/7-608-12-002-p.pdf, accessed June 7, 2012.

[101] "Audit of USAID/Morocco's Economic Competitiveness Project," USAID Office of the Inspector General, Audit Report No. 7-608-12-002-P, December 15, 2011, p. 7. Available at http://transition.usaid.gov/oig/public/fy12rpts/7-608-12-002-p.pdf, accessed June 7, 2012.

[102] "Audit of USAID/Morocco's Economic Competitiveness Project," USAID Office of the Inspector General, Audit Report No. 7-608-12-002-P, December 15, 2011, p. 7. Available at http://transition.usaid.gov/oig/public/fy12rpts/7-608-12-002-p.pdf, accessed June 7, 2012.

[103] "Audit of USAID/Morocco's Economic Competitiveness Project," USAID Office of the Inspector General, Audit Report No. 7-608-12-002-P, December 15, 2011, p. 7. Available at http://transition.usaid.gov/oig/public/fy12rpts/7-608-12-002-p.pdf, accessed June 7, 2012.

[104] "Audit of USAID/Morocco's Economic Competitiveness Project," USAID Office of the Inspector General, Audit Report No. 7-608-12-002-P, December 15, 2011, p. 7. Available at http://transition.usaid.gov/oig/public/fy12rpts/7-608-12-002-p.pdf, accessed June 7, 2012.

[105] "Audit of USAID/Morocco's Economic Competitiveness Project," USAID Office of the Inspector General, Audit Report No. 7-608-12-002-P, December 15, 2011, p. 7. Available at http://transition.usaid.gov/oig/public/fy12rpts/7-608-12-002-p.pdf, accessed June 7, 2012.

[106] "Audit of USAID/Morocco's Economic Competitiveness Project," USAID Office of the Inspector General, Audit Report No. 7-608-12-002-P, December 15, 2011, p. 7. Available at http://transition.usaid.gov/oig/public/fy12rpts/7-608-12-002-p.pdf, accessed June 7, 2012.

[107] "Audit of USAID/Morocco's Economic Competitiveness Project," USAID Office of the Inspector General, Audit Report No. 7-608-12-002-P, December 15, 2011, p. 18. Available at http://transition.usaid.gov/oig/public/fy12rpts/7-608-12-002-p.pdf, accessed June 7, 2012.

[108] Kenny, Adele. "Moroccan Ceramics Are Rich In History," *Antiques and Auction News*, February 3, 2011, http://www.antiquesandauctionnews.net/Article+Display/Moroccan+Ceramics+Are+Rich+In+History/, accessed September 25, 2012.

[109] Plushnick-Masti, Ramit. "The Big Story: NASA builds menu for planned Mars mission in 2030s," Associated Press, July 17, 2012. Available at http://bigstory.ap.org/article/nasa-builds-menu-planned-mars-mission-2030s, accessed September 27, 2012.

[110] Daneman, Matthew. "Mars mission to be simulated to find best menus for trip," *USA Today*, February 20, 2012, http://www.usatoday.com/tech/science/space/story/2012-02-17/research-mars-food-hawaii/53160760/1 , accessed September 24, 2012.

[111] Vergano, Dan. "NASA chief: U.S. won't go it alone on manned Mars mission," *USA Today*, August 1, 2012, http://www.usatoday.com/tech/science/space/story/2012-08-01/NASA-mars-rover/56656270/1, accessed September 27, 2012.

[112] Plushnick-Masti, Ramit. "The Big Story: NASA builds menu for planned Mars mission in 2030s," Associated Press, July 17, 2012. Available at http://bigstory.ap.org/article/nasa-builds-menu-planned-mars-mission-2030s, accessed September 27, 2012.

[113] Atkinson, Nancy. "Dream Job: Go to Hawaii and Eat Astronaut Food," *Universe Today*, February 27, 2012. Available at http://www.universetoday.com/93818/dream-job-go-to-hawaii-and-eat-astronaut-food/, accessed September 24, 2012.

[114] "Compensation, and penalties for early withdrawal," Cornell/University of Hawaii Mars Analogue Mission and Food Study website, accessed October 11, 2012; http://manoa.hawaii.edu/hi-seas/RecruitmentClosed.html .

[115] HI-SEAS program, University of Hawaii website, http://manoa.hawaii.edu/hi-seas/RecruitmentClosed.html, accessed September 24, 2012.

[116] HI-SEAS program, University of Hawaii website, http://manoa.hawaii.edu/hi-seas/RecruitmentClosed.html, accessed September 24, 2012.

[117] Daneman, Matthew. "Mars mission to be simulated to find best menus for trip," *USA Today*, February 20, 2012. Available at http://www.usatoday.com/tech/science/space/story/2012-02-17/research-mars-food-hawaii/53160760/1, accessed September 24, 2012.

[118] Plushnick-Masti, Ramit. "The Big Story: NASA builds menu for planned Mars mission in 2030s," Associated Press, July 17, 2012; http://bigstory.ap.org/article/nasa-builds-menu-planned-mars-mission-2030s.

[119] Plushnick-Masti, Ramit. "The Big Story: NASA builds menu for planned Mars mission in 2030s," Associated Press, July 17, 2012; http://bigstory.ap.org/article/nasa-builds-menu-planned-mars-mission-2030s.

[120] Plushnick-Masti, Ramit. "The Big Story: NASA builds menu for planned Mars mission in 2030s," Associated Press, July 17, 2012. Available at http://bigstory.ap.org/article/nasa-builds-menu-planned-mars-mission-2030s.

[121] Plushnick-Masti, Ramit. "The Big Story: NASA builds menu for planned Mars mission in 2030s," Associated Press, July 17, 2012. Available at http://bigstory.ap.org/article/nasa-builds-menu-planned-mars-mission-2030s.

[122] Plushnick-Masti, Ramit. "The Big Story: NASA builds menu for planned Mars mission in 2030s," Associated Press, July 17, 2012; http://bigstory.ap.org/article/nasa-builds-menu-planned-mars-mission-2030s.

[123] "Award Abstract #0951010: RESUBMISSION Understanding predator-prey signaling interactions: the dynamics of antisnake displays in ground squirrels and kangaroo rats," Website of the National Science Foundation, http://nsf.gov/awardsearch/showAward.do?AwardNumber=0951010, accessed September 24, 2012.

[124] Boyle, Rebecca. "Video: Robot Squirrel Confuses a Snake," *Popular Science*, March 14, 2012. Available at http://www.popsci.com/technology/article/2012-03/video-robot-squirrel-confuses-snake-study-predator-prey-behavior, accessed September 24, 2012.

[125] "Robosquirrels presentations to rattlesnakes," YouTube video, posted February 2, 2012, http://www.youtube.com/watch?v=H0hyursVxG0, accessed August 17, 2012.

[126] Knight, Matthew. "'Robosquirrel' deployed to research relationship with rattlesnakes," CNN, April 4, 2012, http://articles.cnn.com/2012-04-04/tech/tech_robot-squirrel-rattlesnakes_1_snake-attack-robot-squirrels?_s=PM:TECH, accessed September 24, 2012.

[127] Joshi S, R Johnson, A Rundus, R Clark, et al. (2011) "Robotic Squirrel Models: Study of Squirrel-Rattlesnake Interaction in Laboratory and Natural Settings," *IEEE Robotics and Automation Magazine*, 18(4): 65.

[128] Joshi S, R Johnson, A Rundus, R Clark, et al. (2011) "Robotic Squirrel Models: Study of Squirrel-Rattlesnake Interaction in Laboratory and Natural Settings," *IEEE Robotics and Automation Magazine*, 18(4): 60.

[129] "Robosquirrels presentations to rattlesnakes," YouTube video, posted February 2, 2012, http://www.youtube.com/watch?v=H0hyursVxG0, accessed August 17, 2012.

[130] Joshi S, R Johnson, A Rundus, R Clark, et al. (2011) "Robotic Squirrel Models: Study of Squirrel-Rattlesnake Interaction in Laboratory and Natural Settings," *IEEE Robotics and Automation Magazine*, 18(4): 66.

[131] "Award Abstract #0951010: RESUBMISSION Understanding predator-prey signaling interactions: the dynamics of antisnake displays in ground squirrels and kangaroo rats," Website of the National Science Foundation, http://nsf.gov/awardsearch/showAward.do?AwardNumber=0951010, accessed September 24, 2012.

[132] Rodriguez, Sabrina. "Robot Squirrels Versus Rattlesnakes," KTXL-Fox40, April 3, 2012, http://www.fox40.com/news/headlines/ktxl-robot-squirrels-versus-rattlesnakes-20120403,0,7741395.story, accessed September 24, 2012.

[133] Roach, John. "RoboSquirrel vs. rattlesnake: Who wins?," NBC News Tech, March 14, 2012, http://www.nbcnews.com/technology/futureoftech/robosquirrel-vs-rattlesnake-who-wins-441781, accessed September 24, 2012.

[134] Dicou, Natalie. "Ooh La La! The Caviar Next Door," *Times-News*, February 8, 2012, http://magicvalley.com/lifestyles/food-and-cooking/ooh-la-la-the-caviar-next-door/article_7683e269-f8f9-506b-a7b4-66dc68f5d460.html, accessed September 10, 2012.

[135] Sang-Hun, Choe. "Catering to Caviar Tastes From an Unexpected Place," *New York Times*, May 11, 2012. Available at http://www.nytimes.com/2012/05/12/business/global/catering-to-caviar-tastes-from-an-unexpected-place.html?pagewanted=all, accessed September 10, 2012.

[136] Tidwell, John. "Sturgeon Fishes and Caviar Dreams," *Smithsonian Zoogoer*, May/June 2001. Available at http://nationalzoo.si.edu/Publications/ZooGoer/2001/3/sturgeonandcaviar.cfm, accessed September 10, 2012.

[137] Tidwell, John. "Sturgeon Fishes and Caviar Dreams," *Smithsonian Zoogoer*, May/June 2001. Available at http://nationalzoo.si.edu/Publications/ZooGoer/2001/3/sturgeonandcaviar.cfm, accessed October 11, 2012.

[138] Sang-Hun, Choe. "Catering to Caviar Tastes From an Unexpected Place," *New York Times*, May 11, 2012. Available at http://www.nytimes.com/2012/05/12/business/global/catering-to-caviar-tastes-from-an-unexpected-place.html?pagewanted=all, accessed September 10, 2012.

[139] Dicou, Natalie. "Ooh La La! The Caviar Next Door," *Times-News*, February 8, 2012, http://magicvalley.com/lifestyles/food-and-cooking/ooh-la-la-the-caviar-next-door/article_7683e269-f8f9-506b-a7b4-66dc68f5d460.html, accessed September 10, 2012.

[140] Dicou, Natalie. "Ooh La La! The Caviar Next Door," *Times-News*, February 8, 2012, http://magicvalley.com/lifestyles/food-and-cooking/ooh-la-la-the-caviar-next-door/article_7683e269-f8f9-506b-a7b4-66dc68f5d460.html, accessed September 10, 2012.

[141] Hand, Guy. "Idaho Caviar Industry is in the Black," *Northwest Food News*, March 4, 2011, http://www.nwfoodnews.com/2011/03/04/idaho-caviar-industry-is-in-the-black/, accessed September 10, 2012.

[142] Ellis, Sean. "Western innovator: Innovation wells up at fish farm, *Capital Press*, December 15, 2011, http://www.capitalpress.com/idaho/SE-Innovator-Leo-Ray-121611.

[143] Dicou, Natalie. "Ooh La La! The Caviar Next Door," *Times-News*, February 8, 2012, http://magicvalley.com/lifestyles/food-and-cooking/ooh-la-la-the-caviar-next-door/article_7683e269-f8f9-506b-a7b4-66dc68f5d460.html, accessed September 10, 2012.

[144] Hand, Guy. "Idaho Caviar Industry is in the Black," *Northwest Food News*, March 4, 2011, http://www.nwfoodnews.com/2011/03/04/idaho-caviar-industry-is-in-the-black/, accessed September 10, 2012.

[145] Dicou, Natalie. "Ooh La La! The Caviar Next Door," *Times-News*, February 8, 2012, http://magicvalley.com/lifestyles/food-and-cooking/ooh-la-la-the-caviar-next-door/article_7683e269-f8f9-506b-a7b4-66dc68f5d460.html, accessed September 10, 2012.

[146] "Kachemak Bay Ferry: Federally Funded Ferry Was Constructed with Limited Oversight and Faces Future Operating Challenges," Government Accountability Office, GAO-12-559, June 2012, p. 20. Available at http://www.gao.gov/assets/600/591505.pdf, accessed September 24, 2012.

[147] The state ferry – part of Alaska's marine highway system – runs between Seldovia and Homer twice per week and is capable of carrying heavy freight, vehicles, and passengers.

[148] A number of villages scattered along the coast are only reachable by sea and air travel. Homer population is about 5,000 people and Seldovia is 280.

[149] The Kachemak Ferry was paid for with $3.3 million of taxpayer dollars. With slight configuration differences, Stan Stephens Tours of Valdez, Alaska, bought m/v *Valdez Spirit*, the exact same vessel with $2.3 million.

[150] Interview with Tim Cashman, owner of Alaska Coastal Marine Services, August 24, 2012. While the tribe attributes the private tour operator's loses solely to the poor economy, the companies disagree.

[151] Interview with Tim Cashman, owner of Alaska Coastal Marine Services, August 24, 2012. While the tribe attributes the private tour operator's loses solely to the poor economy, the companies disagree.

[152] Interview with Tim Cashman, owner of Alaska Coastal Marine Services, August 24, 2012. While the tribe attributes the private tour operator's loses solely to the poor economy, the companies disagree.

[153] Interview with Jack Montgomery, owner of Rainbow Tours, August 31, 2012.

[154] Interview with Jack Montgomery, owner of Rainbow Tours, August 31, 2012.

[155] Interview with Jack Montgomery, owner of Rainbow Tours, August 31, 2012.

[156] Interview with Pete Zimmerman, Resident of Homer, August 30, 2012.

[157] Interview with Mako Haggerty, Water Taxi operator based in Homer, Alaska, August 29, 2012

[158] Interview with Mako Haggerty, Water Taxi operator based in Homer, Alaska, August 29, 2012

[159] "Kachemak Bay Ferry: Federally Funded Ferry Was Constructed with Limited Oversight and Faces Future Operating Challenges," Government Accountability Office, GAO-12-559, June 2012, p. 15. Available at http://www.gao.gov/assets/600/591505.pdf, accessed September 24, 2012.

[160] "Kachemak Bay Ferry: Federally Funded Ferry Was Constructed with Limited Oversight and Faces Future Operating Challenges," Government Accountability Office, GAO-12-559, June 2012, p. 36. Available at http://www.gao.gov/assets/600/591505.pdf, accessed September 24, 2012.

[161] Email correspondence from Tim Cashman owner of the Alaska Coastal Marine Services, August 25, 2012. Video obtained by the Office of Senator Coburn.

[162] "Kachemak Bay Ferry: Federally Funded Ferry Was Constructed with Limited Oversight and Faces Future Operating Challenges," Government Accountability Office, GAO-12-559, June 2012, p. 12. Available at http://www.gao.gov/assets/600/591505.pdf, accessed September 24, 2012.

[163] "Kachemak Bay Ferry: Federally Funded Ferry Was Constructed with Limited Oversight and Faces Future Operating Challenges," Government Accountability Office, GAO-12-559, June 2012, p. 20. Available at http://www.gao.gov/assets/600/591505.pdf, accessed September 24, 2012.

[164] "Kachemak Bay Ferry: Federally Funded Ferry Was Constructed with Limited Oversight and Faces Future Operating Challenges," Government Accountability Office, GAO-12-559, June 2012, page 20; http://www.gao.gov/assets/600/591505.pdf.

[165] Letter from Tim Cashman to Senator Lisa Murkowski, June 4, 2010.

[166] Letter from Tim Cashman to Senator Lisa Murkowski, June 4, 2010.

[167] Note: As it started operation, the tribe received another $675,000 (including $475,000 in stimulus money) to construct two docks and assist with operating expenses. To date, one of the docks built with the funds is unused. "Kachemak Bay Ferry: Federally Funded Ferry Was Constructed with Limited Oversight and Faces Future Operating Challenges," Government Accountability Office, GAO-12-559, June 2012, p. 14, 33. Available at http://www.gao.gov/assets/600/591505.pdf, accessed September 24, 2012.

[168] Armstrong, Michael. "Ferry or Tour Boat," May 26, 2010, *Homer News*, http://www.homernews.com/stories/052610/news_1_001.shtml#.UD6i5UK5e5Q, accessed August 30, 2012.

[169] Kizzia, Tom. "If they build the Seldovia ferry, will people ride," *Anchorage Daily News*, January 10, 2005: A-1.

[170] "Kachemak Bay Ferry: Federally Funded Ferry Was Constructed with Limited Oversight and Faces Future Operating Challenges," Government Accountability Office, GAO-12-559, June 2012, p. 34. Available at http://www.gao.gov/assets/600/591505.pdf, accessed September 24, 2012.

[171] Using ballpark estimates, at the current $59 round trip ticket, the Seldovia Village Tribe will have sell an estimate of 13,599 extra round-trip tickets to close the 800,000 operating loss GAO estimates for the Kachemak Voyager.

[172] Note: In the first season, the *Kachemak Voyager* made 44 of its journeys without paying customers. 14 passengers is about 10% of the capacity of the Voyager. "Kachemak Bay Ferry: Federally Funded Ferry Was Constructed with Limited Oversight and Faces Future Operating Challenges," Government Accountability Office, GAO-12-559, June 2012, p. 33. Available at http://www.gao.gov/assets/600/591505.pdf, accessed September 24, 2012.

[173] "Kachemak Bay Ferry: Federally Funded Ferry Was Constructed with Limited Oversight and Faces Future Operating Challenges," Government Accountability Office, GAO-12-559, June 2012, page 51; http://www.gao.gov/assets/600/591505.pdf.

[174] "Kachemak Bay Ferry: Federally Funded Ferry Was Constructed with Limited Oversight and Faces Future Operating Challenges," Government Accountability Office, GAO-12-559, June 2012, Highlights page. Available at http://www.gao.gov/assets/600/591505.pdf, accessed September 24, 2012.

[175] "GRANTS MANAGEMENT: Action Needed to Improve the Timeliness of Grant Closeouts by Federal Agencies," Government Accountability Office, April 2012, GAO-12-360, page 19. Available at http://www.gao.gov/assets/600/590926.pdf, accessed September 17, 2012.

[176] "GRANTS MANAGEMENT: Action Needed to Improve the Timeliness of Grant Closeouts by Federal Agencies," Government Accountability Office, April 2012, GAO-12-360, page 19. Available at http://www.gao.gov/assets/600/590926.pdf, accessed September 17, 2012.

[177] "GRANTS MANAGEMENT: Action Needed to Improve the Timeliness of Grant Closeouts by Federal Agencies," Government Accountability Office, April 2012, GAO-12-360, page 19. Available at http://www.gao.gov/assets/600/590926.pdf, accessed September 17, 2012.

[178] "GRANTS MANAGEMENT: Action Needed to Improve the Timeliness of Grant Closeouts by Federal Agencies," Government Accountability Office, April 2012, GAO-12-360, page 19. Available at http://www.gao.gov/assets/600/590926.pdf, accessed September 17, 2012.

[179] "GRANTS MANAGEMENT: Action Needed to Improve the Timeliness of Grant Closeouts by Federal Agencies," Government Accountability Office, April 2012, GAO-12-360, page 19. Available at http://www.gao.gov/assets/600/590926.pdf, accessed September 17, 2012.

[180] Morath, Eric. "Treasury to Cut Costs by Remaking Coins, Replacing Paper," *Wall Street Journal* Real Time Economics blog, March 28, 2012, http://blogs.wsj.com/economics/2012/03/28/treasury-to-cut-costs-by-remaking-coins-replacing-paper/, accessed August 21, 2012.

[181] Morath, Eric. "Treasury to Cut Costs by Remaking Coins, Replacing Paper," *Wall Street Journal* Real Time Economics blog, March 28, 2012, http://blogs.wsj.com/economics/2012/03/28/treasury-to-cut-costs-by-remaking-coins-replacing-paper/, accessed August 21, 2012.

[182] Total production as of September 2012 was 4.8 billion coins (see Coin Production Figures, United States Mint, http://www.usmint.gov/about_the_mint/coin_production/index.cfm?action=production_figures&allCoinsYear=2012, accessed October 11, 2012). At the cost of $.024/penny, production of 5 billion pennies would cost $120 million.

[183] Treasury sells the pennies to the Federal Reserve at face value, a transaction that will generate $50-$60 million, which does not fully offset the at least $120 million cost to produce 5 billion pennies.

[184] Huchzermeyer, Laura. "US May Save Money by Changing the Way It Makes Money," Hoover's Bizmology blog, March 28, 2012, http://bizmology.hoovers.com/2012/03/28/us-may-save-money-by-changing-the-way-it-makes-money/, accessed August 21, 2012.

[185] "Future of the Penny: Congressional Options," Government Accountability Office, July 1996, GAO/T-GGD-96-153, p. 12. Available at http://gao.gov/assets/110/106568.pdf, accessed September 24, 2012.

[186] "Future of the Penny: Congressional Options," Government Accountability Office, July 1996, GAO/T-GGD-96-153, p. 3. Available at http://gao.gov/assets/110/106568.pdf, accessed September 24, 2012.

[187] "Canada's penny withdrawal: All you need to know," *CBC News*, March 30, 2012. Available at http://www.cbc.ca/news/canada/toronto/story/2012/03/30/f-penny-faq.html, accessed August 21, 2012.

[188] "Order Free Cell Phone Service," Expert Choice Cellular website, http://www.mygovernmentcellphone.com/free-government-cell-phone-order.html, accessed September 24, 2012.

[189] "Free Government Cell Phone Service," Expert Choice Cellular website, http://www.mygovernmentcellphone.com/, accessed September 24, 2012.

[190] "What is Universal Service?" Universal Service Administrative Company (USAC) website, http://www.usac.org/about/about/universal-service/faqs.aspx#Q1, accessed September 24, 2012.

[191] Information provided by Universal Service Administrative Company (USAC) to the Office of Senator Tom Coburn, August 27, 2012.

[192] Universal Service Administrative Company (USAC) disbursements to wireless companies from July 2011-June 2012. Information provided by USAC to the Office of Senator Tom Coburn, August 20, 2012.

[193] Sweigart, Josh. "1 million Ohioans using free phone program," *Dayton Daily News*, August 17, 2012, http://www.daytondailynews.com/news/news/subsidized-cell-phone-program-nearly-doubles-in-oh/nRDqC/, accessed August 24, 2012.

[194] In 2008, the first prepaid wireless phone company was approved to participate in the program, leading to significant growth in the number of people in the program. "Improved Management Can Enhance FCC Decision Making for the Universal Service Fund Low-Income Program," Government Accountability Office, October 2010, GAO-11-11, p. 9, 16. Available at http://www.gao.gov/assets/320/312708.pdf, accessed August 24, 2012.

[195] From July 2011-June 2012, Lifeline disbursements totaled $2,066,912,266, of which $1,452,806,857 was disbursed to wireless companies. Of that sum, $832,685,143 was disbursed to prepaid wireless companies. Information provided by USAC to the Office of Senator Tom Coburn, August 21, 2012.

[196] Chiaramonte, Perry. "Carlos Slim, World's Richest Man, Gets Richer Supplying 'Obamaphones' to Poor," FoxNews.com, October 10, 2012, http://www.foxnews.com/us/2012/10/10/carlos-slim-worlds-richest-man-gets-richer-supplying-obamaphones-to-poor/, accessed October 12, 2012.

[197] "Report and Order and Further Notice of Proposed Rulemaking," Federal Communications Commission, released February 6, 2012, FCC 12-11, p. 183. Available at http://www.usac.org/_res/documents/li/pdf/fcc/FCC-12-11.pdf, accessed September 20, 2012.

[198] "The Free Cell Phone & Minutes Program," SafeLink Wireless website, https://www.safelinkwireless.com/Enrollment/Safelink/en/Public/NewHome.html, accessed September 26, 2012.

[199] Information provided by USAC to the Office of Senator Tom Coburn, August 21, 2012.

[200] James, Erin. "Program giving free phones to low-income Yorkers," *The York Dispatch*, August 14, 2012.

[201] Collin, Liz. "Reports of Fraud, Abuse Surround Federal Free Phone Program," *CBS Minnesota*, July 19, 2012, http://minnesota.cbslocal.com/2012/07/19/reports-of-fraud-abuse-surround-federal-free-phone-program/, accessed August 24, 2012.

[202] Nagus, Chris. "More Problems with Free Cell Phone Progarm," December 13, 2011, http://www.kmov.com/news/broke/More-problems-with-free-cell-phone-program-135556583.html, accessed September 26, 2012.

[203] Letter to Sharon Gillett, RE: Results of Lifeline Duplicate In-Depth Data Validations, WC Docket No. 11-42, CC Docket No. 96-45, WC Docket No. 03-109, January 10, 2012, http://apps.fcc.gov/ecfs/document/view.action?id=7021753115, accessed September 24, 2012.

[204] "Report and Order and Further Notice of Proposed Rulemaking," Federal Communications Commission, released February 6, 2012, FCC 12-11, p. 79. Available at http://www.usac.org/_res/documents/li/pdf/fcc/FCC-12-11.pdf, accessed August 24, 2012.

[205] "Telecommunications: Improvement Management Can Enhance FCC Decision Making for the Universal Service Fund Low-Income Program," Government Accountability Office, October 2011, GAO-11-11, p. 35. Available at http://gao.gov/assets/320/312708.pdf, accessed September 17, 2012.

[206] "Report and Order and Further Notice of Proposed Rulemaking," Federal Communications Commission, released February 6, 2012, FCC 12-11, p. 243. Available at http://www.usac.org/_res/documents/li/pdf/fcc/FCC-12-11.pdf, accessed August 24, 2012.

[207] Eyre, Eric. "State Paid $22K Each for Internet Routers," *The Charleston Gazette*, May 5, 2012. Available at http://wvgazette.com/News/201205050057, accessed August 21, 2012.

[208] Eyre, Eric. "State Paid $22K Each for Internet Routers," *The Charleston Gazette*, May 5, 2012. Available at http://wvgazette.com/News/201205050057, accessed August 21, 2012.

[209] Eyre, Eric. "W.Va. router purchases done via routine procedure," *The Charleston Gazette*, August 26, 2012. Available at http://wvgazette.com/News/Business/201208260187, accessed September 5, 2012.

[210] Eyre, Eric. "State Paid $22K Each for Internet Routers," *The Charleston Gazette*, May 5, 2012. Available at http://wvgazette.com/News/201205050057, accessed August 21, 2012.

[211] Eyre, Eric. "State Paid $22K Each for Internet Routers," *The Charleston Gazette*, May 5, 2012. Available at http://wvgazette.com/News/201205050057, accessed August 21, 2012.

[212] Eyre, Eric. "Planning agencies refuse to use expensive Internet routers," *The Charleston Gazette*, June 23, 2012. Available at http://wvgazette.com/News/201206230070, accessed September 5, 2012.

[213] Eyre, Eric. "Planning agencies refuse to use expensive Internet routers," *The Charleston Gazette*, June 23, 2012. Available at http://wvgazette.com/News/201206230070, accessed September 5, 2012.

[214] Eyre, Eric. "Planning agencies refuse to use expensive Internet routers," *The Charleston Gazette*, June 23, 2012. Available at http://wvgazette.com/News/201206230070, accessed September 5, 2012.

[215] Eyre, Eric. "Planning agencies refuse to use expensive Internet routers," *The Charleston Gazette*, June 23, 2012. Available at http://wvgazette.com/News/201206230070, accessed September 5, 2012.

[216] Eyre, Eric. "Planning agencies refuse to use expensive Internet routers," *The Charleston Gazette*, June 23, 2012. Available at http://wvgazette.com/News/201206230070, accessed September 5, 2012.

[217] Eyre, Eric. "Planning agencies refuse to use expensive Internet routers," *The Charleston Gazette*, June 23, 2012. Available at http://wvgazette.com/News/201206230070, accessed September 5, 2012.

[218] Eyre, Eric. "State Paid $22K Each for Internet Routers," *The Charleston Gazette*, May 5, 2012. Available at http://wvgazette.com/News/201205050057, accessed August 21, 2012.

[219] Eyre, Eric. "State Paid $22K Each for Internet Routers," *The Charleston Gazette*, May 5, 2012. Available at http://wvgazette.com/News/201205050057, accessed August 21, 2012.

[220] Eyre, Eric. "State Paid $22K Each for Internet Routers," *The Charleston Gazette*, May 5, 2012. Available at http://wvgazette.com/News/201205050057, accessed August 21, 2012.

[221] Eyre, Eric. "State Paid $22K Each for Internet Routers," *The Charleston Gazette*, May 5, 2012. Available at http://wvgazette.com/News/201205050057, accessed August 21, 2012.

[222] Eyre, Eric. "Internet routers have sat unused for two years," *The Charleston Gazette*, May 6, 2012. Available at http://wvgazette.com/News/201205060065, accessed September 10, 2012.

[223] Eyre, Eric. "State Paid $22K Each for Internet Routers," *The Charleston Gazette*, May 5, 2012. Available at http://wvgazette.com/News/201205050057, accessed August 21, 2012.

[224] Eyre, Eric. "Internet routers have sat unused for two years," *The Charleston Gazette*, May 6, 2012. Available at http://wvgazette.com/News/201205060065, accessed September 10, 2012.

[225] At $22,600 each, 366 routers would cost over $8 million. Eyre, Eric. "Internet routers have sat unused for two years," *The Charleston Gazette*, May 6, 2012. Available at http://wvgazette.com/News/201205060065, accessed September 10, 2012.

[226] Eyre, Eric. "State Paid $22K Each for Internet Routers," *The Charleston Gazette*, May 5, 2012. Available at http://wvgazette.com/News/201205050057, accessed August 21, 2012.

[227] Eyre, Eric. "State Paid $22K Each for Internet Routers," *The Charleston Gazette*, May 5, 2012. Available at http://wvgazette.com/News/201205050057, accessed August 21, 2012.

[228] Messina, Lawrence. "W.Va. officials defend stimulus broadband spending," *Associated Press*, July 12, 2012. Available at http://finance.yahoo.com/news/w-va-officials-defend-stimulus-broadband-spending-120903485--finance.html, accessed September 5, 2012.

[229] Eyre, Eric. "Firm to audit W. Va. Broadband stimulus spending," *The Charleston Gazette*, May 7, 2012. Available at http://wvgazette.com/News/201205070200, accessed October 11, 2012.

[230] Eyre, Eric. "Firm to audit W. Va. Broadband stimulus spending," *The Charleston Gazette*, May 7, 2012. Available at http://wvgazette.com/News/201205070200, accessed October 11, 2012.

[231] Eyre, Eric. "Planning agencies refuse to use expensive Internet routers," *The Charleston Gazette*, June 23, 2012. Available at http://wvgazette.com/News/201206230070, accessed September 5, 2012.

[232] "About," Website of "Prom Week," http://promweek.soe.ucsc.edu/?page_id=9, accessed August 23, 2012.

[233] "UCSC's Prom Week game nominated for gaming awards." *Santa Cruz Sentinel*, February 14, 2012, http://www.santacruzsentinel.com/rss/ci_19964647, accessed September 28, 2012.

[234] "Award Abstract #0747522: CAREER: Automated Support for Novice Authorning[sp] of Interactive Drama," Website of the National Science Foundation, http://nsf.gov/awardsearch/showAward.do?AwardNumber=0747522, accessed September 24, 2012.

[235] "UCSC's Prom Week game nominated for gaming awards." *Santa Cruz Sentinel*, February 14, 2012, http://www.santacruzsentinel.com/rss/ci_19964647, accessed September 28, 2012.

[236] "UCSC's Prom Week game nominated for gaming awards." *Santa Cruz Sentinel*, February 14, 2012, http://www.santacruzsentinel.com/rss/ci_19964647, accessed September 28, 2012.

[237] "Prom Week," Website of the University of California at Santa Cruz, available online at http:/games.soe.ucsc.edu/project/prom-week, accessed October 2, 2012.

[238] "Prom Week Trailer," Youtube, posted May 27, 2011, http://www.youtube.com/watch?v=zc5QEcWGh1U, accessed August 23, 2012.

[239] "Prom Week," Website of the University of California at Santa Cruz, available online at http:/games.soe.ucsc.edu/project/prom-week, accessed September 24, 2012.

[240] "UCSC's Prom Week game nominated for gaming awards." *Santa Cruz Sentinel*, February 14, 2012, http://www.santacruzsentinel.com/rss/ci_19964647, accessed September 28, 2012.

[241] "Award Abstract #0747522: CAREER: Automated Support for Novice Authorning[sp] of Interactive Drama," Website of the National Science Foundation, http://nsf.gov/awardsearch/showAward.do?AwardNumber=0747522, accessed September 24, 2012.

[242] "Prom Week" on Facebook, http://www.facebook.com/promweek/info, accessed August 23, 2012.

[243] "Estimated Revenue Effects of the Revenue Provisions Contained in the Chairman's Modification to S. ___, the 'Highway Investment, Job Creation and Economic Growth Act of 2012,' Scheduled for Markup by the

Committee on Finance on February 7, 2012," Joint Committee on Taxation, February 7, 2012, JCX-12-12. Available at http://www.finance.senate.gov/imo/media/doc/JCX1212.pdf, accessed September 24, 2012.

[244] Mufson, Steven. "Paper industry pushed further into the black by "black liquor" tax credits," *Washington Post*, April 26, 2011, http://www.washingtonpost.com/business/economy/paper-industry-pushed-further-into-the-black-by-black-liquor-tax-credits/2011/04/19/AFdkrMtE_print.html, accessed September 17, 2012.

[245] By making a simple change to the liquor, companies qualified for the credit, which paid out $.50 per gallon.

[246] Note: This original provision was passed in the 2005 Highway Bill and was called the "alternative fuel mixture credit." Mufson, Steven. "Paper industry pushed further into the black by "black liquor" tax credits," *Washington Post*, April 26, 2011, http://www.washingtonpost.com/business/economy/paper-industry-pushed-further-into-the-black-by-black-liquor-tax-credits/2011/04/19/AFdkrMtE_print.html, accessed September 17, 2012.

[247] Sheffield, Christopher. "Black liquor turns solid gold," *Memphis Business Journal*, January 24, 2012. Available at http://www.bizjournals.com/mcmphis/stories/2010/01/25/story2.html?page=all, accessed September 24, 2012.

[248] Kroh, Eric. "Disallowed 'Black Liquor' Tax Credit Soldiers On, at a Cost," *Tax Notes*, March 12, 2012, p. 1367.

[249] Mufson, Steven. "Paper industry pushed further into the black by "black liquor" tax credits," *Washington Post*, April 26, 2011, http://www.washingtonpost.com/business/economy/paper-industry-pushed-further-into-the-black-by-black-liquor-tax-credits/2011/04/19/AFdkrMtE_print.html, accessed September 17, 2012.

[250] Internal Revenue Service Office of Chief Counsel, Letter to Holly L. McCann, Memorandum Number AM2010-002, June 28, 2010. Available at http://www.irs.gov/pub/irs-utl/am2010002.pdf, accessed September 17, 2012.

[251] Kroh, Eric. "Disallowed 'Black Liquor' Tax Credit Soldiers On, at a Cost," *Tax Notes*, March 12, 2012, p. 1367.

[252] "Estimated Revenue Effects of the Revenue Provisions Contained in the Chairman's Modification to S. __, the 'Highway Investment, Job Creation and Economic Growth Act of 2012,' Scheduled for Markup by the Committee on Finance on February 7, 2012," Joint Committee on Taxation, February 7, 2012, JCX-12-12. Available at http://www.finance.senate.gov/imo/media/doc/JCX1212.pdf, accessed September 24, 2012.

[253] Ivry, Bob, and Christopher Donville. "Black Liquor Tax Boondoggle May Net Billions for Papermakers," *Bloomberg News*, April 17, 2009, http://www.bloomberg.com/apps/news?pid=newsarchive&sid=abDjfGgdumh4, accessed September 17, 2012.

[254] Sheffield, Christopher. "Black liquor turns solid gold," *Memphis Business Journal*, January 24, 2012. Available at http://www.bizjournals.com/memphis/stories/2010/01/25/story2.html?page=all, accessed September 24, 2012.

[255] Mufson, Steven. "Paper industry pushed further into the black by "black liquor" tax credits," *Washington Post*, April 26, 2011, http://www.washingtonpost.com/business/economy/paper-industry-pushed-further-into-the-black-by-black-liquor-tax-credits/2011/04/19/AFdkrMtE_print.html, accessed September 17, 2012.

[256] "Highway Investment, Job Creation, and Economic Growth Act of 2012," U.S. Senate Finance Committee, Report No. 112-152, February 27, 2012. Available at http://www.finance.senate.gov/legislation/details/?id=d923f3c4-5056-a032-52f9-cc852968f453, accessed September 13, 2012.

[257] Sullivan, Martin A. "IRS Allows New $25 Billion Tax Break for Paper Industry," *Tax Notes*, October 19, 2009, p. 271-272.

[258] It was added an offset the cost of the transportation bill that passed by Congress in June. Closing the loophole would have prevented paper companies from claiming credits under BCAP for black liquor produced in 2009.

[259] Weisman, Jonathan. "Tax Loopholes Block Efforts to Close Gaping Deficit," *New York Times*, July 20, 2012: A1. Available at http://www.nytimes.com/2012/07/21/us/politics/in-black-liquor-a-cautionary-tale-for-deficit-reduction.html?pagewanted=all, accessed August 17, 2012.

[260] Letter to the Board of Commissioners of the Community Development Corporation of the County of Los Angeles. "Approve Exchange of Community Development Block Grant Funds Between the Cities of Beverly Hills and Hawaiian Gardens," April 3, 2012. Motion adopted by the Commission on April 3, 2012. Available at http://file.lacounty.gov/bos/supdocs/67400.pdf, accessed August 14, 2012.

[261] "Santa Fe Springs sells CDBG funds to La Mirada," *Los Angeles Wave*, April 19, 2012. Available at http://wavenewspapers.com/news/local/east_edition/article_e93777d4-8a5c-11e1-a274-0019bb30f31a.html?_dc=971312522655.3529, accessed August 14, 2012.

[262] Community Development Commission of the County of Los Angeles, "2012-2013 One-year Action Plan, Appendix I: CDBG Allocations," page 1. Available at http://www3.lacdc.org/CDCWebsite/uploadedfiles/CDBG/One%20Year%20Action%20Plan/2012-2013%20One-Year%20Action%20Plan/Volume%20I/Appendix%20I.pdf, accessed August 14, 2012.

[263] State and County Quickfacts, Beverly Hills (city), California. http://quickfacts.census.gov/qfd/states/06/0606308.html, last revised June 6, 2012, accessed August 14, 2012.

[264] Letter to the Board of Commissioners of the Community Development Corporation of the County of Los Angeles. "Approve Exchange of Community Development Block Grant Funds Between the Cities of Beverly Hills and Hawaiian Gardens," April 3, 2012. Motion adopted by the Commission on April 3, 2012. Available at http://file.lacounty.gov/bos/supdocs/67400.pdf, accessed August 14, 2012.

[265] Letter to the Board of Commissioners of the Community Development Corporation of the County of Los Angeles. "Approve Exchange of Community Development Block Grant Funds Between the Cities of Beverly Hills and Hawaiian Gardens," April 3, 2012. Motion adopted by the Commission on April 3, 2012. Available at http://file.lacounty.gov/bos/supdocs/67400.pdf, accessed August 14, 2012.

[266] "Beverly Hills Trades Community Grants for Cash," BetterBike.org, March 7, 2012, http://betterbike.org/2012/03/beverly-hills-trades-community-grants-for-cash/, accessed September 12, 2012.

[267] Letter to the Board of Commissioners of the Community Development Corporation of the County of Los Angeles. "Approve Exchange of Community Development Block Grant Funds Between the Cities of Beverly Hills and Hawaiian Gardens," April 3, 2012. Motion adopted by the Commission on April 3, 2012. Available at http://file.lacounty.gov/bos/supdocs/67400.pdf, accessed August 14, 2012.

[268] Letter to the Board of Commissioners of the Community Development Corporation of the County of Los Angeles. "Approve Exchange of Community Development Block Grant Funds Between the Cities of Beverly Hills and Hawaiian Gardens," April 3, 2012. Motion adopted by the Commission on April 3, 2012. Available at http://file.lacounty.gov/bos/supdocs/67400.pdf, accessed August 14, 2012.

[269] Agenda Report for March 6, 2012, meeting of the Beverly Hills City Council. Available at http://betterbike.org/wp-content/uploads/2012/03/CDBG-trading-staff-report.pdf, accessed September 12, 2012.

[270] "Santa Fe Springs sells CDBG funds to La Mirada," *Los Angeles Wave*, April 19, 2012. Available at http://wavenewspapers.com/news/local/east_edition/article_e93777d4-8a5c-11e1-a274-0019bb30f31a.html?_dc=971312522655.3529, accessed August 14, 2012.

[271] "Santa Fe Springs sells CDBG funds to La Mirada," *Los Angeles Wave*, April 19, 2012. Available at http://wavenewspapers.com/news/local/east_edition/article_e93777d4-8a5c-11e1-a274-0019bb30f31a.html?_dc=971312522655.3529, accessed August 14, 2012.

[272] "Santa Fe Springs sells CDBG funds to La Mirada," *Los Angeles Wave*, April 19, 2012. Available at http://wavenewspapers.com/news/local/east_edition/article_e93777d4-8a5c-11e1-a274-0019bb30f31a.html?_dc=971312522655.3529, accessed August 14, 2012.

[273] "Community Development Block Grant – CDBG," Department of Housing and Urban Development website, http://portal.hud.gov/hudportal/HUD?src=/program_offices/comm_planning/communitydevelopment/programs, accessed August 14, 2012.

[274] "Nuclear Nonproliferation: DOE Needs to Reassess Its Programs to Assist Weapons Scientists in Russia and Other Countries," Government Accountability Office, January 23, 2008, GAO-08-434T, http://www.gao.gov/new.items/d08434t.pdf.

[275] "FY2013 Congressional Budget Request," Department of Energy, National Nuclear Security Administration Office of the Administrator, February 2012, Volume 1, page 391. Available at http://www.cfo.doe.gov/budget/13budget/Content/Volume1.pdf, accessed September 24, 2012. Note, the program is now known as "Global Security through Science Partnerships."

[276] "Nuclear Nonproliferation: DOE Needs to Reassess Its Programs to Assist Weapons Scientists in Russia and Other Countries," Government Accountability Office, January 23, 2008, GAO-08-434T, http://www.gao.gov/new.items/d08434t.pdf.

[277] "Nuclear Nonproliferation: DOE Needs to Reassess Its Programs to Assist Weapons Scientists in Russia and Other Countries," Government Accountability Office, January 23, 2008, GAO-08-434T, http://www.gao.gov/new.items/d08434t.pdf.

[278] "Nuclear Nonproliferation: DOE Needs to Reassess Its Programs to Assist Weapons Scientists in Russia and Other Countries," Government Accountability Office, January 23, 2008, GAO-08-434T, http://www.gao.gov/new.items/d08434t.pdf.

[279] "Nuclear Nonproliferation: DOE Needs to Reassess Its Programs to Assist Weapons Scientists in Russia and Other Countries," Government Accountability Office, January 23, 2008, GAO-08-434T, http://www.gao.gov/new.items/d08434t.pdf.

[280] "Nuclear Nonproliferation: DOE Needs to Reassess Its Programs to Assist Weapons Scientists in Russia and Other Countries," Government Accountability Office, January 23, 2008, GAO-08-434T, http://www.gao.gov/new.items/d08434t.pdf.

[281] "Nuclear Nonproliferation: DOE Needs to Reassess Its Programs to Assist Weapons Scientists in Russia and Other Countries," Government Accountability Office, January 23, 2008, GAO-08-434T, http://www.gao.gov/new.items/d08434t.pdf.

[282] "International Nonproliferation Program," Department of Energy website, http://www.y12.doe.gov/missions/nonproliferation/inp/gipp/initiativesprevention.php, accessed March 21, 2012.

[283] Bhattarai, Abha. "From 'Angry Birds' to multi-player video games, NASA ramps up investment in educational technology," *Washington Post*, September 2, 2012. Available at http://www.washingtonpost.com/business/capitalbusiness/from-angry-birds-to-multi-player-video-games-nasa-ramps-up-investment-in-educational-technology/2012/08/31/c3d9d35c-c46c-11e1-916d-a4bc61efcad8_story.html, accessed September 6, 2012.

[284] Bhattarai, Abha. "From 'Angry Birds' to multi-player video games, NASA ramps up investment in educational technology," *Washington Post*, September 2, 2012. Available at http://www.washingtonpost.com/business/capitalbusiness/from-angry-birds-to-multi-player-video-games-

nasa-ramps-up-investment-in-educational-technology/2012/08/31/c3d9d35c-c46c-11e1-916d-a4bc61efcad8_story.html, accessed September 6, 2012.

[285] Bhattarai, Abha. "From 'Angry Birds' to multi-player video games, NASA ramps up investment in educational technology," *Washington Post*, September 2, 2012. Available at http://www.washingtonpost.com/business/capitalbusiness/from-angry-birds-to-multi-player-video-games-nasa-ramps-up-investment-in-educational-technology/2012/08/31/c3d9d35c-c46c-11e1-916d-a4bc61efcad8_story.html, accessed September 6, 2012.

[286] Bhattarai, Abha. "From 'Angry Birds' to multi-player video games, NASA ramps up investment in educational technology," *Washington Post*, September 2, 2012. Available at http://www.washingtonpost.com/business/capitalbusiness/from-angry-birds-to-multi-player-video-games-nasa-ramps-up-investment-in-educational-technology/2012/08/31/c3d9d35c-c46c-11e1-916d-a4bc61efcad8_story.html, accessed September 6, 2012.

[287] Bhattarai, Abha. "From 'Angry Birds' to multi-player video games, NASA ramps up investment in educational technology," *Washington Post*, September 2, 2012. Available at http://www.washingtonpost.com/business/capitalbusiness/from-angry-birds-to-multi-player-video-games-nasa-ramps-up-investment-in-educational-technology/2012/08/31/c3d9d35c-c46c-11e1-916d-a4bc61efcad8_story.html, accessed September 6, 2012.

[288] Bhattarai, Abha. "From 'Angry Birds' to multi-player video games, NASA ramps up investment in educational technology," *Washington Post*, September 2, 2012. Available at http://www.washingtonpost.com/business/capitalbusiness/from-angry-birds-to-multi-player-video-games-nasa-ramps-up-investment-in-educational-technology/2012/08/31/c3d9d35c-c46c-11e1-916d-a4bc61efcad8_story.html, accessed September 6, 2012.

[289] Though NASA does not support the project financially, one of its employees contributes administratively, costing taxpayers an estimated $7,700.
"Nonreimbursable Space Act Agreement Between RFC Media, LLC. and the National Aeronautics and Space Administration, for 3rd Rock Radio," signed by NASA on October 21, 2011. A copy of the contract was provided by NASA to the Congressional Research Service. The Office of Senator Coburn received the contract by email December 20, 2011.

[290] Third Rock Radio Blog, Website of Third Rock Radio, posted December 12, 2011, http://www.rfcmedia.com/thirdrockradio/, accessed September 24, 2012.

[291] Third Rock Radio Blog, Website of Third Rock Radio, posted December 12, 2011, http://www.rfcmedia.com/thirdrockradio/, accessed September 24, 2012.

[292] "Nonreimbursable Space Act Agreement Between RFC Media, LLC. and the National Aeronautics and Space Administration, for 3rd Rock Radio," signed by NASA on October 21, 2011. A copy of the contract was provided by NASA to the Congressional Research Service. The Office of Senator Coburn received the contract by email December 20, 2011.

[293] "Nonreimbursable Space Act Agreement Between RFC Media, LLC. and the National Aeronautics and Space Administration, for 3rd Rock Radio," signed by NASA on October 21, 2011. A copy of the contract was provided by NASA to the Congressional Research Service. The Office of Senator Coburn received the contract by email December 20, 2011.

[294] Information provided by NASA to the Congressional Research Service, July 30, 2012.

[295] Workman, Robert. "Microsoft and NASA team up for Curiosity Mars rover Xbox Game," *Christian Science Monitor*, August 1, 2012. Available at http://www.csmonitor.com/Science/2012/0801/Microsoft-and-NASA-team-up-for-Curiosity-Mars-rover-Xbox-game-video, accessed August 8, 2012.

[296] Information provided by NASA to the Congressional Research Service, July 30, 2012.

[297] Information provided by NASA to the Congressional Research Service, July 30, 2012.

[298] Information provided by NASA to the Congressional Research Service, July 30, 2012.

[299] Strange, Adario. "NASA Releases Mars Rover Game for Xbox 360," *PCMag.com*, July 17, 2012. Available at http://www.pcmag.com/article2/0,2817,2407219,00.asp, accessed August 8, 2012.

[300] Information provided by NASA to the Congressional Research Service, July 30, 2012.

[301] USASpending.gov, Prime Award Spending Data, Transaction IDs: AG84N8P120130, AG8371P120002, AG82BHP120020 AG91U4P120006, AG8371P120002, AG91U4P120006, AG84N8P120130, AG84N8P120062, AG82ATP120016, AG84N8P120098, AG8371P120002, AG8371P110003 (all fiscal year 2012 transactions for Friends of Smokey Bear Balloon, DUNS Num. 152959636), http://usaspending.gov/search?form_fields=%7B%22search_term%22%3A%22friends+of+smokey+bear+balloon%22%2C%22fyear%22%3A%5B%222012%22%5D%7D, accessed October 11, 2012.

[302] USASpending.gov, Prime Award Spending Data, Contracts awarded to Friends of Smokey Bear Balloon (DUNS Number 152959636), http://usaspending.gov/search?form_fields=%7B%22search_term%22%3A%22friends+of+smokey+bear+balloon%22%7D, accessed August 31, 2012.

[303] USASpending.gov, Prime Award Spending Data, Transaction ID AG91U4P120006, http://usaspending.gov/explore?fiscal_year=all&comingfrom=searchresults&piid=AG91U4P120006&typeofview=complete, accessed September 24, 2012.

[304] KPBS TV website, "2012 Temecula Valley Balloon & Wine Festival," http://www.kpbs.org/events/2012/jun/01/14153/, accessed October 11, 2012.

[305] USASpending.gov, Prime Award Spending Data, Transaction IDs: AG84N8P120130, AG8371P120002, AG82BHP120020 AG91U4P120006, AG8371P120002, AG91U4P120006, AG84N8P120130, AG84N8P120062, AG82ATP120016, AG84N8P120098, AG8371P120002, AG8371P110003 (all fiscal year 2012 transactions for Friends of Smokey Bear Balloon, DUNS Num. 152959636), http://usaspending.gov/search?form_fields=%7B%22search_term%22%3A%22friends+of+smokey+bear+balloon%22%2C%22fyear%22%3A%5B%222012%22%5D%7D, accessed October 11, 2012.

[306] USASpending.gov, Prime Award Spending Data, Transaction ID AG82ATP120016, available at http://usaspending.gov/explore?fiscal_year=all&comingfrom=searchresults&piid=AG82ATP120016&typeofview=complete, accessed October 11, 2012.

[307] USASpending.gov, Prime Award Spending Data, Transaction ID AG447UP100325, available at http://usaspending.gov/explore?fiscal_year=all&comingfrom=searchresults&piid=AG447UP100325&typeofview=complete, accessed September 24, 2012.

[308] USASpending.gov, Prime Award Spending Data, Transaction IDs: AG04GGP120097, AG8156P120017, INA12PX91333, AG8156P120055.

[309] USASpending.gov, Prime Award Spending Data, Transaction IDs: AG84N8P120130, AG8371P120002, AG82BHP120020 AG91U4P120006, AG8371P120002, AG91U4P120006, AG84N8P120130, AG84N8P120062, AG82ATP120016, AG84N8P120098, AG8371P120002, AG8371P110003 (all fiscal year 2012 transactions for Friends of Smokey Bear Balloon, DUNS Num. 152959636).

[310] USASpending.gov, Prime Award Spending Data, Transaction IDs: AG04GGP120097, AG8156P120017, INA12PX91333, AG8156P120055.

[311] National Climate Data Center, "U.S. August Wildfire Activity (2000-2012)," http://www1.ncdc.noaa.gov/pub/data/cmb/images/fire/2012/08/August2012_wildfirecounts.png, accessed October 11, 2012.

[312] Tabak J, V Zayas. (2012) "The Roles of Featural and Configural Face Processing in Snap Judgments of Sexual Orientation," *PLoS One*, 7(5): 1-7.

[313] In exchange for participation in the study, the college students received extra course credit. Tabak J, V Zayas. (2012) "The Roles of Featural and Configural Face Processing in Snap Judgments of Sexual Orientation," *PLoS One*, 7(5): 1-7.

[314] Tabak J, V Zayas. (2012) "The Roles of Featural and Configural Face Processing in Snap Judgments of Sexual Orientation," *PLoS One*, 7(5): 1-7.

[315] Tabak, J and V Zayas. "The Science of 'Gaydar'," *New York Times*, June 3, 2012 (published online June 1, 2012): SR10 [New York print edition]. Available at http://www.nytimes.com/2012/06/03/opinion/sunday/the-science-of-gaydar.html, accessed September 24, 2012.

[316] Tabak, J and V Zayas. "The Science of 'Gaydar'," *New York Times*, June 3, 2012 (published online June 1, 2012): SR10 [New York print edition]. Available at http://www.nytimes.com/2012/06/03/opinion/sunday/the-science-of-gaydar.html, accessed September 24, 2012.

[317] Tabak J, V Zayas. (2012) "The Roles of Featural and Configural Face Processing in Snap Judgments of Sexual Orientation," *PLoS One*, 7(5): 1-7.

[318] Tabak, J and V Zayas. "The Science of 'Gaydar'," *New York Times*, June 3, 2012 (published online June 1, 2012): SR10 [New York print edition]. Available at http://www.nytimes.com/2012/06/03/opinion/sunday/the-science-of-gaydar.html, accessed September 24, 2012.

[319] Tabak J, V Zayas. (2012) "The Roles of Featural and Configural Face Processing in Snap Judgments of Sexual Orientation," *PLoS One*, 7(5): 1-7.

[320] Tabak, J and V Zayas. "The Science of 'Gaydar'," *New York Times*, June 3, 2012 (published online June 1, 2012): SR10 [New York print edition]. Available at http://www.nytimes.com/2012/06/03/opinion/sunday/the-science-of-gaydar.html, accessed September 24, 2012.

[321] Tabak J, V Zayas. (2012) "The Roles of Featural and Configural Face Processing in Snap Judgments of Sexual Orientation," *PLoS One*, 7(5): 1-7.

[322] Tabak J, V Zayas. (2012) "The Roles of Featural and Configural Face Processing in Snap Judgments of Sexual Orientation," *PLoS One*, 7(5): 1-7.

[323] Tabak, J and V Zayas. "The Science of 'Gaydar'," *New York Times*, June 3, 2012 (published online June 1, 2012): SR10 [New York print edition]. Available at http://www.nytimes.com/2012/06/03/opinion/sunday/the-science-of-gaydar.html, accessed September 24, 2012.

[324] Information provided by the National Science Foundation to the Congressional Research Service, May 31, 2012.

[325] "Strategic Sourcing: Improved and Expanded Use Could Save Billions in Annual Procurement Costs," Government Accountability Office, September 2012, GAO-12-919, p. 1. Available at http://www.gao.gov/assets/650/648644.pdf, accessed October 15, 2012.

[326] "Strategic Sourcing: Improved and Expanded Use Could Save Billions in Annual Procurement Costs," Government Accountability Office, September 2012, GAO-12-919, p. 1, 35. Available at http://www.gao.gov/assets/650/648644.pdf, accessed October 15, 2012.

[327] "Strategic Sourcing: Improved and Expanded Use Could Save Billions in Annual Procurement Costs," Government Accountability Office, September 2012, GAO-12-919, p. 3. Available at http://www.gao.gov/assets/650/648644.pdf, accessed October 15, 2012.

[328] "Strategic Sourcing: Improved and Expanded Use Could Save Billions in Annual Procurement Costs," Government Accountability Office, September 2012, GAO-12-919, Highlights page. Available at http://www.gao.gov/assets/650/648644.pdf, accessed October 15, 2012.

[329] "Strategic Sourcing: Improved and Expanded Use Could Save Billions in Annual Procurement Costs," Government Accountability Office, September 2012, GAO-12-919, Highlights page. Available at http://www.gao.gov/assets/650/648644.pdf, accessed October 15, 2012.

[330] DOD saved .06 percent on its overall spending from strategic sourcing, 5.8 percent of which went through strategic sourcing. "Strategic Sourcing: Improved and Expanded Use Could Save Billions in Annual Procurement Costs," Government Accountability Office, September 2012, GAO-12-919, p. 9. Available at http://www.gao.gov/assets/650/648644.pdf, accessed October 15, 2012.

[331] DHS sent 19.8 percent of its spending through strategic sourcing, and saved a total of 2.28 percent of its budget. See Figure 3. "Strategic Sourcing: Improved and Expanded Use Could Save Billions in Annual Procurement Costs," Government Accountability Office, September 2012, GAO-12-919, p. 9. Available at http://www.gao.gov/assets/650/648644.pdf, accessed October 15, 2012.

[332] "Strategic Sourcing: Improved and Expanded Use Could Save Billions in Annual Procurement Costs," Government Accountability Office, September 2012, GAO-12-919, p. 10. Available at http://www.gao.gov/assets/650/648644.pdf, accessed October 15, 2012.

[333] "Strategic Sourcing: Improved and Expanded Use Could Save Billions in Annual Procurement Costs," Government Accountability Office, September 2012, GAO-12-919, p. 14. Available at http://www.gao.gov/assets/650/648644.pdf, accessed October 15, 2012.

[334] "Strategic Sourcing: Improved and Expanded Use Could Save Billions in Annual Procurement Costs," Government Accountability Office, September 2012, GAO-12-919, p. 23. Available at http://www.gao.gov/assets/650/648644.pdf, accessed October 15, 2012.

[335] "Strategic Sourcing: Improved and Expanded Use Could Save Billions in Annual Procurement Costs," Government Accountability Office, September 2012, GAO-12-919, p. 1. Available at http://www.gao.gov/assets/650/648644.pdf, accessed October 15, 2012.

[336] "Strategic Sourcing: Improved and Expanded Use Could Save Billions in Annual Procurement Costs," Government Accountability Office, September 2012, GAO-12-919, p. 35. Available at http://www.gao.gov/assets/650/648644.pdf, accessed October 15, 2012.

[337] "Strategic Sourcing: Improved and Expanded Use Could Save Billions in Annual Procurement Costs," Government Accountability Office, September 2012, GAO-12-919, p. 1. Available at http://www.gao.gov/assets/650/648644.pdf, accessed October 15, 2012.

[338] "National Endowment for the Arts Announces $1 Million in Grants for The Big Read," National Endowment for the Arts website, http://www.nea.gov/news/news12/big-read-grants-2012-2013.html, accessed October 11, 2012.

[339] National Endowment for the Arts website, "National Endowment for the Arts Announces $1 Million in Grants for The Big Read," http://www.nea.gov/news/news12/big-read-grants-2012-2013.html, accessed October 11, 2012.

[340] "The Big Read: September 2012-June 2013," National Endowment for the Arts website, http://www.nea.gov/national/bigread/press/bigread2013list.php?sortby=alpha, accessed September 10, 2012.

[341] Corcoran, Lindsay. "Third Shrewsbury Big Read Planned for April 2013," *Shrewsbury Daily Voice*, July 19, 2012. Available at http://shrewsbury.dailyvoice.com/neighbors/third-shrewsbury-big-read-planned-april-2013, accessed September 10, 2012.

[342] "2012-13 Calendar of Events," Storytelling & Arts Center of the Southeast, http://www.storyartscenter.org/calendar.htm, accessed October 4, 2012

[343] "Staten Island OutLOUD to host NEA's The Big Read for second year in a row," *Staten Island Advance*, July 18, 2012, http://www.silive.com/entertainment/arts/index.ssf/2012/07/staten_island_outloud_to_host.html, accessed September 10, 2012.

[344] "Ready to Read in Camden: NEA Selects Rutgers—Camden for The Big Read, One of Two Sites in the City," Rutgers, the State University of New Jersey, Press Release, July 13, 2012, http://news.rutgers.edu/medrel/news-releases/2012/07/ready-to-read-in-cam-20120713/, accessed September 10, 2012.

[345] "50 Fest Kicks Off CENTERSTAGE 50th Anniversary Season, 9/27-30," *BroadwayWorld.com*, August 15, 2012, http://baltimore.broadwayworld.com/article/50-Fest-Kicks-Off-CENTERSTAGE-50th-Anniversary-Season-927-30-20120815, accessed August 20, 2012.

[346] "Big Read 2012," Massillon Museum website, http://www.massillonmuseum.org/eventprog_thebigread.html, accessed October 4, 2012.

[347] "Gov. Heineman Awards $505,000 in CDBG Funds For Sarpy County Expansion," State of Nebraska website, March 19, 2012, http://www.governor.nebraska.gov/news/2012/03/19_sarpy_co.html, accessed October 2, 2012.

[348] "Governor Heineman Awards $500,000 for Nebraska Pet Care Company," WOWT-6, http://www.wowt.com/home/headlines/Govenor_Heineman_Awards_500000_for_Sarpy_County_Expansion_143396536.html, accessed October 2, 2012.

[349] "Governor Heineman Awards $500,000 for Nebraska Pet Care Company," WOWT-6, http://www.wowt.com/home/headlines/Govenor_Heineman_Awards_500000_for_Sarpy_County_Expansion_143396536.html, accessed October 2, 2012.

[350] Product Catalog, Website of Sergeant's Pet Care Products, Inc., http://www.sergeants.com/products/ProductCatalog.asp?one=18&two=35&three=120&pr=1044 , accessed October 2, 2012.

[351] Product Catalog, Website of Sergeant's Pet Care Products, Inc., http://www.sergeants.com/products/ProductCatalog.asp?one=52&two=154, October 2, 2012.

[352] Product Catalog, Website of Sergeant's Pet Care Products, Inc., http://www.sergeants.com/products/ProductCatalog.asp?one=1&two=103&three=154, accessed April 17, 2012.

[353] Gonzalez, Cindy. "Sergeant's adds jobs at new headquarters," *The Omaha World Herald*, March 20, 2012; http://www.omaha.com/article/20120320/MONEY/703209965 .

[354] Overley, Jeff. "Morgan Lewis Helps Perrigo Fetch Pet Care Co. For $285M," Morgan Lewis website, September 13, 2012, http://www.morganlewis.com/pubs/Law360_PerrigoWin_13sept12.pdf, accessed October 2, 2012.

[355] Senator Tom Coburn, "Treasure MAP: The Market Access Program's Bounty of Waste, Loot and Spoils Plundered from Taxpayers," June 2012, http://www.coburn.senate.gov/public/index.cfm?a=Files.Serve&File_id=5c2568d4-ae96-40bc-b3d8-19e7a259f749, p. 15, accessed October 2, 2012.

[356] "Schumer Secures $199k in Federal Funds for Key Infrastructure Work in Genesee County – New Access Road will Help Pave the Way for Pepsi's Muller Quaker Greek Yogurt Factory," Website of U.S. Senator Charles E. Schumer, Press Release, August 20, 2012, http://www.schumer.senate.gov/Newsroom/record.cfm?id=337479, accessed August 22, 2012.

[357] "The Power of PepsiCo," PepsiCo Inc. 2011 Annual Report, http://www.pepsico.com/annual11/downloads/PEP_AR11_2011_Annual_Report.pdf, accessed August 22, 2012.

[358] Ring, Niamh. "Pepsi to Sell Yogurt in U.S. in Venture With Muller," Bloomberg News, July 9, 2012, http://www.businessweek.com/news/2012-07-09/pepsi-to-sell-yogurt-in-u-dot-s-dot-in-venture-with-muller, accessed August 22, 2012.

[359] "Schumer Secures $199k in Federal Funds for Key Infrastructure Work in Genesee County – New Access Road will Help Pave the Way for Pepsi's Muller Quaker Greek Yogurt Factory," Website of U.S. Senator Charles E. Schumer, Press Release, August 20, 2012, http://www.schumer.senate.gov/Newsroom/record.cfm?id=337479, accessed August 22, 2012.

[360] "Schumer Secures $199k in Federal Funds for Key Infrastructure Work in Genesee County – New Access Road will Help Pave the Way for Pepsi's Muller Quaker Greek Yogurt Factory," Website of U.S. Senator Charles E. Schumer, Press Release, August 20, 2012, http://www.schumer.senate.gov/Newsroom/record.cfm?id=337479, accessed August 22, 2012.

[361] "Genesee County, Genessee Valley Agri-Business Park, Schumer, Yogurt Plant," WGRZ-TV, August 20, 2012, http://www.wgrz.com/news/local/story.aspx?odyssey=topicpage&storyid=178585, accessed September 10, 2012.

[362] "Schumer Secures $199k in Federal Funds for Key Infrastructure Work in Genesee County – New Access Road will Help Pave the Way for Pepsi's Muller Quaker Greek Yogurt Factory," Website of U.S. Senator Charles E. Schumer, Press Release, August 20, 2012, http://www.schumer.senate.gov/Newsroom/record.cfm?id=337479, accessed August 22, 2012.

[363] "Pepsi latest to enter fast-growing yogurt market," Associated Press, July 9, 2012. Available at http://www.usatoday.com/money/industries/food/story/2012-07-09/pepsi-selling-yogurt/56111492/1, accessed August 22, 2012.

[364] Kaplan, Thomas. "Another Yogurt Factory Planned for Upstate," The New York Times City Room blog, February 24, 2012, http://cityroom.blogs.nytimes.com/2012/02/24/another-yogurt-factory-is-set-to-open-upstate/, accessed August 22, 2012.

[365] Strom, Stephanie. "PepsiCo, Shifting Aim, Sees Promise in Yogurt," The New York Times, July 8, 2012. Available at http://www.nytimes.com/2012/07/09/business/pepsico-with-muller-by-quaker-yogurt-aims-at-a-surging-market.html?pagewanted=all, accessed August 22, 2012.

[366] Neuman, William. "Greek Yogurt a Boon for New York State," The New York Times, January 12, 2012. Available at http://www.nytimes.com/2012/01/13/business/demand-for-greek-style-helps-form-a-yogurt-cluster-in-new-york.html, accessed August 22, 2012.

[367] "Study: Golfers Can Improve Their Putt with a Different Look," Purdue University website, April 3, 2012. Available online at http://www.purdue.edu/newsroom/research/2012/120403WittGolf.html, accessed September 24, 2012.

[368] "Award Abstract #0957051: Action's Effect on Perception," Website of the National Science Foundation, http://nsf.gov/awardsearch/showAward.do?AwardNumber=0957051, accessed September 24, 2012.

[369] "Fear in the Eye of the Beholder: Fear and the Perception of Spatial Layout," National Institutes of Health, Project no. 1R01MH075781, http://projectreporter.nih.gov/project_info_history.cfm?aid=7617737&icde=12528748, accessed September 24, 2012.

[370] Witt J, S Linkenauger, and D Proffit. (2012) "Get Me Out of This Slump! Visual Illusions Improve Sports Performance," Psychological Science, 23(4):397.

[371] Witt J, S Linkenauger, and D Proffit. (2012) "Get Me Out of This Slump! Visual Illusions Improve Sports Performance," Psychological Science, 23(4):397.

[372] Witt J, S Linkenauger, and D Proffit. (2012) "Get Me Out of This Slump! Visual Illusions Improve Sports Performance," Psychological Science, 23(4):397.

[373] Witt J, S Linkenauger, and D Proffit. (2012) "Get Me Out of This Slump! Visual Illusions Improve Sports Performance," *Psychological Science*, 23(4):398.

[374] Balentine, John. "Mural a vision of sustainability," *Keep Me Current*, April 6, 2012. Available at http://www.keepmecurrent.com/lakes_region_weekly/news/mural-a-vision-of-sustainability/article_09d8317e-7fed-11e1-b490-001a4bcf887a.html, accessed August 31, 2012.

[375] American Recovery and Reinvestment Act of 2009, PL 111-5, 123 Stat. 180. Available at http://www.gpo.gov/fdsys/pkg/PLAW-111publ5/pdf/PLAW-111publ5.pdf, accessed September 17, 2012.

[376] Balentine, John. "Mural a vision of sustainability," *Keep Me Current*, April 6, 2012. Available at http://www.keepmecurrent.com/lakes_region_weekly/news/mural-a-vision-of-sustainability/article_09d8317e-7fed-11e1-b490-001a4bcf887a.html, accessed August 31, 2012.

[377] Balentine, John. "Mural a vision of sustainability," *Keep Me Current*, April 6, 2012. Available at http://www.keepmecurrent.com/lakes_region_weekly/news/mural-a-vision-of-sustainability/article_09d8317e-7fed-11e1-b490-001a4bcf887a.html, accessed August 31, 2012..

[378] Balentine, John. "Mural a vision of sustainability," *Keep Me Current*, April 6, 2012. Available at http://www.keepmecurrent.com/lakes_region_weekly/news/mural-a-vision-of-sustainability/article_09d8317e-7fed-11e1-b490-001a4bcf887a.html, accessed August 31, 2012.

[379] American Recovery and Reinvestment Act of 2009, p. 66, http://www.gpo.gov/fdsys/pkg/BILLS-111hr1enr/pdf/BILLS-111hr1enr.pdf#page=66

[380] "Communities Putting Prevention to Work: CDC awards $372.8 Million to 44 Communities," Centers for Disease Control and Prevention website, posted March 29, 2010, http://www.cdc.gov/features/chronicpreventiongrants/index.html, accessed October 12, 2012.

[381] Cost per free school lunch is $2.86. See "National School Lunch Program," US Department of Agriculture website, http://www.fns.usda.gov/cnd/lunch/AboutLunch/NSLPFactSheet.pdf, accessed August 20, 2012.

[382] "The Fix We're In For: The State of Our Nation's Busiest Bridges," Transportation for America (T4 America), October 2011. Available at http://t4america.org/docs/bridgereport/bridgereport-metros.pdf, accessed September 6, 2012.

[383] Kelley, Jeremy and Sharahn D. Boykin. "Unused bridge gets $500k federal grant," *Dayton Daily News*, August 19, 2012. Available at http://www.daytondailynews.com/news/news/local-govt-politics/unused-bridge-gets-500k-federal-grant/nRFS8/, accessed September 6, 2012.

[384] Kelley, Jeremy and Sharahn D. Boykin. "Unused bridge gets $500k federal grant," *Dayton Daily News*, August 19, 2012. Available at http://www.daytondailynews.com/news/news/local-govt-politics/unused-bridge-gets-500k-federal-grant/nRFS8/, accessed September 6, 2012.

[385] "2012 Discretionary Grant Program Fact Sheet," Federal Highway Administration website, updated August 20, 2012, http://www.fhwa.dot.gov/discretionary/2012nhcbp.cfm, accessed September 6, 2012.

[386] Kelley, Jeremy and Sharahn D. Boykin. "Unused bridge gets $500k federal grant," *Dayton Daily News*, August 19, 2012. Available at http://www.daytondailynews.com/news/news/local-govt-politics/unused-bridge-gets-500k-federal-grant/nRFS8/, accessed September 6, 2012.

[387] Kelley, Jeremy and Sharahn D. Boykin. "Unused bridge gets $500k federal grant," *Dayton Daily News*, August 19, 2012. Available at http://www.daytondailynews.com/news/news/local-govt-politics/unused-bridge-gets-500k-federal-grant/nRFS8/, accessed September 6, 2012.

[388] Kelley, Jeremy and Sharahn D. Boykin. "Unused bridge gets $500k federal grant," *Dayton Daily News*, August 19, 2012. Available at http://www.daytondailynews.com/news/news/local-govt-politics/unused-bridge-gets-500k-federal-grant/nRFS8/, accessed September 6, 2012.

[389] Kelley, Jeremy and Sharahn D. Boykin. "Unused bridge gets $500k federal grant," *Dayton Daily News*, August 19, 2012. Available at http://www.daytondailynews.com/news/news/local-govt-politics/unused-bridge-gets-500k-federal-grant/nRFS8/, accessed September 6, 2012.

[390] Kelley, Jeremy and Sharahn D. Boykin. "Unused bridge gets $500k federal grant," *Dayton Daily News*, August 19, 2012. Available at http://www.daytondailynews.com/news/news/local-govt-politics/unused-bridge-gets-500k-federal-grant/nRFS8/, accessed September 6, 2012.

[391] Kelley, Jeremy and Sharahn D. Boykin. "Unused bridge gets $500k federal grant," *Dayton Daily News*, August 19, 2012. Available at http://www.daytondailynews.com/news/news/local-govt-politics/unused-bridge-gets-500k-federal-grant/nRFS8/, accessed September 6, 2012.

[392] Kelley, Jeremy and Sharahn D. Boykin. "Unused bridge gets $500k federal grant," *Dayton Daily News*, August 19, 2012. Available at http://www.daytondailynews.com/news/news/local-govt-politics/unused-bridge-gets-500k-federal-grant/nRFS8/, accessed September 6, 2012.

[393] Kelley, Jeremy and Sharahn D. Boykin. "Unused bridge gets $500k federal grant," *Dayton Daily News*, August 19, 2012. Available at http://www.daytondailynews.com/news/news/local-govt-politics/unused-bridge-gets-500k-federal-grant/nRFS8/, accessed September 6, 2012.

[394] Kelley, Jeremy and Sharahn D. Boykin. "Unused bridge gets $500k federal grant," *Dayton Daily News*, August 19, 2012. Available at http://www.daytondailynews.com/news/news/local-govt-politics/unused-bridge-gets-500k-federal-grant/nRFS8/, accessed September 6, 2012.

[395] Kelley, Jeremy and Sharahn D. Boykin. "Unused bridge gets $500k federal grant," *Dayton Daily News*, August 19, 2012. Available at http://www.daytondailynews.com/news/news/local-govt-politics/unused-bridge-gets-500k-federal-grant/nRFS8/, accessed September 6, 2012.

[396] Trivedi AN, RC Grebla, L Jiang, J Yoon, V Mor, and KW Kizer. (2012) "Duplicate Federal Payments for Dual Enrollees in Medicare Advantage Plans and the Veterans Affairs Health Care System," *Journal of the American Medical Association*, 308(1):69.

[397] Personal communication with study's lead author, August 21, 2012.

[398] Trivedi AN, RC Grebla, L Jiang, J Yoon, V Mor, and KW Kizer. (2012) "Duplicate Federal Payments for Dual Enrollees in Medicare Advantage Plans and the Veterans Affairs Health Care System," *Journal of the American Medical Association*, 308(1):69.

[399] Trivedi AN, RC Grebla, L Jiang, J Yoon, V Mor, and KW Kizer. (2012) "Duplicate Federal Payments for Dual Enrollees in Medicare Advantage Plans and the Veterans Affairs Health Care System," *Journal of the American Medical Association*, 308(1):70.

[400] Trivedi AN, RC Grebla, L Jiang, J Yoon, V Mor, and KW Kizer. (2012) "Duplicate Federal Payments for Dual Enrollees in Medicare Advantage Plans and the Veterans Affairs Health Care System," *Journal of the American Medical Association*, 308(1):70.

[401] Trivedi AN, RC Grebla, L Jiang, J Yoon, V Mor, and KW Kizer. (2012) "Duplicate Federal Payments for Dual Enrollees in Medicare Advantage Plans and the Veterans Affairs Health Care System," *Journal of the American Medical Association*, 308(1):70.

[402] Ten percent of VA/NA dual enrollees did not use their MA plan at all. One option for savings would be to recover any MA costs on behalf of these enrollees. The lead author of the Trivedi et al. (2012) estimates that actual savings are over $1 billion.

[403] Personal communication with study's lead author, August 21, 2012.

[404] Information provided by the Indianapolis Public Transportation Corporation to the Congressional Research Service, July 9, 2012.

[405] Website of the Indianapolis Public Transportation Corporation, "IndyGo Fare Pricing." Available online at http://www.indygo.net/pages/fare-information, accessed September 24, 2012.

[406] Russell, John. "As Super Bowl 2012 looms, Indy cab drivers get tips on welcoming an estimated 150,000 football fans," *Indianapolis Star*, January 22, 2012. Available at http://www.indystar.com/article/20120122/NEWS11/201220338/As-Super-Bowl-2012-looms-Indy-cab-drivers-get-tips-welcoming-an-estimated-150-000-football-fans, accessed September 24, 2012.

[407] Russell, John. "As Super Bowl 2012 looms, Indy cab drivers get tips on welcoming an estimated 150,000 football fans," *Indianapolis Star*, January 22, 2012. Available at http://www.indystar.com/article/20120122/NEWS11/201220338/As-Super-Bowl-2012-looms-Indy-cab-drivers-get-tips-welcoming-an-estimated-150-000-football-fans, accessed September 24, 2012.

[408] Rovell, Darren. "The top Super Bowl ticket myths," *ESPN.com*, January 31, 2006, http://sports.espn.go.com/espn/page2/story?page=rovell/060131, accessed August 30, 2012. Ticket price averages are for those sold in the secondary market.

[409] Shipp, Brett. "New questions over DISD's $57,000 trip to the movies," WFAA-TV, March 9, 2012, http://www.wfaa.com/news/investigates/New-questions-over-DISDs-57000-trip-to-the-movies-141987013.html, accessed August 30, 2012.

[410] Haag, Matthew, *The Dallas Morning News* Education Blog, August 10, 2012"Friday document dump: Read the feds' review of Dallas ISD's boys-only field trip to Red Tails," http://educationblog.dallasnews.com/2012/08/friday-document-dump-read-the-feds-review-of-dallas-isds-boys-only-field-trip-to-red-tails.html/, accessed October 11, 2012.

[411] Haag, Matthew, "Dallas ISD must provide gender equality training after boys-only field trip to see 'Red Tails'," *The Dallas Morning News*, July 20, 2012, http://www.dallasnews.com/news/education/headlines/20120720-dallas-isd-must-provide-gender-equality-training-after-boys-only-field-trip-to-see-red-tails.ece, accessed October 11, 2012.

[412] Shipp, Brett. "New questions over DISD's $57,000 trip to the movies," WFAA-TV, March 9, 2012, http://www.wfaa.com/news/investigates/New-questions-over-DISDs-57000-trip-to-the-movies-141987013.html, accessed August 30, 2012.

[413] Shipp, Brett. "New questions over DISD's $57,000 trip to the movies," WFAA-TV, March 9, 2012, http://www.wfaa.com/news/investigates/New-questions-over-DISDs-57000-trip-to-the-movies-141987013.html, accessed August 30, 2012.

[414] Shipp, Brett. "New questions over DISD's $57,000 trip to the movies," WFAA-TV, March 9, 2012, http://www.wfaa.com/news/investigates/New-questions-over-DISDs-57000-trip-to-the-movies-141987013.html, accessed August 30, 2012.

[415] Shipp, Brett. "DISD questioned over $57,000 field trip using federal funds," WFAA-TV, February 9, 2012, http://www.wfaa.com/news/education/DISD-questioned-over-32000-field-trip-using-federal-funds-139058539.html, accessed August 30, 2012.

[416] DISD internal emails published on Scribd.com, http://www.scribd.com/doc/84341974/Dallas-ISD-Red-Tails-emails, accessed August 30, 2012.

[417] "State, Federal Agencies Investigating DISD For Discrimination," CBSDFW.com, March 7, 2012, http://dfw.cbslocal.com/2012/03/07/state-federal-agencies-investigating-disd-for-discrimination/, accessed August 30, 2012/

[418] Haag, Matthew. "Friday document dump: Read the feds' review of Dallas ISD's boys-only field trip to Red Tails," *Dallas Morning News* Education Blog, August 10, 2012, http://educationblog.dallasnews.com/2012/08/friday-document-dump-read-the-feds-review-of-dallas-isds-boys-only-field-trip-to-red-tails.html/, accessed August 30, 2012.

[419] "Editorial: DISD's Teflon Administrator," *Dallas Morning News*, July 31, 2012. Available at http://www.dallasnews.com/opinion/editorials/20120731-editorial-disds-teflon-administrator.ece, accessed August 30, 2012.

[420] Hayden, Eric. "Thoreau's Walden: The Video Game," *Time* NewsFeed, April 30, 2012, available at http://newsfeed.time.com/2012/04/30/thoreaus-walden-the-video-game, accessed August 23, 2012.

[421] "Walden, A Game," Website of the University of Southern California, http://cinema.usc.edu/interactive/research/walden.cfm, accessed August 23, 2012.

[422] "Walden, A Game," Website of the University of Southern California, http://cinema.usc.edu/interactive/research/walden.cfm, accessed August 23, 2012.

[423] Hayden, Eric. "Thoreau's Walden: The Video Game," *Time* NewsFeed, April 30, 2012, available at http://newsfeed.time.com/2012/04/30/thoreaus-walden-the-video-game, accessed August 23, 2012.

[424] Hayden, Eric. "Thoreau's Walden: The Video Game," *Time* NewsFeed, April 30, 2012, available at http://newsfeed.time.com/2012/04/30/thoreaus-walden-the-video-game, accessed August 23, 2012.

[425] Temple, Emily. "There's Going To Be A Henry David Thoreau Video Game" *FlavorWire.com*, April 26, 2012, http://www.flavorwire.com/284117/theres-going-to-be-a-henry-david-thoreau-video-game, accessed August 23, 2012.

[426] Baldwin, Roberto. "Urinal Cake Delivers PSA on Drunk Driving," *Wired* Gadget Lab Blog, July 3, 2012, http://www.wired.com/gadgetlab/2012/07/urinal-cake-takes-the-piss-out-of-drunk-driving/, accessed September 24, 2012.

[427] Information provided the State of Michigan to the Congressional Research Service, July 24, 2012.

[428] "Mich. Deploys Talking Urinal Cakes in DUI Fight," Associated Press Video at Youtube.com, posted July 2, 2012, http://www.youtube.com/watch?v=4UCrf3tmkwo, accessed July 10, 2012.

[429] "Mich. Deploys Talking Urinal Cakes in DUI Fight," Associated Press Video at Youtube.com, posted July 2, 2012, http://www.youtube.com/watch?v=4UCrf3tmkwo, accessed July 10, 2012.

[430] "Mich. Deploys Talking Urinal Cakes in DUI Fight," Associated Press Video at Youtube.com, posted July 2, 2012, http://www.youtube.com/watch?v=4UCrf3tmkwo, accessed July 10, 2012.

[431] "Mich. Deploys Talking Urinal Cakes in DUI Fight," Associated Press Video at Youtube.com, posted July 2, 2012, http://www.youtube.com/watch?v=4UCrf3tmkwo, accessed July 10, 2012.

[432] "Talking Urinal Fights Drunk Driving," CNN Video at Youtube.com, posted July 2, 2012, http://www.youtube.com/watch?v=QUy7XWRql6w&feature=related, accessed July 10, 2012.

[433] Schwartz, Terri. "'Avengers' Becomes Third-Highest-Grossing Movie Ever," *MTV News*, June 1, 2012, http://www.mtv.com/news/articles/1686345/avengers-box-office-gross.jhtml, accessed October 2, 2012.

[434] Hernandez, Marjorie. "Comic book stores owners see hope as comic sales numbers rebound; Comic book industry enjoys post-recession comeback," *Ventura County Star*, June 9, 2012, http://www.vcstar.com/news/2012/jun/09/comic-book-stores-owners-see-hope-as-comic-sales/#ixzz285L2Tef7, accessed October 2, 2012.

[435] "CCS Awarded $255,000 Community Development Grant," Website of Center for Cartoon Studies, http://www.cartoonstudies.org/index.php/2011/06/29/ccs-awarded-255000-community-development-grant/, accessed October 1, 2012.

[436] "Who Should Attend?" Website of Center for Cartoon Studies, http://www.cartoonstudies.org/index.php/about/who-should-attend/, accessed August 14, 2012.

[437] "CCS Awarded $255,000 Community Development Grant," Website of Center for Cartoon Studies, http://www.cartoonstudies.org/index.php/2011/06/29/ccs-awarded-255000-community-development-grant/, accessed August 14, 2012.

[438] "Governor Shumlin Announces $2.1 in Community Development Grants," Website of Vermont State Government, June 28, 2011, http://www.vermont.gov/portal/government/article.php?news=2692, accessed August 14, 2012.

[439] "CCS Awarded $255,000 Community Development Grant," website of Center for Cartoon Studies, http://www.cartoonstudies.org/index.php/2011/06/29/ccs-awarded-255000-community-development-grant/, accessed August 14, 2012.

[440] "Governor Shumlin Announces $2.1 in Community Development Grants," Website of Vermont State Government, June 28, 2011, http://www.vermont.gov/portal/government/article.php?news=2692, accessed August 14, 2012.

441 "FAQs," Website of Center for Cartoon Studies, http://www.cartoonstudies.org/index.php/about/faqs/, accessed October 2, 2012.

442 "FAQs," Website of Center for Cartoon Studies, http://www.cartoonstudies.org/index.php/about/faqs/, accessed October 2, 2012.

443 "The Center for Cartoon Studies; Report of an Evaluation Team to the Committee on Accreditation & Certification of the Vermont Higher Education Council," Vermont Higher Education Council, May 18, 2011, http://education.vermont.gov/new/pdfdoc/board/packet_archives/2011/09-20/EDU-SBE_Item_E3_VHEC_Evaluation_September_20_2011.pdf, accessed October 2, 2012.

444 "The Center for Cartoon Studies; Report of an Evaluation Team to the Committee on Accreditation & Certification of the Vermont Higher Education Council," Vermont Higher Education Council, May 18, 2011, http://education.vermont.gov/new/pdfdoc/board/packet_archives/2011/09-20/EDU-SBE_Item_E3_VHEC_Evaluation_September_20_2011.pdf, accessed October 2, 2012.

445 Mahan, Shannon M. "Federal Pell Grant Program of the Higher Education Act: How the Program Works, Recent Legislative Changes, and Current Issues," Congressional Research Service, March 27, 2012, R42446.

446 The State Department's Police Development Program in Iraq has $118.2 million available to it in FY2010 and FY2011 funds, and expects to receive $76 million in FY2012 funds. Additionally, the program wasted $206 million in building the Baghdad Police College Annex and the Basra facility, both of which turned out to be "*de facto* waste, the IG said. They will be handed over to the Government of Iraq this year. See "Iraq Police Development Program: Lack of Iraqi Support and Security Problems Raise Question about the Continued Viability of the Program," Office of the Special Inspector General for Iraq Reconstruction, Audit Report No. SIGIR 12-020, July 30, 2012, Summary page, http://www.sigir.mil/files/audits/12-020.pdf, accessed August 1, 2012.

447 "Iraqi Police Development Program: Opportunities for Improved Program Accountability and Budget Transparency," Office of the Special Inspector General for Iraq Reconstruction, Audit Report No. SIGIR 12-006, October 24, 2011, p. 8, http://www.sigir.mil/files/audits/12-006.pdf#view=fit, accessed August 1, 2012.

448 "Iraq Police Development Program: Lack of Iraqi Support and Security Problems Raise Question about the Continued Viability of the Program," Office of the Special Inspector General for Iraq Reconstruction, Audit Report No. SIGIR 12-080, July 30, 2012, p. 19, http://www.sigir.mil/files/audits/12-020.pdf, accessed August 1, 2012.

449 "Iraqi Police Development Program: Opportunities for Improved Program Accountability and Budget Transparency," Office of the Special Inspector General for Iraq Reconstruction, Audit Report No. SIGIR 12-006, October 24, 2011, p.9, http://www.sigir.mil/files/audits/12-006.pdf#view=fit, accessed August 1, 2012.

450 "Iraq Police Development Program: Lack of Iraqi Support and Security Problems Raise Question about the Continued Viability of the Program," Office of the Special Inspector General for Iraq Reconstruction, Audit Report No. SIGIR 12-020, July 30, 2012, p. 22, http://www.sigir.mil/files/audits/12-020.pdf, accessed August 1, 2012.

451 "Iraq Police Development Program: Lack of Iraqi Support and Security Problems Raise Question about the Continued Viability of the Program," Office of the Special Inspector General for Iraq Reconstruction, Audit Report No. SIGIR 12-020, July 30, 2012, p. 12, http://www.sigir.mil/files/audits/12-020.pdf, accessed August 1, 2012.

452 "Iraqi Police Development Program: Opportunities for Improved Program Accountability and Budget Transparency," Office of the Special Inspector General for Iraq Reconstruction, Audit Report No. SIGIR 12-006, October 24, 2011, p. 6, http://www.sigir.mil/files/audits/12-006.pdf#view=fit, accessed August 1, 2012.

453 "Iraqi Police Development Program: Opportunities for Improved Program Accountability and Budget Transparency," Office of the Special Inspector General for Iraq Reconstruction, Audit Report No. SIGIR 12-006, October 24, 2011, p.8, http://www.sigir.mil/files/audits/12-006.pdf#view=fit, accessed August 1, 2012.

[454] "Iraq Police Development Program: Lack of Iraqi Support and Security Problems Raise Question about the Continued Viability of the Program," Office of the Special Inspector General for Iraq Reconstruction, Audit Report No. SIGIR 12-020, July 30, 2012, p. 12, http://www.sigir.mil/files/audits/12-020.pdf, accessed August 1, 2012.

[455] "Iraq Police Development Program: Lack of Iraqi Support and Security Problems Raise Question about the Continued Viability of the Program," Office of the Special Inspector General for Iraq Reconstruction, Audit Report No. SIGIR 12-020, July 30, 2012, p. 10, http://www.sigir.mil/files/audits/12-020.pdf, accessed August 1, 2012.

[456] Arango, Tim. "U.S. May Scrap Costly Efforts to Train Iraqi Police," *New York Times*, May 13, 2012.

[457] "Iraq Police Development Program: Lack of Iraqi Support and Security Problems Raise Question about the Continued Viability of the Program," Office of the Special Inspector General for Iraq Reconstruction, Audit Report No. SIGIR 12-020, July 30, 2012, p. 11, http://www.sigir.mil/files/audits/12-020.pdf, accessed August 1, 2012.

[458] "Iraq Police Development Program: Lack of Iraqi Support and Security Problems Raise Question about the Continued Viability of the Program," Office of the Special Inspector General for Iraq Reconstruction, Audit Report No. SIGIR 12-020, July 30, 2012, p. 16, http://www.sigir.mil/files/audits/12-020.pdf, accessed August 1, 2012.

[459] "Iraq Police Development Program: Lack of Iraqi Support and Security Problems Raise Question about the Continued Viability of the Program," Office of the Special Inspector General for Iraq Reconstruction, Audit Report No. SIGIR 12-020, July 30, 2012, p. 15, http://www.sigir.mil/files/audits/12-020.pdf, accessed August 1, 2012.

[460] "Iraq Police Development Program: Lack of Iraqi Support and Security Problems Raise Question about the Continued Viability of the Program," Office of the Special Inspector General for Iraq Reconstruction, Audit Report No. SIGIR 12-020, July 30, 2012, p. 18, http://www.sigir.mil/files/audits/12-020.pdf, accessed August 1, 2012.

[461] "Iraq Police Development Program: Lack of Iraqi Support and Security Problems Raise Question about the Continued Viability of the Program," Audit Report No. SIGIR 12-020, Office of the Special Inspector General for Iraq Reconstruction, July 30, 2012, p. 15, http://www.sigir.mil/files/audits/12-020.pdf, accessed August 1, 2012.

[462] O'Keefe, Ed. "State Department's police training program in Iraq lacks planning, report says," *The Washington Post*, October 24, 2011.

[463] "Award Abstract #1010974 The Great Immensity," Website of the National Science Foundation, http://nsf.gov/awardsearch/showAward.do?AwardNumber=1010974, accessed September 19, 2012.

[464] Tamblyn, Jeff. " 'Great Immensity' at Kansas City Repertory Theatre, Review," Kansas City infoZine, February 27, 2012. Available online at: http://www.infozine.com/news/infozine/50914.html, accessed September 19, 2012.

[465] Website of "The Great Immensity," www.thegreatimmensity.org/about, accessed October 15, 2012.

[466] Tamblyn, Jeff. " 'Great Immensity' at Kansas City Repertory Theatre, Review," Kansas City infoZine, February 27, 2012. Available online at: http://www.infozine.com/news/infozine/50914.html, accessed September 19, 2012.

[467] Tamblyn, Jeff. " 'Great Immensity' at Kansas City Repertory Theatre, Review," Kansas City infoZine, February 27, 2012. Available online at: http://www.infozine.com/news/infozine/50914.html, accessed September 19, 2012.

[468] Tamblyn, Jeff. " 'Great Immensity' at Kansas City Repertory Theatre, Review," Kansas City infoZine, February 27, 2012. Available online at: http://www.infozine.com/news/infozine/50914.html, accessed September 19, 2012.

[469] Tamblyn, Jeff. " 'Great Immensity' at Kansas City Repertory Theatre, Review," Kansas City infoZine, February 27, 2012. Available online at: http://www.infozine.com/news/infozine/50914.html, accessed September 19, 2012.

[470] Hirsch, Deborah. "*The Great Immensity* at KC Rep takes on global warming," *The Pitch*, February 28, 2012, http://www.pitch.com/kansascity/the-great-immensity-kc-rep-civilians/Content?oid=2800953, accessed October 4, 2012.

[471] Gillerman, Margaret. "Federal agency approves grant for Delmar Loop trolley," *St. Louis Post-Dispatch*, September 6, 2012, http://www.stltoday.com/federal-agency-approves-grant-for-delmar-loop-trolley/article_b52b3116-f7e3-11e1-8c73-0019bb30f31a.html, accessed September 24, 2012.

[472] "St. Louis Loop Trolley Project," American Public Transportation Association website, http://www.apta.com/resources/hottopics/circulators/Documents/St-Louis-Trolley-Fact-Sheet.pdf, accessed September 24, 2012.

[473] "Transportation Improvement Program: Fiscal years 2013 through 2016," East-West Gateway Council of Governments, http://www.ewgateway.org/pdffiles/Library/trans/tip/FY2013-2016/tip-fy2013-2016-final.pdf, accessed October 11, 2012.

[474] "Transportation Improvement Program: Fiscal years 2013 through 2016," East-West Gateway Council of Governments, http://www.ewgateway.org/pdffiles/Library/trans/tip/FY2013-2016/tip-fy2013-2016-final.pdf, accessed October 11, 2012.

[475] Gillerman, Margaret. "Federal agency approves grant for Delmar Loop trolley," *St. Louis Post-Dispatch*, September 6, 2012, http://www.stltoday.com/federal-agency-approves-grant-for-delmar-loop-trolley/article_b52b3116-f7e3-11e1-8c73-0019bb30f31a.html, accessed September 24, 2012.

[476] Gillerman, Margaret. "Federal agency approves grant for Delmar Loop trolley," *St. Louis Post-Dispatch*, September 6, 2012, http://www.stltoday.com/federal-agency-approves-grant-for-delmar-loop-trolley/article_b52b3116-f7e3-11e1-8c73-0019bb30f31a.html, accessed September 24, 2012.

[477] Gillerman, Margaret. "Federal agency approves grant for Delmar Loop trolley," *St. Louis Post-Dispatch*, September 6, 2012, http://www.stltoday.com/federal-agency-approves-grant-for-delmar-loop-trolley/article_b52b3116-f7e3-11e1-8c73-0019bb30f31a.html, accessed September 24, 2012.

[478] Thakkar, Neel. "Federal decision on Loop trolley funding expected soon," *St. Louis Beacon*, September 4, 2012, https://www.stlbeacon.org/#!/content/26792/loop_trolley_update_083012, accessed September 24, 2012.

[479] Thakkar, Neel. "Federal decision on Loop trolley funding expected soon," *St. Louis Beacon*, September 4, 2012, https://www.stlbeacon.org/#!/content/26792/loop_trolley_update_083012, accessed September 24, 2012.

[480] Thakkar, Neel. "Federal decision on Loop trolley funding expected soon," *St. Louis Beacon*, September 4, 2012, https://www.stlbeacon.org/#!/content/26792/loop_trolley_update_083012, accessed September 24, 2012.

[481] Thakkar, Neel. "Federal decision on Loop trolley funding expected soon," *St. Louis Beacon*, September 4, 2012, https://www.stlbeacon.org/#!/content/26792/loop_trolley_update_083012, accessed September 24, 2012.

[482] O'Rourke, Ronald, "Navy Littoral Combat Ship (LCS) Program: Background, Issues, and Options for Congress," Congressional Research Service, June 13, 2012, RL33741, p. 6.

[483] O'Rourke, Ronald, "Navy Littoral Combat Ship (LCS) Program: Background, Issues, and Options for Congress," Congressional Research Service, June 13, 2012, RL33741, p. 85.

[484] The Congressional Budget Office estimates the additional cost of building 20 ships under the dual-award strategy will be $740 million, or $37 million per ship. For just four ships currently being constructed, the additional cost is roughly $148 million. See O'Rourke, Ronald, "Navy Littoral Combat Ship (LCS) Program:

Background, Issues, and Options for Congress," Congressional Research Service, June 13, 2012, RL33741, p. 79, 85.

[485] O'Rourke, Ronald, "Navy Littoral Combat Ship (LCS) Program: Background, Issues, and Options for Congress," Congressional Research Service, August 10, 2012, RL33741, p. 83.

[486] O'Rourke, Ronald, "Navy Littoral Combat Ship (LCS) Program: Background, Issues, and Options for Congress," Congressional Research Service, June 13, 2012, RL33741, p. 85.

[487] "Defense Acquisitions: Assessments of Selected Weapons Programs," Government Accountability Office, March 2012, GAO-12-400SP, p. 107. Available at http://gao.gov/products/GAO-12-400SP, accessed September 24, 2012.

[488] "Defense Acquisitions: Assessments of Selected Weapons Programs," Government Accountability Office, March 2012, GAO-12-400SP, p. 108. Available at http://gao.gov/products/GAO-12-400SP, accessed September 24, 2012.

[489] "Defense Acquisitions: Assessments of Selected Weapons Programs," Government Accountability Office, March 2012, GAO-12-400SP, p. 108. Available at http://gao.gov/products/GAO-12-400SP, accessed September 24, 2012.

[490] Cavas, Christopher. "U.S. Navy Boosting LCS Core Crew Up to 95%," *Defense News*, July 2, 2012. Available at http://www.defensenews.com/apps/pbcs.dll/article?AID=2012307020001, accessed August 27, 2012.

[491] O'Rourke, Ronald, "Navy Littoral Combat Ship (LCS) Program: Background, Issues, and Options for Congress," Congressional Research Service, June 13, 2012, RL33741, p. 6.

[492] By 2016, the Navy plans on purchasing 24 LCS, but it will not have a single fully capable mission module at that time. See "Defense Acquisitions: Assessments of Selected Weapons Programs," Government Accountability Office, March 2012, GAO-12-400SP, p. 109. Available at http://gao.gov/products/GAO-12-400SP, accessed September 24, 2012.

[493] Cavas, Christopher. "Past imperfect," *Armed Forces Journal*, April 2011. Available at http://www.armedforcesjournal.com/2011/04/5848053, accessed August 27, 2012.

[494] Grant Numbers X1 – 97206712-0 and X1 – 97206712-1, "Students Against Trash," Environmental Protection Agency website, Available at http://yosemite.epa.gov/oarm/igms_egf.nsf/AllGrantsNarrow?OpenView, accessed August 10, 2012.

[495] Grant Number X1 – 97206712-0, "Students Against Trash," Environmental Protection Agency website, Available at http://yosemite.epa.gov/oarm/igms_egf.nsf/AllGrantsNarrow?OpenView, accessed August 10, 2012.

[496] "Environment Poster Design Contest," Environmental Finance Center -- Syracuse University, http://efc.syracusecoe.org/efc/projects.html?skuvar=27, accessed August 10, 2012.

[497] Grant Number X1 – 97206712-0, "Students Against Trash," Environmental Protection Agency website, Available at http://yosemite.epa.gov/oarm/igms_egf.nsf/AllGrantsNarrow?OpenView, accessed August 10, 2012.

[498] "Environment Poster Design Contest," Environmental Finance Center -- Syracuse University, http://efc.syracusecoe.org/efc/projects.html?skuvar=27, accessed August 10, 2012.

[499] Scoring guidelines on http://www.studentsvstrash.com/, accessed August 10, 2012.

[500] "Contest Details," http://www.studentsvstrash.com/resources.html, accessed August 10, 2012.

[501] Poster finalists at http://www.studentsvstrash.com/finalists.html, accessed August 10, 2012.

[502] Poster finalists at http://www.studentsvstrash.com/finalists.html, accessed August 10, 2012.

[503] The $388,000 in federal money consisted of $65,000 from the American Recovery and Reinvestment Act (the "stimulus bill") and $323,000 from the Congestion Mitigation and Air Quality (CMAQ) program, which is paid for from the federal Highway Trust Fund. Information provided by Grants Pass grants specialist to Office of Senator Tom Coburn, May 7, 2012.

[504] Minutes of the January 18, 2012, Grants Pass City Conucil meeting, page 8. Available at http://www.grantspassoregon.gov/Modules/ShowDocument.aspx?documentid=18262, accessed September 6, 2012.

[505] Minutes of the February 1, 2012, Grants Pass City Council meeting, pages 4-5. Available at http://www.grantspassoregon.gov/Modules/ShowDocument.aspx?documentid=18451, accessed September 6, 2012.

[506] Minutes of the January 18, 2012, Grants Pass City Conucil meeting, page 9. Available at http://www.grantspassoregon.gov/Modules/ShowDocument.aspx?documentid=18262, accessed September 6, 2012.

[507] Millman, Joel. "Six-Figure Bus Shelter Stirs Cries to Stop It," *Wall Street Journal*, January 18, 2012. Available at http://online.wsj.com/article/SB10001424052970204468004577167201198731144.html#articleTabs%3Darticle, accessed September 6, 2012.

[508] The median price of homes in Grants Pass is about $167,000, according to Zillow.com information for Grants Pass, Oregon: http://www.zillow.com/local-info/OR-Grants-Pass/r_31829/, accessed October 13, 2012.

[509] Information provided by Grants Pass grants specialist to Office of Senator Tom Coburn, May 7, 2012.

[510] Information provided by Grants Pass grants specialist to Office of Senator Tom Coburn, May 7, 2012.

[511] Minutes of the January 18, 2012, Grants Pass City Council meeting, page 9. Available at http://www.grantspassoregon.gov/Modules/ShowDocument.aspx?documentid=18262, accessed September 6, 2012.

[512] Information provided by Grants Pass grants specialist to Office of Senator Tom Coburn, May 7, 2012.

[513] Minutes of the February 1, 2012, Grants Pass City Council meeting, pages 4-5. Available at http://www.grantspassoregon.gov/Modules/ShowDocument.aspx?documentid=184510, accessed September 6, 2012.

[514] "Implementation of Federal Prize Authority: Progress Report," White House Office of Science and Technology Policy, March 2012. Available at http://www.whitehouse.gov/sites/default/files/microsites/ostp/competes_report_on_prizes_final.pdf, accessed September 24, 2012.

[515] "Implementation of Federal Prize Authority: Progress Report," White House Office of Science and Technology Policy, March 2012. Available at http://www.whitehouse.gov/sites/default/files/microsites/ostp/competes_report_on_prizes_final.pdf, accessed September 24, 2012.

[516] "Implementation of Federal Prize Authority: Progress Report," White House Office of Science and Technology Policy, March 2012. Available at http://www.whitehouse.gov/sites/default/files/microsites/ostp/competes_report_on_prizes_final.pdf, accessed September 24, 2012.

[517] "The 'Fruit and Veggie Pokey,'" Youtube.com, http://www.youtube.com/watch?v=wWGO_8p1dxI&feature=player_embedded, accessed September 12, 2012.

[518] "Implementation of Federal Prize Authority: Progress Report," White House Office of Science and Technology Policy, March 2012. Available at http://www.whitehouse.gov/sites/default/files/microsites/ostp/competes_report_on_prizes_final.pdf, accessed September 24, 2012.

[519] "FEMA's Decisions to Replace Rather than Repair Buildings at the University of Iowa," Department of Homeland Security Office of Inspector General, Audit Report Number DD-12-17, June 19, 2012, p. 20, http://www.oig.dhs.gov/assets/GrantReports/OIG_DD-12-17_Jun12.pdf, accessed July 20, 2012.

[520] "FEMA's Decisions to Replace Rather than Repair Buildings at the University of Iowa," Department of Homeland Security Office of Inspector General, Audit Report Number DD-12-17, June 19, 2012, p. 3, http://www.oig.dhs.gov/assets/GrantReports/OIG_DD-12-17_Jun12.pdf, accessed July 20, 2012.

[521] "FEMA's Decisions to Replace Rather than Repair Buildings at the University of Iowa," Department of Homeland Security Office of Inspector General, Audit Report Number DD-12-17, June 19, 2012, p. 7, http://www.oig.dhs.gov/assets/GrantReports/OIG_DD-12-17_Jun12.pdf, accessed July 20, 2012.

[522] "FEMA's Decisions to Replace Rather than Repair Buildings at the University of Iowa," Department of Homeland Security Office of Inspector General, Audit Report Number DD-12-17, June 19, 2012, p. 8, http://www.oig.dhs.gov/assets/GrantReports/OIG_DD-12-17_Jun12.pdf, accessed July 20, 2012.

[523] "FEMA's Decisions to Replace Rather than Repair Buildings at the University of Iowa," Department of Homeland Security Office of Inspector General, Audit Report Number DD-12-17, June 19, 2012, p. 9, http://www.oig.dhs.gov/assets/GrantReports/OIG_DD-12-17_Jun12.pdf, accessed July 20, 2012.

[524] "FEMA's Decisions to Replace Rather than Repair Buildings at the University of Iowa," Department of Homeland Security Office of Inspector General, Audit Report Number DD-12-17, June 19, 2012, p. 11, http://www.oig.dhs.gov/assets/GrantReports/OIG_DD-12-17_Jun12.pdf, accessed July 20, 2012.

[525] "FEMA's Decisions to Replace Rather than Repair Buildings at the University of Iowa," Department of Homeland Security Office of Inspector General, Audit Report Number DD-12-17, June 19, 2012, p. 13, http://www.oig.dhs.gov/assets/GrantReports/OIG_DD-12-17_Jun12.pdf, accessed July 20, 2012.

[526] "FEMA's Decisions to Replace Rather than Repair Buildings at the University of Iowa," Department of Homeland Security Office of Inspector General, Audit Report Number DD-12-17, June 19, 2012, p. 20, http://www.oig.dhs.gov/assets/GrantReports/OIG_DD-12-17_Jun12.pdf, accessed July 20, 2012.

[527] "The Strong Receives Museums for America Grant from Institute of Museum and Library Services," Website of The Strong, Press Release, July 26, 2012, http://www.thestrong.org/press/releases/2012/07/4364-strong-receives-museums-america-grant-imls, accessed July 31, 2012.

[528] "The Strong Receives Museums for America Grant from Institute of Museum and Library Services," Website of The Strong, Press Release, July 26, 2012, http://www.thestrong.org/press/releases/2012/07/4364-strong-receives-museums-america-grant-imls, accessed July 31, 2012.

[529] "eGameRevolution," Website of the National Museum of Play, http://www.museumofplay.org/see-do/exhibits/egamerevolution?utm_source=homepage&utm_medium=panel&utm_campaign=home-panels-general, accessed July 31, 2012.

[530] "eGameRevolution," Website of the National Museum of Play, http://www.museumofplay.org/see-do/exhibits/egamerevolution?utm_source=homepage&utm_medium=panel&utm_campaign=home-panels-general, accessed July 31, 2012.

[531] "eGameRevolution," Website of the National Museum of Play, http://www.museumofplay.org/see-do/exhibits/egamerevolution?utm_source=homepage&utm_medium=panel&utm_campaign=home-panels-general, accessed July 31, 2012.

[532] Prices are listed on the home website of the National Museum of Play, http://www.museumofplay.org/, accessed October 15, 2012.

[533] "Game Collections," Website of the National Museum of Play, http://www.museumofplay.org/collections/game, accessed July 31, 2012.

[534] "Game Collections," Website of the National Museum of Play, http://www.museumofplay.org/collections/game, accessed July 31, 2012.

[535] "Game Collections," Website of the National Museum of Play, http://www.museumofplay.org/collections/game, accessed July 31, 2012.

[536] Wyland, Scott. "'Sidewalk to nowhere' in Indian River County is $1M waste of taxpayer money, some say," *TCPalm*, June 12, 2012, http://www.tcpalm.com/news/2012/jun/12/sidewalk-to-nowhere-in-indian-river-county-is-1m/?partner=RSS, accessed September 24, 2012.

[537] Wyland, Scott. "'Sidewalk to nowhere' in Indian River County is $1M waste of taxpayer money, some say," *TCPalm*, June 12, 2012, http://www.tcpalm.com/news/2012/jun/12/sidewalk-to-nowhere-in-indian-river-county-is-1m/?partner=RSS, accessed September 24, 2012.

[538] Wyland, Scott. "'Sidewalk to nowhere' in Indian River County is $1M waste of taxpayer money, some say," *TCPalm*, June 12, 2012, http://www.tcpalm.com/news/2012/jun/12/sidewalk-to-nowhere-in-indian-river-county-is-1m/?partner=RSS, accessed September 24, 2012.

[539] Wyland, Scott. "'Sidewalk to nowhere' in Indian River County is $1M waste of taxpayer money, some say," *TCPalm*, June 12, 2012, http://www.tcpalm.com/news/2012/jun/12/sidewalk-to-nowhere-in-indian-river-county-is-1m/?partner=RSS, accessed September 24, 2012.

[540] "Editorial: 'Sidewalk to nowhere' in Indian River County raises legitimate questions about decision-making process," *TCPalm*, August 19, 2012, http://www.tcpalm.com/news/2012/aug/19/editorial-sidewalk-to-nowhere-in-indian-river/, accessed October 4, 2012.

[541] Wyland, Scott. "'Sidewalk to nowhere' in Indian River County is $1M waste of taxpayer money, some say," *TCPalm*, June 12, 2012, http://www.tcpalm.com/news/2012/jun/12/sidewalk-to-nowhere-in-indian-river-county-is-1m/?partner=RSS, accessed September 24, 2012.

[542] Wyland, Scott. "'Sidewalk to nowhere' in Indian River County is $1M waste of taxpayer money, some say," *TCPalm*, June 12, 2012, http://www.tcpalm.com/news/2012/jun/12/sidewalk-to-nowhere-in-indian-river-county-is-1m/?partner=RSS, accessed September 24, 2012.

[543] Wyland, Scott. "'Sidewalk to nowhere' in Indian River County is $1M waste of taxpayer money, some say," *TCPalm*, June 12, 2012, http://www.tcpalm.com/news/2012/jun/12/sidewalk-to-nowhere-in-indian-river-county-is-1m/?partner=RSS, accessed September 24, 2012.

[544] Wyland, Scott. "'Sidewalk to nowhere' in Indian River County is $1M waste of taxpayer money, some say," *TCPalm*, June 12, 2012, http://www.tcpalm.com/news/2012/jun/12/sidewalk-to-nowhere-in-indian-river-county-is-1m/?partner=RSS, accessed September 24, 2012.

[545] Wyland, Scott. "'Sidewalk to nowhere' in Indian River County is $1M waste of taxpayer money, some say," *TCPalm*, June 12, 2012, http://www.tcpalm.com/news/2012/jun/12/sidewalk-to-nowhere-in-indian-river-county-is-1m/?partner=RSS, accessed September 24, 2012.

[546] Wyland, Scott. "'Sidewalk to nowhere' in Indian River County is $1M waste of taxpayer money, some say," *TCPalm*, June 12, 2012, http://www.tcpalm.com/news/2012/jun/12/sidewalk-to-nowhere-in-indian-river-county-is-1m/?partner=RSS, accessed September 24, 2012.

[547] Wyland, Scott. "'Sidewalk to nowhere' in Indian River County is $1M waste of taxpayer money, some say," *TCPalm*, June 12, 2012, http://www.tcpalm.com/news/2012/jun/12/sidewalk-to-nowhere-in-indian-river-county-is-1m/?partner=RSS, accessed September 24, 2012.

[548] McMillin, Zane. "See why the 'sidewalk to nowhere' has one Kent County resident riled," *MLive.com*, July 17, 2012, http://www.mlive.com/news/grand-rapids/index.ssf/2012/07/see_why_the_sidewalk_to_nowher.html, accessed October 4, 2012.

[549] McMillin, Zane. "See why the 'sidewalk to nowhere' has one Kent County resident riled," *MLive.com*, July 17, 2012, http://www.mlive.com/news/grand-rapids/index.ssf/2012/07/see_why_the_sidewalk_to_nowher.html, accessed October 4, 2012.

[550] McMillin, Zane. "See why the 'sidewalk to nowhere' has one Kent County resident riled," *MLive.com*, July 17, 2012, http://www.mlive.com/news/grand-rapids/index.ssf/2012/07/see_why_the_sidewalk_to_nowher.html, accessed October 4, 2012.

[551] McMillin, Zane. "See why the 'sidewalk to nowhere' has one Kent County resident riled," *MLive.com*, July 17, 2012, http://www.mlive.com/news/grand-rapids/index.ssf/2012/07/see_why_the_sidewalk_to_nowher.html, accessed October 4, 2012.

[552] McMillin, Zane. "See why the 'sidewalk to nowhere' has one Kent County resident riled," *MLive.com*, July 17, 2012, http://www.mlive.com/news/grand-rapids/index.ssf/2012/07/see_why_the_sidewalk_to_nowher.html, accessed October 4, 2012.

[553] Minutes of April 24, 2012, Meeting of the Board of County Road Commissioners of the County of Kent, available at http://www.kentcountyroads.net/Meetings/Minutes/2012/Board/12april24.pdf, accessed October 5, 2012.

[554] McMillin, Zane. "See why the 'sidewalk to nowhere' has one Kent County resident riled," *MLive.com*, July 17, 2012, http://www.mlive.com/news/grand-rapids/index.ssf/2012/07/see_why_the_sidewalk_to_nowher.html, accessed October 4, 2012.

[555] Information provided by NASA to the Congressional Research Service, June 25, 2012.

[556] NASA Office of Inspector General, "Review of NASA's Learned Lesson Information System," Report No. IG-12-012, March 6, 2012, p. iii. Available online at: http://oig.nasa.gov/audits/reports/FY12/IG-12-012.pdf, accessed September 24, 2012.

[557] NASA Office of Inspector General, "Review of NASA's Learned Lesson Information System," Report No. IG-12-012, March 6, 2012, p. V. Available online at: http://oig.nasa.gov/audits/reports/FY12/IG-12-012.pdf, accessed September 24, 2012.

[558] NASA Office of Inspector General, "Review of NASA's Learned Lesson Information System," Report No. IG-12-012, March 6, 2012, p. 2. Available online at: http://oig.nasa.gov/audits/reports/FY12/IG-12-012.pdf, accessed September 24, 2012.

[559] NASA Office of Inspector General, "Review of NASA's Learned Lesson Information System," Report No. IG-12-012, March 6, 2012, p. 15. Available online at: http://oig.nasa.gov/audits/reports/FY12/IG-12-012.pdf, accessed September 24, 2012.

[560] NASA Office of Inspector General, "Review of NASA's Learned Lesson Information System," Report No. IG-12-012, March 6, 2012, p. iv. Available online at: http://oig.nasa.gov/audits/reports/FY12/IG-12-012.pdf, accessed September 24, 2012.

[561] NASA Office of Inspector General, "Review of NASA's Learned Lesson Information System," Report No. IG-12-012, March 6, 2012, p. iv. Available online at: http://oig.nasa.gov/audits/reports/FY12/IG-12-012.pdf, accessed September 24, 2012.

[562] NASA Office of Inspector General, "Review of NASA's Learned Lesson Information System," Report No. IG-12-012, March 6, 2012, p. iv. Available online at: http://oig.nasa.gov/audits/reports/FY12/IG-12-012.pdf, accessed September 24, 2012.

[563] NASA Office of Inspector General, "Review of NASA's Learned Lesson Information System," Report No. IG-12-012, March 6, 2012. Available online at: http://oig.nasa.gov/audits/reports/FY12/IG-12-012.pdf, accessed September 24, 2012.

[564] Information provided by the Federal Transit Administration to the Congressional Research Service, September 10, 2012.

[565] Information provided by the Federal Transit Administration to the Congressional Research Service, September 10, 2012.

[566] "Alaska Railroad Passenger Services," Website of the Alaska Railroad Corporation, published May 16, 2012. Available at http://alaskarailroad.com/Portals/6/pdf/pr/2012_05_16_Passenger_FS_PR.pdf, accessed July 10, 2012.

[567] "Coastal Classic Train Information," Website of the Alaska Railroad Corporation, http://alaskarailroad.com/OurTrains/CoastalClassic/tabid/100/Default.aspx, accessed October 11, 2012.

568 "Glacier Discovery Route Information," Website of the Alaska Railroad Corporation, http://alaskarailroad.com/OurTrains/GlacierDiscovery/tabid/101/Default.aspx, accessed July 10, 2012.

569 "2011 Annual Report," Alaska Railroad Corporation, http://alaskarailroad.com/LinkClick.aspx?fileticket=x9sos0_PYOM%3d&tabid=466, accessed July 10, 2012.

570 Figure calculated by dividing $36 million by 412,200 passengers. "Alaska Railroad Passenger Services," Website of the Alaska Railroad Corporation, published May 16, 2012. Available at http://alaskarailroad.com/Portals/6/pdf/pr/2012_05_16_Passenger_FS_PR.pdf, accessed July 10, 2012.

571 Mallet, William J. "Federal Support of Public Transit Operating Expenditures: Trends and Policy Issues," Congressional Research Service, March 16, 2011, R41695.

572 "Fact Sheet," StarTran website, http://www.lincoln.ne.gov/city/pworks/startran/factsht.htm, accessed September 5, 2012.

573 "FY 2011 Grant-by-Grant Information," Federal Transit Administration website, http://www.fta.dot.gov/documents/Grant_by_Grant_Information_FY2011.xlsx, accessed September 11, 2012.

574 "FTA Funding Information," Alaska Railroad Corporation website, http://alaskarailroad.com/Community/TransitInformation/FTAFundingInformation/tabid/621/Default.aspx, accessed September 4, 2012.

575 "FTA Funding Information," Alaska Railroad Corporation website, http://alaskarailroad.com/Community/TransitInformation/FTAFundingInformation/tabid/621/Default.aspx, accessed September 4, 2012.

576 Allen, Jonathan, and Jessica Meyers. "Don Young's Railroad to Nowhere," *Politico*, July 10, 2012. Available at http://www.politico.com/news/stories/0712/78318.html, accessed August 10, 2012.

577 "FTA Funding Information," Alaska Railroad Corporation website, http://alaskarailroad.com/Community/TransitInformation/FTAFundingInformation/tabid/621/Default.aspx, accessed September 4, 2012.

578 Allen, Jonathan, and Jessica Meyers. "Don Young's Railroad to Nowhere," *Politico*, July 10, 2012. Available at http://www.politico.com/news/stories/0712/78318.html, accessed August 10, 2012.

579 Allen, Jonathan, and Jessica Meyers. "Don Young's Railroad to Nowhere," *Politico*, July 10, 2012. Available at http://www.politico.com/news/stories/0712/78318.html, accessed August 10, 2012.

580 Federal Award IDs: RO48399 20891, BP1093664, BP1097171, BP1097993, BP1091640, BP1093673, BP1097213, BP1099761, USASpending.gov, accessed September 27, 2012.

581 "USDA Rural Development Announces Business Assistance Grant- Jackson Winery DBC Belle Joli'," U.S. Department of Agriculture website, February 16, 2012, http://www.rurdev.usda.gov/STELPRD4015228_print.html, accessed June 7, 2012.

582 "USDA Rural Development Announces Business Assistance Grant- Jackson Winery DBC Belle Joli'," U.S. Department of Agriculture website, February 16, 2012, http://www.rurdev.usda.gov/STELPRD4015228_print.html, accessed June 7, 2012.

583 "Olde Chautauqua Vineyards on of three WNY farms receiving federal funds," *The Observer*, February 4, 2012, http://www.observertoday.com/page/content.detail/id/568245/Olde-Chautauqua-Vineyards-one-of-three-WNY-farms-receiving--federal-funds.html?nav=5007, accessed June 7, 2012.

584 "USDA Rural Development Provides Over Half a Million Dollars to Support Business Development and Marketing Opportunities in Western New York," U.S. Department of Agriculture website, February 3, 2012, http://www.rurdev.usda.gov/STELPRD4014590.html, accessed June 7, 2012.

585 "View Finder: The Vineyard at Dodon Farm," *The Edgewater-Davidsonville Patch*, April 21, 2011, http://edgewater.patch.com/articles/view-finder-the-vineyard-at-dodon-farm, accessed June 7, 2012.

586 Federal Award ID: BP1097171, USASpending.gov, available at http://usaspending.gov/explore?frompage=assistance&tab=By%20Prime%20Awardee&comingfrom=search

results&federal_award_id=BP1097171&federal_award_mod=0183&fiscal_year=all&typeofview=complete, accessed October 11, 2012.

[587] Federal Award ID: BP1097171, USASpending.gov, available at http://usaspending.gov/explore?frompage=assistance&tab=By%20Prime%20Awardee&comingfrom=search results&federal_award_id=BP1097171&federal_award_mod=0183&fiscal_year=all&typeofview=complete, accessed September 27, 2012.

[588] Federal Award IDs: BP1091640, BP1093673, USASpending.gov, accessed September 27, 2012.

[589] Over 40% of the unpaid taxes were payroll taxes such as contributions to Social Security and Medicare. "Medicaid: Providers in Three States with Unpaid Federal Taxes Received Over $6 Billion in Medicaid Reimbursements," Government Accountability Office, July 2012, GAO-12-857, p. 7. Available at http://gao.gov/assets/600/593095.pdf, accessed September 24, 2012.

[590] "Medicaid: Providers in Three States with Unpaid Federal Taxes Received Over $6 Billion in Medicaid Reimbursements," Government Accountability Office, July 2012, GAO-12-857, p. 15. Available at http://gao.gov/assets/600/593095.pdf, accessed September 24, 2012.

[591] "Medicaid: Providers in Three States with Unpaid Federal Taxes Received Over $6 Billion in Medicaid Reimbursements," Government Accountability Office, July 2012, GAO-12-857, p. 15. Available at http://gao.gov/assets/600/593095.pdf, accessed September 24, 2012.

[592] "Medicaid: Providers in Three States with Unpaid Federal Taxes Received Over $6 Billion in Medicaid Reimbursements," Government Accountability Office, July 2012, GAO-12-857, p. 32. Available at http://gao.gov/assets/600/593095.pdf, accessed September 24, 2012.

[593] "Medicaid: Providers in Three States with Unpaid Federal Taxes Received Over $6 Billion in Medicaid Reimbursements," Government Accountability Office, July 2012, GAO-12-857, p. 15. Available at http://gao.gov/assets/600/593095.pdf, accessed September 24, 2012.

[594] "Medicaid: Providers in Three States with Unpaid Federal Taxes Received Over $6 Billion in Medicaid Reimbursements," Government Accountability Office, July 2012, GAO-12-857, p. 15. Available at http://gao.gov/assets/600/593095.pdf, accessed September 24, 2012.

[595] If the IRS could implement continuous levies, savings to taxpayers would likely many times this figure. "Medicaid: Providers in Three States with Unpaid Federal Taxes Received Over $6 Billion in Medicaid Reimbursements," Government Accountability Office, July 2012, GAO-12-857, p. 19. Available at http://gao.gov/assets/600/593095.pdf, accessed September 24, 2012.

[596] Website of the U.S. Federal Business Opportunities, https://www.fbo.gov/index?s=opportunity&mode=form&tab=core&id=e7a1344f6e6efb1acb1058ad76b52e19&_cview=0, accessed March 27, 2012.

[597] Website of the U.S. Federal Business Opportunities, https://www.fbo.gov/index?s=opportunity&mode=form&tab=core&id=e7a1344f6e6efb1acb1058ad76b52e19&_cview=0, accessed March 27, 2012.

[598] Simon, Richard. "Construction plans for downtown L.A. federal courthouse announced," *The Los Angeles Times*, January 20, 2012. Available at http://articles.latimes.com/2012/jan/20/local/la-me-downtown-courthouse-20120120, accessed March 28, 2012.

[599] Statement of Mr. Robert A. Peck, Commissioner of the Public Building Service, Before the Committee on Transportation and Infrastructure, Hearing on the Los Angeles Courthouse, http://www.gsa.gov/portal/content/120151, accessed March 28, 2012.

[600] Simon, Richard. "Construction plans for downtown L.A. federal courthouse announced," *The Los Angeles Times*, January 20, 2012. Available at http://articles.latimes.com/2012/jan/20/local/la-me-downtown-courthouse-20120120, accessed March 28, 2012.

[601] "FEDERAL COURTHOUSE CONSTRUCTION: Nationwide Space and Cost Issues Are Applicable to L.A. Courthouse Project," *Government Accountability Office,* GAO-12-98T, November 2011. Available at http://www.gao.gov/assets/590/586085.pdf, accessed March 28, 2012.

[602] "FEDERAL COURTHOUSE CONSTRUCTION: Nationwide Space and Cost Issues Are Applicable to L.A. Courthouse Project," *Government Accountability Office,* GAO-12-98T, November 2011. Available at http://www.gao.gov/assets/590/586085.pdf, accessed March 28, 2012.

[603] Letter to GSA Administrator Martha Johnson, October 21, 2011. Available at http://republicans.transportation.house.gov/Media/file/112th/EDPBEM/2011-10-21-DenhamNortonLetter.pdf, accessed March 30, 2012.

[604] "FEDERAL COURTHOUSE CONSTRUCTION: Nationwide Space and Cost Issues Are Applicable to L.A. Courthouse Project," *Government Accountability Office,* GAO-12-98T, November 2011. Available at http://www.gao.gov/assets/590/586085.pdf, accessed March 28, 2012.

[605] Statement of Mr. Robert A. Peck, Commissioner of the Public Building Service, Before the Committee on Transportation and Infrastructure, Hearing on the Los Angeles Courthouse, http://www.gsa.gov/portal/content/120151, accessed March 28, 2012.

[606] "L.A. COURTHOUSE: Initial Project Justification Is Outdated and Flawed," *Government Accountability Office*, GAO-12-968T, August 17, 2012. Available at http://www.gao.gov/assets/600/593799.pdf, accessed August 28, 2012.

[607] This sum represents the amount spent by the U.S. Department of Agriculture and the Department of Housing and Urban Development on projects related to beef and trout jerky, and a conservative portion of the funds the Department of Defense has used to study the new meat snacks.

[608] "Department of Defense Fiscal Year (FY) 2013 President's Budget Submission," Justification Book Volume 3, Research, Development, Test & Evaluation, Defense-Wide, Office of Secretary of Defense, volume 3, February 2012, page 724. Available at http://comptroller.defense.gov/defbudget/fy2013/budget_justification/pdfs/03_RDT_and_E/Office_Secretar_of_Defense_PB_2013_1.pdf, accessed October 13, 2012.

"Department of Defense Fiscal Year (FY) 2012 Budget Estimates," Justification Book Volume 3, Research, Development, Test & Evaluation, Defense-Wide, Office of Secretary of Defense, Volume 3, February 2011, page 855. Available at http://comptroller.defense.gov/defbudget/fy2012/budget_justification/pdfs/03_RDT_and_E/OSD.pdf, accessed October 13, 2012.

"Department of Defense Fiscal Year (FY) 2011 Budget Estimates," Volume 3B, Research, Development, Test and Evaluation, Defense-Wide, Office of Secretary of Defense, Volume 3, February 2010, page 459. Available at http://comptroller.defense.gov/defbudget/fy2011/budget_justification/pdfs/03_RDT_and_E/OSD%20RDTE_PB_2011_Volume%203B.pdf, accessed October 13, 2012.

[609] "Foreign Comparative Testing (FCT) Program," U.S. Navy website, http://www.onr.navy.mil/Science-Technology/Directorates/Transition/Technology-Transition-Initiatives-03TTX/Foreign-Comparative-Testing-FCT.aspx, accessed October 9, 2012.

[610] "Foreign Comparative Testing (FCT) Program," U.S. Navy website, http://www.onr.navy.mil/Science-Technology/Directorates/Transition/Technology-Transition-Initiatives-03TTX/Foreign-Comparative-Testing-FCT.aspx, accessed October 9, 2012.

[611] Teel, Roger. "DOD considers foreign technologies to save dollars," U.S. Army website, June 22, 2012, http://www.army.mil/article/82386/DOD_considers_foreign_technologies_to_save_dollars/, accessed October 9, 2012.

[612] Teel, Roger. "'Where's the beef?' -- DoD finds answers in osmotic dehydration process," U.S. Army website, September 17, 2012, http://www.army.mil/article/87419/_Where_s_the_beef_____DoD_finds_answers_in_osmotic_dehydration_process/, accessed October 10, 2012.

[613] Teel, Roger. "'Where's the beef?' -- DoD finds answers in osmotic dehydration process," U.S. Army website, September 17, 2012, http://www.army.mil/article/87419/_Where_s_the_beef_____DoD_finds_answers_in_osmotic_dehydration_process/, accessed October 10, 2012.

[614] Teel, Roger. "'Where's the beef?' -- DoD finds answers in osmotic dehydration process," U.S. Army website, September 17, 2012, http://www.army.mil/article/87419/_Where_s_the_beef_____DoD_finds_answers_in_osmotic_dehydration_process/, accessed October 10, 2012.

[615] "Department of Defense Fiscal Year (FY) 2011 Budget Estimates," Volume 3B, Research, Development, Test and Evaluation, Defense-Wide, Office of the Secretary of Defense (OSD), Office of Secretary Of Defense, Volume 3, page 459, February 2010; http://comptroller.defense.gov/defbudget/fy2011/budget_justification/pdfs/03_RDT_and_E/OSD%20RDTE_PB_2011_Volume%203B.pdf.

[616] Teel, Roger. "'Where's the beef?' -- DoD finds answers in osmotic dehydration process," U.S. Army website, September 17, 2012, http://www.army.mil/article/87419/_Where_s_the_beef_____DoD_finds_answers_in_osmotic_dehydration_process/, accessed October 10, 2012.

[617] Teel, Roger. "'Where's the beef?' -- DoD finds answers in osmotic dehydration process," U.S. Army website, September 17, 2012, http://www.army.mil/article/87419/_Where_s_the_beef_____DoD_finds_answers_in_osmotic_dehydration_process/, accessed October 10, 2012.

[618] "Gourmet flavors beef up beef jerky," Snack Food and Wholesale Bakery Magazine, September 28, 2012, http://www.snackandbakery.com/articles/85997-gourmet-flavors-beef-up-beef-jerky, accessed October 9, 2012.

[619] "Minong receives Community Development Block Grant," Wisconsin Economic Development Corporation, November 28, 2011, http://inwisconsin.com/blog/2011/11/28/minong-community-development-grant/, accessed October 13, 2012.

[620] "Grant to help pave way for Jack Link's expansion in Minong," Duluth News Tribune, December 5, 2011, http://www.duluthnewstribune.com/event/article/id/216379/, accessed October 9, 2012.

[621] "ABOUT US: Our History," Jack Link's Snacks Inc. website, http://www.jacklinks.com/#SubChannel_AboutUs_OurHistory, accessed October 10, 2012.

[622] "SUNBURST TROUT ADDS SMOKER WITH NCVACS, USDA AWARDS," North Carolina State University website, posted February 22, 2012, http://plantsforhumanhealth.ncsu.edu/2012/02/22/sunburst-trout-farms/, accessed October 9, 2012.

[623] The federal School Improvement Grants (SIG) program authorized under the No Child Left Behind Act awards three-year grants to states and local school districts to improve student achievement in the lowest-performing schools. Schools may choose from a limited set of turn-around plans to improve performance. "Education Should Take Additional Steps to Ensure Accountability for Schools and Contractors," *Government Accountability Office*, April 2012, GAO-12-373, Highlights page. Available at http://gao.gov/assets/600/590054.pdf, accessed September 24, 2012.

[624] "School Improvement Grants (SIG): Federal Title I School Improvement Grants, Cohort II, 2010-2011 School Year," State of Washington Office of Superintendent of Public Instruction website, http://www.k12.wa.us/Improvement/SIG/CohortII.aspx, accessed September 4, 2012.

[625] School Improvement Grant MAP: Washington, U.S. Department of Education website, http://www2.ed.gov/programs/sif/map/wa.html, accessed August 15, 2012.

[626] "Tinkering Toward Transformation: A Look at Federal School Improvement Grant Implementation." The Center on Reinventing Public Education, March 2012, p. 27. Available at http://www.crpe.org/sites/default/files/pub_SIG_Tinkering_mar12_0.pdf, accessed August 15, 2012.

[627] "Tinkering Toward Transformation: A Look at Federal School Improvement Grant Implementation." The Center on Reinventing Public Education, March 2012, p. 26. Available at http://www.crpe.org/sites/default/files/pub_SIG_Tinkering_mar12_0.pdf, accessed August 15, 2012.

[628] "Tinkering Toward Transformation: A Look at Federal School Improvement Grant Implementation." The Center on Reinventing Public Education, March 2012, p. 2. Available at http://www.crpe.org/sites/default/files/pub_SIG_Tinkering_mar12_0.pdf, accessed August 15, 2012.

[629] "Tinkering Toward Transformation: A Look at Federal School Improvement Grant Implementation." The Center on Reinventing Public Education, March 2012, p. 16. Available at http://www.crpe.org/sites/default/files/pub_SIG_Tinkering_mar12_0.pdf, accessed August 15, 2012.

[630] "Tinkering Toward Transformation: A Look at Federal School Improvement Grant Implementation." The Center on Reinventing Public Education, March 2012, p. 9. Available at http://www.crpe.org/sites/default/files/pub_SIG_Tinkering_mar12_0.pdf, accessed August 15, 2012.

[631] "Tinkering Toward Transformation: A Look at Federal School Improvement Grant Implementation." The Center on Reinventing Public Education, March 2012, p. 11. Available at http://www.crpe.org/sites/default/files/pub_SIG_Tinkering_mar12_0.pdf, accessed August 15, 2012.

[632] "Tinkering Toward Transformation: A Look at Federal School Improvement Grant Implementation." The Center on Reinventing Public Education, March 2012, p. 14. Available at http://www.crpe.org/sites/default/files/pub_SIG_Tinkering_mar12_0.pdf, accessed August 15, 2012.

[633] Rosenthal, Brian. "UW report: Large federal grants yielding mostly small changes in struggling schools." *The Seattle Times*, March 29, 2012. Available at http://blogs.seattletimes.com/today/2012/03/uw-report-large-federal-grants-yielding-mostly-small-changes-in-struggling-schools, accessed August 15, 2012.

[634] "Tinkering Toward Transformation: A Look at Federal School Improvement Grant Implementation." The Center on Reinventing Public Education, March 2012, p. 22. Available at http://www.crpe.org/sites/default/files/pub_SIG_Tinkering_mar12_0.pdf, accessed August 15, 2012.

[635] "Tinkering Toward Transformation: A Look at Federal School Improvement Grant Implementation." The Center on Reinventing Public Education, March 2012, p. 22. Available at http://www.crpe.org/sites/default/files/pub_SIG_Tinkering_mar12_0.pdf, accessed August 15, 2012.

[636] "Tinkering Toward Transformation: A Look at Federal School Improvement Grant Implementation." The Center on Reinventing Public Education, March 2012, p. 22. Available at http://www.crpe.org/sites/default/files/pub_SIG_Tinkering_mar12_0.pdf, accessed August 15, 2012.

[637] "There Are Billions of Dollars in Undetected Tax Refund Fraud Resulting From Identity Theft," Treasury Inspector General for Tax Administration, Audit Report No. 2012-42-080, July 19, 2012, p. 26. Available at http://www.treasury.gov/tigta/auditreports/2012reports/201242080fr.pdf, accessed August 7, 2012.

[638] "There Are Billions of Dollars in Undetected Tax Refund Fraud Resulting From Identity Theft," Treasury Inspector General for Tax Administration, Audit Report No. 2012-42-080, July 19, 2012, p. 26. Available at http://www.treasury.gov/tigta/auditreports/2012reports/201242080fr.pdf, accessed August 7, 2012.

[639] "There Are Billions of Dollars in Undetected Tax Refund Fraud Resulting From Identity Theft," Treasury Inspector General for Tax Administration, Audit Report No. 2012-42-080, July 19, 2012, p. 2. Available at http://www.treasury.gov/tigta/auditreports/2012reports/201242080fr.pdf, accessed August 7, 2012.

[640] "There Are Billions of Dollars in Undetected Tax Refund Fraud Resulting From Identity Theft," Treasury Inspector General for Tax Administration, Audit Report No. 2012-42-080, July 19, 2012, p. 11. Available at http://www.treasury.gov/tigta/auditreports/2012reports/201242080fr.pdf, accessed August 7, 2012.

[641] "There Are Billions of Dollars in Undetected Tax Refund Fraud Resulting From Identity Theft," Treasury Inspector General for Tax Administration, Audit Report No. 2012-42-080, July 19, 2012, p. 11. Available at http://www.treasury.gov/tigta/auditreports/2012reports/201242080fr.pdf, accessed August 7, 2012.

[642] "There Are Billions of Dollars in Undetected Tax Refund Fraud Resulting From Identity Theft," Treasury Inspector General for Tax Administration, Audit Report No. 2012-42-080, July 19, 2012, p. 10. Available at http://www.treasury.gov/tigta/auditreports/2012reports/201242080fr.pdf, accessed August 7, 2012.

[643] "There Are Billions of Dollars in Undetected Tax Refund Fraud Resulting From Identity Theft," Treasury Inspector General for Tax Administration, Audit Report No. 2012-42-080, July 19, 2012, p. 10. Available at http://www.treasury.gov/tigta/auditreports/2012reports/201242080fr.pdf, accessed August 7, 2012.

[644] "There Are Billions of Dollars in Undetected Tax Refund Fraud Resulting From Identity Theft," Treasury Inspector General for Tax Administration, Audit Report No. 2012-42-080, July 19, 2012, p. 16. Available at http://www.treasury.gov/tigta/auditreports/2012reports/201242080fr.pdf, accessed August 7, 2012.

[645] "There Are Billions of Dollars in Undetected Tax Refund Fraud Resulting From Identity Theft," Treasury Inspector General for Tax Administration, Audit Report No. 2012-42-080, July 19, 2012, p. 9. Available at http://www.treasury.gov/tigta/auditreports/2012reports/201242080fr.pdf, accessed August 7, 2012.

[646] "There Are Billions of Dollars in Undetected Tax Refund Fraud Resulting From Identity Theft," Treasury Inspector General for Tax Administration, Audit Report No. 2012-42-080, July 19, 2012, p. 4. Available at http://www.treasury.gov/tigta/auditreports/2012reports/201242080fr.pdf, accessed August 7, 2012.

[647] "Abington Library 'Star Wars' event Sept. 8," *Wicked Local* Abington, August 28, 2012, http://www.wickedlocal.com/abington/news/x1405835107/Abington-Library-Star-Wars-event-Sept-8#axzz26kuWASZZ, accessed September 17, 2012.

[648] "News and Events," Abington Public Library website, http://www.abingtonpl.org/news.shtml, accessed October 13, 2012.

[649] "Abington Library 'Star Wars' event Sept. 8," *Wicked Local* Abington, August 28, 2012, http://www.wickedlocal.com/abington/news/x1405835107/Abington-Library-Star-Wars-event-Sept-8#axzz26kuWASZZ, accessed September 17, 2012.

[650] Abington Public Library Facebook page, posted September 8, 2012, http://www.facebook.com/photo.php?fbid=395808713806873&set=a.395808640473547.92594.163402140380866&type=3&permPage=1, accessed October 13, 2012.

[651] Information provided by the Abingdon Public Library, October 15, 2012.

[652] "Board Awards Over $800,000 in Grants," Massachusetts Board of Library Commissioners website, News release, July 15, 2010, http://mblc.state.ma.us/mblc/news/releases/past-releases/2010/nr100715.php, accessed September 17, 2012.

[653] Meeting Minutes of the Abington Public Library Board of Trustees, July 30, 2012, http://www.abingtonpl.org/documents/Minutes073012.pdf, accessed October 13, 2012.

[654] "Box Office History for Star Wars Movies," Nash Information Services website, http://www.the-numbers.com/movies/series/StarWars.php, accessed September 17, 2012.

[655] "Box Office History for Star Wars Movies," Nash Information Services website, http://www.the-numbers.com/movies/series/StarWars.php, accessed September 17, 2012.

[656] Information provided by NASA to the Congressional Research Service, May 29, 2012.

[657] Information provided by NASA to the Congressional Research Service, May 29, 2012.

[658] Bartlett, Tony. "Stennis Space Center targets tourists," *Travel Weekly*, November 15, 2000. Available online at http://www.travelweekly.com/print.aspx?id=155152, accessed September 24, 2012.

[659] According to information provided by NASA to the Congressional Research Service on April 5, 2012, NASA spent $500,000 of its non-appropriated funds on the remodel.

[660] Bartlett, Tony. "Stennis Space Center targets tourists," *Travel Weekly*, November 15, 2000. Available online at http://www.travelweekly.com/print.aspx?id=155152, accessed September 24, 2012.

[661] Information provided by NASA to the Congressional Research Service, May 29, 2012.

[662] Website of the Infinity Space Center, "History." Available online at http://www.visitinfinity.com/about-us/history/, accessed May 1, 2012.

[663] Information provided by NASA to the Congressional Research Service, May 29, 2012.

[664] Information provided by NASA to the Congressional Research Service, May 29, 2012.

[665] "Hancock County Tapped to Manage and Market INFINITY," Infinity Science Center website, March 30, 2012, http://www.visitinfinity.com/news-events/hancock-chamber-tapped-to-manage-and-market-infinity/, accessed October 13, 2012.

[666] Information provided by NASA to the Congressional Research Service, May 29, 2012.

[667] "Visitor Info," Website of the Infinity Space Center, http://www.visitinfinity.com/visitor-info/, accessed May 1, 2012.

[668] Information provided by NASA to the Congressional Research Service, May 29, 2012.

[669] Vargas, Ramon Antonio. "Stennis Space Center in Mississippi launches new visitor center," *The Times-Picayune*, April 10, 2012. Available at http://www.nola.com/business/index.ssf/2012/04/stennis_space_center_in_missis.html, accessed October 15, 2012.

[670] "Visitor Info," Website of the Infinity Space Center, http://www.visitinfinity.com/about-us/, accessed May 1, 2012.

[671] USASpending.gov, Federal Award Identifiers 10-5100-8022 and 11-5100-8065.

[672] "2012 Grant Awards: Art Works," National Endowment for the Arts website, http://www.nea.gov/grants/recent/12grants/12AAE2.php?CAT=Art%20Works&DIS=Arts%20Education, accessed June 18, 2012.

[673] "2012 Grant Awards: Art Works," National Endowment for the Arts website, http://www.nea.gov/grants/recent/12grants/12AAE2.php?CAT=Art%20Works&DIS=Arts%20Education, accessed June 18, 2012.

[674] "Course Descriptions," Website of Circus Harmony, http://www.circusday.org/wp-content/uploads/2012/08/2012-Fall-Winter-Camps-and-Classes-proof-2.pdf, accessed August 15, 2012.

[675] "What We Offer," Website of everydaycircus, inc., http://everydaycircus.net/indexOffer.html, accessed August 15, 2012.

[676] Saldi, Sara. "Need willpower? Watch your favorite TV rerun," *Futurity.org*, September 6, 2012, http://www.futurity.org/society-culture/need-willpower-watch-your-favorite-tv-rerun/, accessed September 13, 2012.

[677] "Alcohol, Relationship Conflict, and Intimate Partner Violence," National Institutes of Health, project no. 5R01AA 016127-05, http://projectreporter.nih.gov/project_info_description.cfm?aid=8094418&icde=13772340, accessed September 13, 2012. Grant was acknowledged in the research paper as supporting the work.

[678] "Research Training on Alchohol Etiology and Treatment" (sp), National Institutes of Health, project no. 5T32AA007583-13, http://projectreporter.nih.gov/pr_Prj_info_desc_dtls.cfm?aid=8263059&icde=13771655, accessed September 13, 2012. Grant was acknowledged in the research paper as supporting the work.

[679] Saldi, Sara. "Need willpower? Watch your favorite TV rerun," *Futurity.org*, September 6, 2012, http://www.futurity.org/society-culture/need-willpower-watch-your-favorite-tv-rerun/, accessed September 13, 2012.

[680] Saldi, Sara. "Need willpower? Watch your favorite TV rerun," *Futurity.org*, September 6, 2012, http://www.futurity.org/society-culture/need-willpower-watch-your-favorite-tv-rerun/, accessed September 13, 2012.

[681] Derrick, Jaye. "Energized by Television: Familiar Fictional Worlds Restore Self-Control," *Social Psychological and Personality Science*, published online first August 8, 2012, p.3.

[682] Derrick, Jaye. "Energized by Television: Familiar Fictional Worlds Restore Self-Control," *Social Psychological and Personality Science*, published online first August 8, 2012, p.7.

[683] Derrick, Jaye. "Energized by Television: Familiar Fictional Worlds Restore Self-Control," *Social Psychological and Personality Science*, published online first August 8, 2012, p.7.

[684] "Alcohol, Relationship Conflict, and Intimate Partner Violence," National Institutes of Health, project no. 5R01AA 016127-05, http://projectreporter.nih.gov/project_info_description.cfm?aid=8094418&icde=13772340, accessed September 13, 2012.

[685] "Research Training on Alchohol Etiology and Treatment" (sp), National Institutes of Health, project no. 5T32AA007583-13, http://projectreporter.nih.gov/pr_Prj_info_desc_dtls.cfm?aid=8263059&icde=13771655, accessed September 13, 2012.

[686] "Fiscal Year 2013: Cuts, Consolidations, and Savings," White House Office of Management and Budget, page 153.

[687] "Fiscal Year 2013: Cuts, Consolidations, and Savings," White House Office of Management and Budget, page 153.

[688] McBride, Dara. "Drexel law professor creates a virtual venue for getting real-world experience," *Philadelphia Inquirer*, August 14, 2012. Available at http://articles.philly.com/2012-08-14/news/33183315_1_law-school-users-new-program, accessed September 14, 2012.

[689] "Award Abstract #1229941: SBIR Phase II: Crowd Sourcing Apprenticeship Learning: LawMeet – A Web Platform for Teaching Entrepreneurial Lawyering," Website of the National Science Foundation, http://nsf.gov/awardsearch/showAward.do?AwardNumber=1229941, accessed September 14, 2012.

[690] Wecker, Menachem. "Law Students Study as 'Virtual Apprentices'," *US News and World Report*, August 24, 2012. Available at http://www.usnews.com/education/best-graduate-schools/top-law-schools/articles/2012/08/24/law-students-study-as-virtual-apprentices, accessed September 14, 2012.

[691] Wecker, Menachem. "Law Students Study as 'Virtual Apprentices'," *US News and World Report*, August 24, 2012. Available at http://www.usnews.com/education/best-graduate-schools/top-law-schools/articles/2012/08/24/law-students-study-as-virtual-apprentices, accessed September 14, 2012.

[692] Wecker, Menachem. "Law Students Study as 'Virtual Apprentices'," *US News and World Report*, August 24, 2012. Available at http://www.usnews.com/education/best-graduate-schools/top-law-schools/articles/2012/08/24/law-students-study-as-virtual-apprentices, accessed September 14, 2012.

[693] Wecker, Menachem. "Law Students Study as 'Virtual Apprentices'," *US News and World Report*, August 24, 2012. Available at http://www.usnews.com/education/best-graduate-schools/top-law-schools/articles/2012/08/24/law-students-study-as-virtual-apprentices, accessed September 14, 2012.

[694] McBride, Dara. "Drexel law professor creates a virtual venue for getting real-world experience," *Philadelphia Inquirer*, August 14, 2012. Available at http://articles.philly.com/2012-08-14/news/33183315_1_law-school-users-new-program, accessed September 14, 2012.

[695] McBride, Dara. "Drexel law professor creates a virtual venue for getting real-world experience," *Philadelphia Inquirer*, August 14, 2012. Available at http://articles.philly.com/2012-08-14/news/33183315_1_law-school-users-new-program, accessed September 14, 2012.

[696] "Opportunity Exists to Strengthen Acquisitions by Reducing Concurrency," Government Accountability Office, April 20, 2012, GAO-12-486, p. 2. Available at http://www.gao.gov/products/GAO-12-486, accessed September 24, 2012.

[697] The system is a network of sensors and rocket interceptors based in land, sea, and space "The Ballistic Missile Defense System (BMDS)," Missile Defense Agency, http://www.mda.mil/system/system.html

[698] "Opportunity Exists to Strengthen Acquisitions by Reducing Concurrency," Government Accountability Office, April 20, 2012, GAO-12-486, p. 19. Available at http://www.gao.gov/products/GAO-12-486, accessed September 24, 2012.

[699] "Opportunity Exists to Strengthen Acquisitions by Reducing Concurrency," Government Accountability Office, April 20, 2012, GAO-12-486, p. 14. Available at http://www.gao.gov/products/GAO-12-486, accessed September 24, 2012.

[700] The system is designed to defend against ballistic missile attacks from North Korea and the Middle East.

[701] "Opportunity Exists to Strengthen Acquisitions by Reducing Concurrency," Government Accountability Office, April 20, 2012, GAO-12-486, p. 77. Available at http://www.gao.gov/products/GAO-12-486, accessed September 24, 2012.

[702] "DEFENSE ACQUISITIONS: Missile Defense Transition Provides Opportunity to Strengthen Acquisition Approach," *Government Accountability Office*, GAO-10-311, February 2010, p. 21. Available at http://www.gao.gov/assets/310/301067.pdf, accessed September 24, 2012.

[703] "DEFENSE ACQUISITIONS: Missile Defense Transition Provides Opportunity to Strengthen Acquisition Approach," *Government Accountability Office*, GAO-10-311, February 2010, p. 21. Available at http://www.gao.gov/assets/310/301067.pdf, accessed September 24, 2012.

[704] "Opportunity Exists to Strengthen Acquisitions by Reducing Concurrency," Government Accountability Office, April 20, 2012, GAO-12-486, p. 78. Available at http://www.gao.gov/products/GAO-12-486, accessed September 24, 2012.

[705] "Opportunity Exists to Strengthen Acquisitions by Reducing Concurrency," Government Accountability Office, April 20, 2012, GAO-12-486, p. 5. Available at http://www.gao.gov/products/GAO-12-486, accessed September 24, 2012.

[706] "Opportunity Exists to Strengthen Acquisitions by Reducing Concurrency," Government Accountability Office, April 20, 2012, GAO-12-486, p. 77. Available at http://www.gao.gov/products/GAO-12-486, accessed September 24, 2012.

[707] "Opportunity Exists to Strengthen Acquisitions by Reducing Concurrency," Government Accountability Office, April 20, 2012, GAO-12-486, p. 18. Available at http://www.gao.gov/products/GAO-12-486, accessed September 24, 2012.

[708] Two interceptors were destroyed in flight tests. "Opportunity Exists to Strengthen Acquisitions by Reducing Concurrency," Government Accountability Office, April 20, 2012, GAO-12-486, p. 76. Available at http://www.gao.gov/products/GAO-12-486, accessed September 24, 2012.

[709] "Opportunity Exists to Strengthen Acquisitions by Reducing Concurrency," Government Accountability Office, April 20, 2012, GAO-12-486, p. 18. Available at http://www.gao.gov/products/GAO-12-486, accessed September 24, 2012.

[710] "Opportunity Exists to Strengthen Acquisitions by Reducing Concurrency," Government Accountability Office, April 20, 2012, GAO-12-486, p. 17. Available at http://www.gao.gov/products/GAO-12-486, accessed September 24, 2012.

[711] This figure reflects the $740 million in additional funds spent on testing after the failure of the first test, plus the $421 million cost of the interceptor used after the first test. Retrofitting may also cost taxpayers at least $600 million.

[712] "Opportunity Exists to Strengthen Acquisitions by Reducing Concurrency," Government Accountability Office, April 20, 2012, GAO-12-486, p. 18. Available at http://www.gao.gov/products/GAO-12-486, accessed September 24, 2012.

[713] "Opportunity Exists to Strengthen Acquisitions by Reducing Concurrency," Government Accountability Office, April 20, 2012, GAO-12-486, p. 29. Available at http://www.gao.gov/products/GAO-12-486, accessed September 24, 2012.

[714] Szydlowski, Joseph. "Gateway district will use grant to buy high-tech exercise gear," *The Record Searchlight*, July 18, 2012. Available at http://www.redding.com/news/2012/jul/18/gateway-district-will-use-grant-to-buy-high-tech/, accessed August 9, 2012.

[715] Szydlowski, Joseph. "Gateway district will use grant to buy high-tech exercise gear," *The Record Searchlight*, July 18, 2012. Available at http://www.redding.com/news/2012/jul/18/gateway-district-will-use-grant-to-buy-high-tech/, accessed August 9, 2012.

[716] Szydlowski, Joseph. "Gateway district will use grant to buy high-tech exercise gear," *The Record Searchlight*, July 18, 2012. Available at http://www.redding.com/news/2012/jul/18/gateway-district-will-use-grant-to-buy-high-tech/, accessed August 9, 2012.

[717] Szydlowski, Joseph. "Gateway district will use grant to buy high-tech exercise gear," *The Record Searchlight*, July 18, 2012. Available at http://www.redding.com/news/2012/jul/18/gateway-district-will-use-grant-to-buy-high-tech/, accessed August 9, 2012.

[718] Szydlowski, Joseph. "Gateway district will use grant to buy high-tech exercise gear," *The Record Searchlight*, July 18, 2012. Available at http://www.redding.com/news/2012/jul/18/gateway-district-will-use-grant-to-buy-high-tech/, accessed August 9, 2012.

[719] Szydlowski, Joseph. "Gateway district will use grant to buy high-tech exercise gear," *The Record Searchlight*, July 18, 2012. Available at http://www.redding.com/news/2012/jul/18/gateway-district-will-use-grant-to-buy-high-tech/, accessed August 9, 2012.

[720] Ross, Bruce. "$100,000 for fitness video games" *The Record-Searchlight* Bruce Ross' blog, July 18, 2012, http://blogs.redding.com/bross/archives/2012/07/100000-for-fitn.html, accessed September 4, 2012.

[721] Energy.gov. "Energy Department Launches Apps for Energy," March 22, 2012. Available at http://energy.gov/articles/energy-department-launches-apps-energy, accessed September 17, 2012.

[722] "Apps for Energy: Rules," Challenge.gov, http://appsforenergy.challenge.gov/rules, accessed September 17, 2012.

[723] Van Grove, Jennifer. "Facebook app promotes energy conservation with peer pressure," *VentureBeat.com*, April 3, 2012, http://venturebeat.com/2012/04/03/facebook-social-energy/, accessed September 5, 2012.

[724] Van Grove, Jennifer. "Facebook app promotes energy conservation with peer pressure," *VentureBeat.com*, April 3, 2012, http://venturebeat.com/2012/04/03/facebook-social-energy/, accessed September 5, 2012.

[725] Borel, Brooke. "Track Household Electricity Use with Web-Connected Monitors," *Popular Science*, December 9, 2009. Available at http://www.popsci.com/gadgets/article/2009-12/track-household-electricity-use-web-connected-monitors, accessed September 5, 2012.

[726] EnergySaver is an Android app, and UTracker, EnergyTracker, and SD Energy are iPhone apps. All were available as September 5, 2012.

[727] The city reported it spent $18,410 in the first quarter of FY2012 to the New York State Housing Finance Agency. See "October 1, 2011 thru December 31, 2011 Performance Report" from State of New York, Grant No. B-08-DN-36-0001, https://hudnsphelp.info/media/GAReports/Q_B-08-DN-36-0001_2011_Q4.pdf, p. 13-15.

[728] "NSP Round 1 Grantees," New York State Homes and Community Renewal website, http://www.nyshcr.org/Topics/Municipalities/NSP/NSPRound1Awards.htm, accessed October 12, 2012.

[729] Robbins, Christopher. "Ogdensburg council approves sale of problem properties," *The Journal*, March 1, 2012. Available at http://www.ogd.com/article/20120301/OGD01/703019919/, accessed August 2, 2012.
[730] Robbins, Christopher. "Ogdensburg council approves sale of problem properties," *The Journal*, March 1, 2012. Available at http://www.ogd.com/article/20120301/OGD01/703019919/, accessed August 2, 2012.
[731] Robbins, Christopher. "Ogdensburg council members call housing rehabilitation work substandard," *The Journal*, February 10, 2012. Available at
http://www.watertowndailytimes.com/article/20120210/NEWS05/702109862/0/NEWS03, accessed August 2, 2012.
[732] Robbins, Christopher. "Ogdensburg council members call housing rehabilitation work substandard," *The Journal*, February 10, 2012. Available at
http://www.watertowndailytimes.com/article/20120210/NEWS05/702109862/0/NEWS03, accessed August 2, 2012.
[733] Robbins, Christopher. "Ogdensburg council approves sale of problem properties," *The Journal*, March 1, 2012. Available at http://www.ogd.com/article/20120301/OGD01/703019919/, accessed August 2, 2012.
[734] Robbins, Christopher. "Ogdensburg council members call housing rehabilitation work substandard," *The Journal*, February 10, 2012. Available at
http://www.watertowndailytimes.com/article/20120210/NEWS05/702109862/0/NEWS03, accessed August 2, 2012.
[735] Minutes of Ogdensburg City Council Meeting, January 23, 2012: p. 28. Available at
http://www.ogdensburg.org/archives/35/23Jan12%20Council%20minutes.pdf, accessed August 2, 2012.
[736] Minutes of Ogdensburg City Council Meeting, January 23, 2012: p. 27. Available at
http://www.ogdensburg.org/archives/35/23Jan12%20Council%20minutes.pdf, accessed August 2, 2012.
[737] Minutes of Ogdensburg City Council Meeting, January 23, 2012: p. 27-28. Available at
http://www.ogdensburg.org/archives/35/23Jan12%20Council%20minutes.pdf, accessed August 2, 2012.
[738] Robbins, Christopher. "Ogdensburg Residents Agitate on Housing Problems," *Watertown Daily Times*, February 14, 2012. Available at
http://www.watertowndailytimes.com/article/20120214/NEWS05/702149847, accessed August 2, 2012.
[739] Robbins, Christopher. "Ogdensburg council approves sale of problem properties," *The Journal*, March 1, 2012. Available at http://www.ogd.com/article/20120301/OGD01/703019919/, accessed August 2, 2012.
[740] Minutes of Ogdensburg City Council Meeting, January 23, 2012: p. 28. Available at
http://www.ogdensburg.org/archives/35/23Jan12%20Council%20minutes.pdf, accessed August 2, 2012.
[741] Robbins, Christopher. "Ogdensburg House Sale Turning Into Nightmare," *Daily Courier-Observer*, January 24, 2012. Available at http://www.wdt.net/article/20120124/DCO01/120129921, accessed August 2, 2012.
[742] Robbins, Christopher. "Ogdensburg council approves sale of problem properties," *The Journal*, March 1, 2012. Available at http://www.ogd.com/article/20120301/OGD01/703019919/, accessed August 2, 2012.
[743] Minutes of Ogdensburg City Council Meeting, January 23, 2012: p. 31. Available at
http://www.ogdensburg.org/archives/35/23Jan12%20Council%20minutes.pdf, accessed August 2, 2012.
[744] Information provided by the USDA to the Congressional Research Service, May 1, 2012
[745] Stinnet, Jon. "Arch installed downtown," *The Cottage Grove Sentinel*, March 13, 2012. Available at
http://www.cgsentinel.com/v2_news_articles.php?heading=0&story_id=5343&page=72, accessed May 2, 2012.
[746] Stinnet, Jon. "Large crowd attends Saturday arch dedication," *The Cottage Grove Sentinel*, March 20, 2012. Available at http://www.cgsentinel.com/v2_news_articles.php?heading=0&page=72&story_id=5353, accessed August 31, 2012.
[747] The IG questioned as much as $1.3 million in spending by the Paul Simon Job Corps Center. "MANAGEMENT & TRAINING CORPORATION DID NOT ENSURE BEST VALUE IN AWARDING SUB-

CONTRACTS AT THE PAUL SIMON JOB CORPS CENTER," U.S. Department of Labor Office of Inspector General, 26-12-002-03-370, March 30, 2012. Available at http://www.oig.dol.gov/public/reports/oa/2012/26-12-002-03-370.pdf, accessed September 24, 2012.

[748] The IG questioned as much as $3.3 million in spending by the Clearfield Job Corps Center. "MANAGEMENT & TRAINING CORPORATION DID NOT ENSURE BEST VALUE IN AWARDING SUB-CONTRACTS AT THE CLEARFIELD JOB CORPS CENTER," U.S. Department of Labor, Office of Inspector General, 26-12-003-03-370, March 30, 2012, http://www.oig.dol.gov/public/reports/oa/2012/26-12-003-03-370.pdf.

[749] Job Corps is a residential job training program for disadvantaged youth. MTC also manages several contracts for recruiting students into the Job Corps program, and is responsible for placing students in jobs, higher education, or the military upon their graduation from the program. Management and Training Corporation Website, "Job Corps" web page, http://www.mtctrains.com/job-corps, accessed June 15, 2012.

[750] "MANAGEMENT & TRAINING CORPORATION DID NOT ENSURE BEST VALUE IN AWARDING SUB-CONTRACTS AT THE PAUL SIMON JOB CORPS CENTER," U.S. Department of Labor Office of Inspector General, 26-12-002-03-370, March 30, 2012. Available at http://www.oig.dol.gov/public/reports/oa/2012/26-12-002-03-370.pdf, accessed September 24, 2012.

[751] "MANAGEMENT & TRAINING CORPORATION DID NOT ENSURE BEST VALUE IN AWARDING SUB-CONTRACTS AT THE CLEARFIELD JOB CORPS CENTER," U.S. Department of Labor, Office of Inspector General, 26-12-003-03-370, March 30, 2012, http://www.oig.dol.gov/public/reports/oa/2012/26-12-003-03-370.pdf.

[752] "MANAGEMENT & TRAINING CORPORATION DID NOT ENSURE BEST VALUE IN AWARDING SUB-CONTRACTS AT THE PAUL SIMON JOB CORPS CENTER," U.S. Department of Labor Office of Inspector General, 26-12-002-03-370, March 30, 2012, p. 3. Available at http://www.oig.dol.gov/public/reports/oa/2012/26-12-002-03-370.pdf, accessed September 24, 2012.

[753] "MANAGEMENT & TRAINING CORPORATION DID NOT ENSURE BEST VALUE IN AWARDING SUB-CONTRACTS AT THE CLEARFIELD JOB CORPS CENTER," U.S. Department of Labor, Office of Inspector General, 26-12-003-03-370, March 30, 2012, p. 4, http://www.oig.dol.gov/public/reports/oa/2012/26-12-003-03-370.pdf.

[754] "MANAGEMENT & TRAINING CORPORATION DID NOT ENSURE BEST VALUE IN AWARDING SUB-CONTRACTS AT THE PAUL SIMON JOB CORPS CENTER," U.S. Department of Labor Office of Inspector General, 26-12-002-03-370, March 30, 2012, p. 3. Available at http://www.oig.dol.gov/public/reports/oa/2012/26-12-002-03-370.pdf, accessed September 24, 2012.

[755] "MANAGEMENT & TRAINING CORPORATION DID NOT ENSURE BEST VALUE IN AWARDING SUB-CONTRACTS AT THE CLEARFIELD JOB CORPS CENTER," U.S. Department of Labor, Office of Inspector General, 26-12-003-03-370, March 30, 2012, p. 4, http://www.oig.dol.gov/public/reports/oa/2012/26-12-003-03-370.pdf.

[756] "MANAGEMENT & TRAINING CORPORATION DID NOT ENSURE BEST VALUE IN AWARDING SUB-CONTRACTS AT THE PAUL SIMON JOB CORPS CENTER," U.S. Department of Labor Office of Inspector General, 26-12-002-03-370, p. 11, March 30, 2012. Available at http://www.oig.dol.gov/public/reports/oa/2012/26-12-002-03-370.pdf, accessed September 24, 2012.

[757] "MANAGEMENT & TRAINING CORPORATION DID NOT ENSURE BEST VALUE IN AWARDING SUB-CONTRACTS AT THE PAUL SIMON JOB CORPS CENTER," U.S. Department of Labor Office of Inspector General, 26-12-002-03-370, p. 11, March 30, 2012. Available at http://www.oig.dol.gov/public/reports/oa/2012/26-12-002-03-370.pdf, accessed September 24, 2012.

[758] "US Department of State Announces Basketball Envoy Program in Venezuela," US Department of State website, May 24, 2012, http://www.state.gov/r/pa/prs/ps/2012/05/190825.htm, accessed September 10, 2012.

[759] The program started in 2002 under then-President Bush.
[760] Information provided by the State Department to the Congressional Research Service, August 6, 2012.
[761] "US Department of State Announces Basketball Envoy Program in Venezuela," US Department of State website, May 24, 2012, http://www.state.gov/r/pa/prs/ps/2012/05/190825.htm, accessed accessed September 27, 2012.
[762] "Major League Soccer Envoys Bring Olympic-size Excitement to Camp in Eastern Ethiopia," USAID website, August 2, 2012, http://blog.usaid.gov/2012/08/olympic-size-excitement-to-camp-in-eastern-ethiopia/, accessed accessed September 27, 2012.
[763] "Past Basketball Programs," US Department of State website, http://exchanges.state.gov/sports/all-basketball.html, accessed accessed September 27, 2012.
[764] "US Department of State Announces Basketball Envoy Program in Venezuela," US Department of State website, May 24, 2012, http://www.state.gov/r/pa/prs/ps/2012/05/190825.htm, accessed September 27, 2012.
[765] Davis, Kelli. "Tunisian Swimmers Make a Splash in the United States," State Department's DipNote blog, July 28, 2012, http://blogs.state.gov/index.php/site/entry/tunisian_swimmers_splash_us, accessed September 27, 2012.
[766] Facebook.com page of SportsUnited, US Department of State. Wall Post on June 27, 2012, http://www.facebook.com/pages/SportsUnited-US-Department-of-State/10150101343025475, accessed September 24, 2012.
[767] "US Department of State Announces Soccer Envoy Program in Ethiopia," US Department of State website, Press Release, July 10, 2012: http://www.state.gov/r/pa/prs/ps/2012/07/194809.htm, accessed July 30, 2012.
[768] "Basketball Programs," US Department of State website, http://exchanges.state.gov/sports/basketball.html, accessed July 30, 2012.
[769] "U.S. Department of State Announces Two Youth Sports Exchange Programs with Russia," U.S. Department of State website, http://www.state.gov/r/pa/prs/ps/2012/07/194534.htm, accessed September 24, 2012.

[770] "Award Abstract #0904456: Collaborative Research: Hand-Mounted Tactile Displays for Haptically Identifying Shape and Dexterous Manipulation," Website of the National Science Foundation, http://nsf.gov/awardsearch/showAward.do?AwardNumber=0904456, accessed March 23, 2012.

[771] "Award Abstract #0746914: CAREER: HCC: Haptic Guidance Systems," Website of the National Science Foundation. http://nsf.gov/awardsearch/showAward.do?AwardNumber=0746914, accessed March 23, 2012.
[772] Amini, Tina. "How Stretching Your Thumbs Could Make Your Games Feel Better," Kotaku, March 6, 2012. Available online at: http://kotaku.com/5890659/how-stretching-your-thumbs-could-make-your-games-feel-better, accessed April 2, 2012.
[773] Horiuchi, Vince. "University of Utah professor invents new video game controller (video)," *The Salt Lake Tribune*, March 6, 2012. Available at http://www.sltrib.com/sltrib/lifestyle/53651096-80/feedback-game-video-professor.html.csp, accessed August 23, 2012.
[774] BBC News, "Thumb-stretching controller pitched to console makers," March 5, 2012. Available online at: http://www.bbc.co.uk/news/technology-17257316, accessed April 2, 2012.
[775] Horiuchi, Vince. "University of Utah professor invents new video game controller (video)," *The Salt Lake Tribune*, March 6, 2012. Available at http://www.sltrib.com/sltrib/lifestyle/53651096-80/feedback-game-video-professor.html.csp, accessed August 23, 2012.
[776] BBC News, "Thumb-stretching controller pitched to console makers," March 5, 2012. Available online at: http://www.bbc.co.uk/news/technology-17257316, accessed April 2, 2012.

[777] BBC News, "Thumb-stretching controller pitched to console makers," March 5, 2012. Available online at: http://www.bbc.co.uk/news/technology-17257316, accessed April 2, 2012.

[778] "Billions of Dollars in Education Credits Appear to Be Erroneous," Treasury Inspector General for Tax Administration, Reference Num. 2011-41-083, September 16, 2012, p. 3. Available at http://www.treasury.gov/tigta/auditreports/2011reports/201141083fr.pdf, accessed September 24, 2012.

[779] "Billions of Dollars in Education Credits Appear to Be Erroneous," Treasury Inspector General for Tax Administration, Reference Num. 2011-41-083, September 16, 2012, p. 3. Available at http://www.treasury.gov/tigta/auditreports/2011reports/201141083fr.pdf, accessed September 24, 2012.

[780] The tax credit is available through 2012.

[781] "Billions of Dollars in Education Credits Appear to Be Erroneous," Treasury Inspector General for Tax Administration, Reference Num. 2011-41-083, September 16, 2012, p. 1. Available at http://www.treasury.gov/tigta/auditreports/2011reports/201141083fr.pdf, accessed September 24, 2012.

[782] "Billions of Dollars in Education Credits Appear to Be Erroneous," Treasury Inspector General for Tax Administration, Reference Num. 2011-41-083, September 16, 2012, p. 3,16. Available at http://www.treasury.gov/tigta/auditreports/2011reports/201141083fr.pdf, accessed September 24, 2012.

[783] "Billions of Dollars in Education Credits Appear to Be Erroneous," Treasury Inspector General for Tax Administration, Reference Num. 2011-41-083, September 16, 2012, p. 16. Available at http://www.treasury.gov/tigta/auditreports/2011reports/201141083fr.pdf, accessed September 24, 2012.

[784] "Billions of Dollars in Education Credits Appear to Be Erroneous," Treasury Inspector General for Tax Administration, Reference Num. 2011-41-083, September 16, 2012, p. 3. Available at http://www.treasury.gov/tigta/auditreports/2011reports/201141083fr.pdf, accessed September 24, 2012.

[785] "Billions of Dollars in Education Credits Appear to Be Erroneous," Treasury Inspector General for Tax Administration, Reference Num. 2011-41-083, September 16, 2012, p. 11. Available at http://www.treasury.gov/tigta/auditreports/2011reports/201141083fr.pdf, accessed September 24, 2012.

[786] "Billions of Dollars in Education Credits Appear to Be Erroneous," Treasury Inspector General for Tax Administration, Reference Num. 2011-41-083, September 16, 2012, p. 11. Available at http://www.treasury.gov/tigta/auditreports/2011reports/201141083fr.pdf, accessed September 24, 2012.

[787] "Billions of Dollars in Education Credits Appear to Be Erroneous," Treasury Inspector General for Tax Administration, Reference Num. 2011-41-083, September 16, 2012, p. 8. Available at http://www.treasury.gov/tigta/auditreports/2011reports/201141083fr.pdf, accessed September 24, 2012.

[788] "Billions of Dollars in Education Credits Appear to Be Erroneous," Treasury Inspector General for Tax Administration, Reference Num. 2011-41-083, September 16, 2012, p. 3. Available at http://www.treasury.gov/tigta/auditreports/2011reports/201141083fr.pdf, accessed September 24, 2012.

[789] "Billions of Dollars in Education Credits Appear to Be Erroneous," Treasury Inspector General for Tax Administration, Reference Num. 2011-41-083, September 16, 2012, p. 3. Available at http://www.treasury.gov/tigta/auditreports/2011reports/201141083fr.pdf, accessed September 24, 2012.

[790] "US to send Indian-American comedy group to India," *The Economic Times*, December 30, 2011. Available at http://articles.economictimes.indiatimes.com/2011-12-30/news/30572993_1_indian-american-religious-tolerance-rajiv-satyal, accessed August 8, 2012.

[791] Epstein, Susan B., and Marian Leonardo Lawson. "State, Foreign Operations, and Related Programs: FY2012 Budget and Appropriations," Congressional Research Service, R41905, January 6, 2012, p. 5.

[792] "US to send Indian-American comedy group to India," *The Economic Times*, December 30, 2011. Available at http://articles.economictimes.indiatimes.com/2011-12-30/news/30572993_1_indian-american-religious-tolerance-rajiv-satyal, accessed August 8, 2012.

[793] Chatterjee, Madhurima. "Make Fun Not War," *The Telegraph (Calcutta, India)*, January 17, 2012. Available at http://www.telegraphindia.com/1120117/jsp/entertainment/story_15013069.jsp#.UCK2KfZlSo0, accessed August 8, 2012.

[794] Wayne, Alex. "Medicaid Fraud Audits Cost Five Times Amount U.S. Found," *Bloomberg Businessweek*, June 14, 2012. Available at http://www.businessweek.com/news/2012-06-14/medicaid-fraud-audits-cost-five-times-amount-u-dot-s-dot-found, accessed September 6, 2012.

[795] "National Medicaid Audit Program: CMS Should Improve Reporting and Focus on Audit Collaboration with States," *Government Accountability Office*, June 2012, GAO-12-627, p. 21. Available at http://www.gao.gov/assets/600/591601.pdf, accessed September 24, 2012.

[796] The report states the audit program takes about 40 percent of the Medicaid Integrity Group's $75 million budget for program integrity. "National Medicaid Audit Program: CMS Should Improve Reporting and Focus on Audit Collaboration with States," *Government Accountability Office*, June 2012, GAO-12-627, p. 2. Available at http://www.gao.gov/assets/600/591601.pdf, accessed September 24, 2012.

[797] "National Medicaid Audit Program: CMS Should Improve Reporting and Focus on Audit Collaboration with States," *Government Accountability Office*, June 2012, GAO-12-627, p. 13. Available at http://www.gao.gov/assets/600/591601.pdf, accessed September 24, 2012.

[798] "National Medicaid Audit Program: CMS Should Improve Reporting and Focus on Audit Collaboration with States," *Government Accountability Office*, June 2012, GAO-12-627, p. 26-7. Available at http://www.gao.gov/assets/600/591601.pdf, accessed September 24, 2012.

[799] "National Medicaid Audit Program: CMS Should Improve Reporting and Focus on Audit Collaboration with States," *Government Accountability Office*, June 2012, GAO-12-627, p. 15. Available at http://www.gao.gov/assets/600/591601.pdf, accessed September 24, 2012.

[800] "National Medicaid Audit Program: CMS Should Improve Reporting and Focus on Audit Collaboration with States," *Government Accountability Office*, June 2012, GAO-12-627, p. 16. Available at http://www.gao.gov/assets/600/591601.pdf, accessed September 24, 2012.

[801] "National Medicaid Audit Program: CMS Should Improve Reporting and Focus on Audit Collaboration with States," *Government Accountability Office*, June 2012, GAO-12-627, p. 15. Available at http://www.gao.gov/assets/600/591601.pdf, accessed September 24, 2012.

[802] "National Medicaid Audit Program: CMS Should Improve Reporting and Focus on Audit Collaboration with States," *Government Accountability Office*, June 2012, GAO-12-627, p. 16. Available at http://www.gao.gov/assets/600/591601.pdf, accessed September 24, 2012.

[803] "National Medicaid Audit Program: CMS Should Improve Reporting and Focus on Audit Collaboration with States," *Government Accountability Office*, June 2012, GAO-12-627, p. 15. Available at http://www.gao.gov/assets/600/591601.pdf, accessed September 24, 2012.

[804] "National Medicaid Audit Program: CMS Should Improve Reporting and Focus on Audit Collaboration with States," *Government Accountability Office*, June 2012, GAO-12-627, p. 16. Available at http://www.gao.gov/assets/600/591601.pdf, accessed September 24, 2012.

[805] "National Medicaid Audit Program: CMS Should Improve Reporting and Focus on Audit Collaboration with States," *Government Accountability Office*, June 2012, GAO-12-627, p. 10. Available at http://www.gao.gov/assets/600/591601.pdf, accessed September 24, 2012.

[806] "National Medicaid Audit Program: CMS Should Improve Reporting and Focus on Audit Collaboration with States," *Government Accountability Office*, June 2012, GAO-12-627, p. 16. Available at http://www.gao.gov/assets/600/591601.pdf, accessed September 24, 2012.

[807] "National Medicaid Audit Program: CMS Should Improve Reporting and Focus on Audit Collaboration with States," *Government Accountability Office*, June 2012, GAO-12-627, p. 21. Available at http://www.gao.gov/assets/600/591601.pdf, accessed September 24, 2012.

[808] Baggett, Connie. "Baldwin County gives green light on courthouse camera purchases," *Press-Register*, March 27, 2012. Available at http://blog.al.com/live/2012/03/baldwin_county_gives_green_lig.html, accessed June 6, 2012.

[809] Baggett, Connie. "Baldwin County gives green light on courthouse camera purchases," *Press-Register*, March 27, 2012. Available at http://blog.al.com/live/2012/03/baldwin_county_gives_green_lig.html, accessed June 6, 2012.

[810] Baggett, Connie. "Baldwin County gives green light on courthouse camera purchases," *Press-Register*, March 27, 2012. Available online at http://blog.al.com/live/2012/03/baldwin_county_gives_green_lig.html, accessed June 6, 2012.

[811] "News Release: Baldwin County Matter," Department of Justice website, Press Release May 11, 2012. Available at http://www.justice.gov/usao/als/news/2012/051112-1.html, accessed June 6, 2012.

[812] Kuo TK, JY Yew, TY Fedina, et al. (2012) "Aging modulates cuticular hydrocarbons and sexual attractiveness in *Drosophila melanogaster*," *Journal of Experimental Biology*, 215:814-21.

[813] Baylor College of Medicine, "Fruit flies drawn to the sweet smell of youth." February 9, 2012. http://www.bcm.edu/news/item.cfm?newsID=5203

[814] Baylor College of Medicine, "Fruit flies drawn to the sweet smell of youth." February 9, 2012. http://www.bcm.edu/news/item.cfm?newsID=5203

[815] Baylor College of Medicine, "Fruit flies drawn to the sweet smell of youth." February 9, 2012. http://www.bcm.edu/news/item.cfm?newsID=5203

[816] "Mechanisms of Olfactory Modulation of Aging in Drosophila," Website of the National Institutes of Health, NIH project number 5R01AG030593-05, http://projectreporter.nih.gov/project_info_details.cfm?aid=8074411&icde=12015135, accessed April 4, 2012. Grant was acknowledged as supporting the study in the researchers' publication.

[817] "Mechanisms of Dietary Restriction in Drosophila," Website of the National Institutes of Health, NIH project number 5R01AG023166-07, http://projectreporter.nih.gov/project_info_description.cfm?aid=8149821&icde=12015172&ddparam=&ddvalue=&ddsub=&cr=1&csb=default&cs=ASC, accessed April 4, 2012. Grant was acknowledged as supporting the study in the researchers' publication.

[818] "Hormonal Modulation of Aggression in Drosophila," Website of the National Institutes of Health, NIH project number 2R01GM074675-05A1, http://projectreporter.nih.gov/project_info_description.cfm?aid=8040316&icde=12015208&ddparam=&ddvalue=&ddsub=&cr=1&csb=default&cs=ASC, accessed April 4, 2012. Grant was acknowledged as supporting the study in the researchers' publication.

[819] NSF Award Abstract #0751650: Interactions Between Neurohormonal Systems: Studies at the Cellular and Genetic Level, http://nsf.gov/awardsearch/showAward.do?AwardNumber=0751650, accessed April 4, 2012.

[820] McGowan, Dan, "Providence Stiffed for Millions in Loan Money," *GoLocalProv*, October 24, 2011. Available at http://www.golocalprov.com/news/pedp-loans/, accessed August 14, 2012.

[821] McGowan, Dan, "Providence Stiffed for Millions in Loan Money," *GoLocalProv*, October 24, 2011. Available at http://www.golocalprov.com/news/pedp-loans/, accessed August 14, 2012.

[822] McGowan, Dan, "Providence Stiffed for Millions in Loan Money," *GoLocalProv*, October 24, 2011. Available at http://www.golocalprov.com/news/pedp-loans/, accessed August 14, 2012.

[823] McGowan, Dan, "Providence Stiffed for Millions in Loan Money," *GoLocalProv*, October 24, 2011. Available at http://www.golocalprov.com/news/pedp-loans/, accessed August 14, 2012.

[824] McGowan, Dan, "Providence Stiffed for Millions in Loan Money," *GoLocalProv*, October 24, 2011. Available at http://www.golocalprov.com/news/pedp-loans/, accessed August 14, 2012.

[825] "HUD questions Providence's use of grant money," *Associated Press*, July 20, 2012. Available at http://www.boston.com/news/local/rhode_island/articles/2012/07/20/hud_questions_providences_use_of_grant_money/, accessed August 20, 2012.

[826] "HUD questions Providence's use of grant money," *Associated Press*, July 20, 2012. Available at http://www.boston.com/news/local/rhode_island/articles/2012/07/20/hud_questions_providences_use_of_grant_money/, accessed August 20, 2012.

[827] "HUD questions Providence's use of grant money," *Associated Press*, July 20, 2012. Available at http://www.boston.com/news/local/rhode_island/articles/2012/07/20/hud_questions_providences_use_of_grant_money/, accessed August 20, 2012.

[828] "Effects of Federal Tax Credits for the Purchase of Electric Vehicles," *Congressional Budget Office*, September 2012, p. IV. Available at http://www.cbo.gov/publication/43576, accessed October 5, 2012.

[829] "Estimated Budget Effects of the Revenue Provisions Contained in the Conference Agreement for H.R. 1, the "American Recovery and Reinvestment Tax Act of 2009," JCX-19-09, February 12, 2009, p. 3.

[830] "Effects of Federal Tax Credits for the Purchase of Electric Vehicles," *Congressional Budget Office*, September 2012, p. 12. Available at http://www.cbo.gov/publication/43576, accessed October 5, 2012.

[831] "Effects of Federal Tax Credits for the Purchase of Electric Vehicles," *Congressional Budget Office*, September 2012, p. IV, 3. Available at http://www.cbo.gov/publication/43576, accessed October 5, 2012.

[832] "Effects of Federal Tax Credits for the Purchase of Electric Vehicles," *Congressional Budget Office*, September 2012, p. 3. Available at http://www.cbo.gov/publication/43576, accessed October 5, 2012.

[833] "Effects of Federal Tax Credits for the Purchase of Electric Vehicles," *Congressional Budget Office*, September 2012, p. 6. Available at http://www.cbo.gov/publication/43576, accessed October 5, 2012.

[834] A car manufacturer meets the standards based on the mix of vehicles it sells in a given year. "Effects of Federal Tax Credits for the Purchase of Electric Vehicles," *Congressional Budget Office*, September 2012, p. 14. Available at http://www.cbo.gov/publication/43576, accessed October 5, 2012.

[835] A car manufacturer meets the standards based on the mix of vehicles it sells in a given year. "Effects of Federal Tax Credits for the Purchase of Electric Vehicles," *Congressional Budget Office*, September 2012, p. 14. Available at http://www.cbo.gov/publication/43576, accessed October 5, 2012.

[836] "Effects of Federal Tax Credits for the Purchase of Electric Vehicles," *Congressional Budget Office*, September 2012, p. 15. Available at http://www.cbo.gov/publication/43576, accessed October 5, 2012.

[837] "Effects of Federal Tax Credits for the Purchase of Electric Vehicles," *Congressional Budget Office*, September 2012, p. 18. Available at http://www.cbo.gov/publication/43576, accessed October 5, 2012.

[838] "Effects of Federal Tax Credits for the Purchase of Electric Vehicles," *Congressional Budget Office*, September 2012, p. 18. Available at http://www.cbo.gov/publication/43576, accessed October 5, 2012.

[839] "Effects of Federal Tax Credits for the Purchase of Electric Vehicles," *Congressional Budget Office*, September 2012, p. 27. Available at http://www.cbo.gov/publication/43576, accessed October 5, 2012.

[840] "Effects of Federal Tax Credits for the Purchase of Electric Vehicles," *Congressional Budget Office*, September 2012, p. 18. Available at http://www.cbo.gov/publication/43576, accessed October 5, 2012.

[841] "Effects of Federal Tax Credits for the Purchase of Electric Vehicles," *Congressional Budget Office*, September 2012, p. 24. Available at http://www.cbo.gov/publication/43576, accessed October 5, 2012.

[842] "Effects of Federal Tax Credits for the Purchase of Electric Vehicles," *Congressional Budget Office*, September 2012, p. 24. Available at http://www.cbo.gov/publication/43576, accessed October 5, 2012.

[843] Cronin, Patrick. "Smuttynose gains support from town," *SeacoastOnline.com*, April 6, 2012. Available online at: http://www.seacoastonline.com/articles/20120406-NEWS-204060361, accessed September 10, 2012.

[844] Cronin, Patrick, "Smuttynose move gets financing," *SeacostOnline.com*, August 10, 2012, http://www.seacoastonline.com/articles/20120810-BIZ-208100375, accessed September 5, 2012.

[845] Cronin, Patrick. "Smuttynose gains support from town," *SeacoastOnline.com*, April 6, 2012. Available online at: http://www.seacoastonline.com/articles/20120406-NEWS-204060361, accessed September 10, 2012.

[846] Cronin, Patrick, "Smuttynose move gets financing," *SeacostOnline.com*, August 10, 2012, http://www.seacoastonline.com/articles/20120810-BIZ-208100375, accessed September 5, 2012.

[847] "Smuttynose excels in micro-brew market," Seacoastonline.com, April 25, 2010. Available online at: http://www.seacoastonline.com/articles/20100425-BIZ-4250309, accessed September 10, 2012.

[848] Cronin, Patrick. "Town of Hampton aids in Smuttynose Brewery's move," *SeacoastOnline.com*, June 5, 2009, http://www.seacoastonline.com/articles/20090605-NEWS-906050372, accessed September 5, 2012.

[849] McCord, Michael. "Smuttynose project still brewing in Hampton," *SeaCoastOnline.com*, September 16, 2011. Available at: www.seacoastonline.com/articles/20110916-NEWS-109160357, accessed September 10, 2012.

[850] Klipp, Liz. "Musical Robot Companion Enhances Listener Experience," Georgia Tech website, June 26, 2012, http://www.gatech.edu/newsroom/release.html?nid=137351, accessed September 27, 2012.

[851] Klipp, Liz. "Musical Robot Companion Enhances Listener Experience," Georgia Tech website, June 26, 2012, http://www.gatech.edu/newsroom/release.html?nid=137351, accessed September 27, 2012.

[852] "Music Technology Robot - Tovbot Shimi – Commercial," Youtube.com, posted September 7, 2012, http://www.youtube.com/watch?v=hzxQ2X_HQXI&feature=related, accessed September 27, 2012.

[853] "Update: What can Shimi do for you," Kickstarter.com, http://www.kickstarter.com/projects/143402057/shimi-a-smart-musical-robot-for-your-iphone/posts?page=2, accessed October 11, 2012.

[854] Lewis, Cali. "Shimi Robot DJ: A Dancing Robot Speaker System on Kickstarter," GeekBeat.tv, September 11, 2012, http://geekbeat.tv/shimi-robot-dj-a-dancing-robot-speaker-system-on-kickstarter/, accessed September 27, 2012.

[855] "Award Abstract #1017169: HCC: Small: Multi Modal Intelligence for Robotic Musicianship," Website of the National Science Foundation, http://nsf.gov/awardsearch/showAward.do?AwardNumber=1017169, accessed September 27, 2012.

[856] "Shimi – A Music Robot For Your Smartphone," Kickstarter.com, http://www.kickstarter.com/projects/143402057/shimi-a-smart-musical-robot-for-your-iphone, accessed September 27, 2012.

[857] Tam, Donna. "Shimi: Your personal robotic DJ," *CNET.com*, September 10, 2012, http://news.cnet.com/8301-10797_3-57510009-235/shimi-your-personal-robotic-dj/, accessed October 11, 2012.

[858] Kliff, Sarah. "Will Philadelphia's experiment in eradicating 'food deserts' work?" *The Washington Post* WonkBlog, June 8, 2012, http://www.washingtonpost.com/blogs/ezra-klein/post/will-philadelphias-experiment-in-eradicating-food-deserts-work/2012/06/08/gJQAU9snNV_blog.html, accessed August 29, 2012.

[859] "Healthy Food Financing Initiative FY12 Appropriations Funding," Website of National Sustainable Agriculture Coalition, December 22, 2011, http://sustainableagriculture.net/blog/hffi-fy12-approps/, accessed July 24, 2012.

[860] "Healthy Food Financing Initative," Department of Health and Human Services website, posted January 18, 2011, http://www.acf.hhs.gov/programs/ocs/resource/healthy-food-financing-initiative-0, accessed October 12, 2012.

[861] Kliff, Sarah. "Will Philadelphia's experiment in eradicating 'food deserts' work?" *The Washington Post* WonkBlog, June 8, 2012, http://www.washingtonpost.com/blogs/ezra-klein/post/will-philadelphias-experiment-in-eradicating-food-deserts-work/2012/06/08/gJQAU9snNV_blog.html, accessed August 29, 2012.

[862] Kliff, Sarah. "Will Philadelphia's experiment in eradicating 'food deserts' work?" *The Washington Post* WonkBlog, June 8, 2012, http://www.washingtonpost.com/blogs/ezra-klein/post/will-philadelphias-experiment-in-eradicating-food-deserts-work/2012/06/08/gJQAU9snNV_blog.html, accessed August 29, 2012.

[863] "Fast Food Restaurants and Food Stores: Longitudinal Associations With Diet in Young to Middle-aged Adults: The CARDIA Study," *Arch Intern Med.* 2011;171(13):1162-1170.

[864] "Fast Food Restaurants and Food Stores: Longitudinal Associations With Diet in Young to Middle-aged Adults: The CARDIA Study," *Arch Intern Med.* 2011;171(13):1162-1170.

[865] "Access to Affordable and Nutritious Food-Measuring and Understanding Food Deserts and their Consequences: Report to Congress," USDA Economic Research Service, June 2009, page 56, http://www.ers.usda.gov/publications/ap/ap036/, accessed August 29, 2012.

[866] Kliff, Sarah. "Will Philadelphia's experiment in eradicating 'food deserts' work?" *The Washington Post* WonkBlog, June 8, 2012, http://www.washingtonpost.com/blogs/ezra-klein/post/will-philadelphias-experiment-in-eradicating-food-deserts-work/2012/06/08/gJQAU9snNV_blog.html, accessed August 29, 2012.

[867] Kliff, Sarah. "Will Philadelphia's experiment in eradicating 'food deserts' work?" *The Washington Post* WonkBlog, June 8, 2012, http://www.washingtonpost.com/blogs/ezra-klein/post/will-philadelphias-experiment-in-eradicating-food-deserts-work/2012/06/08/gJQAU9snNV_blog.html, accessed August 29, 2012.

[868] "NEH Enduring Questions Course on 'What Is the Nature of Happiness'," Website of the National Endowment for the Humanities, https://securegrants.neh.gov/publicquery/main.aspx?q=1&a=0&n=1&ln=walker&fn=mark&o=0&k=0&f=0&s=0&p=0&d=0&y=0&prd=0&cov=0&prz=0&wp=0&pg=0&ob=year&or=DESC, accessed October 11, 2012.

[869] Suther, Tonya. "Should we want to be happy? New NMSU course will explore that question," New Mexico State University website, http://artsci.nmsu.edu/newsletter/should-we-want-to-be-hap.html, accessed October 11, 2012.

[870] "NEH Enduring Questions Course on 'What Is the Nature of Happiness'," Website of the National Endowment for the Humanities, https://securegrants.neh.gov/publicquery/main.aspx?q=1&a=0&n=1&ln=walker&fn=mark&o=0&k=0&f=0&s=0&p=0&d=0&y=0&prd=0&cov=0&prz=0&wp=0&pg=0&ob=year&or=DESC, accessed October 15, 2012.

[871] "NEH Enduring Questions Course on 'What Is the Nature of Happiness'," Website of the National Endowment for the Humanities, https://securegrants.neh.gov/publicquery/main.aspx?q=1&a=0&n=1&ln=walker&fn=mark&o=0&k=0&f=0&s=0&p=0&d=0&y=0&prd=0&cov=0&prz=0&wp=0&pg=0&ob=year&or=DESC, accessed October 11, 2012.

[872] "NEH Enduring Questions Course on 'What Is the Nature of Happiness'," Website of the National Endowment for the Humanities, https://securegrants.neh.gov/publicquery/main.aspx?q=1&a=0&n=1&ln=walker&fn=mark&o=0&k=0&f=0&s=0&p=0&d=0&y=0&prd=0&cov=0&prz=0&wp=0&pg=0&ob=year&or=DESC, accessed October 11, 2012.

[873] "NEH Enduring Questions Course on 'What Is the Nature of Happiness'," Website of the National Endowment for the Humanities, https://securegrants.neh.gov/publicquery/main.aspx?q=1&a=0&n=1&ln=walker&fn=mark&o=0&k=0&f=0&s=0&p=0&d=0&y=0&prd=0&cov=0&prz=0&wp=0&pg=0&ob=year&or=DESC, October 15, 2012.

[874] "Enduring Questions," Website of the National Endowment for the Humanities, http://www.neh.gov/files/grants/enduring-questions-sept-13-2012.pdf, accessed October 15, 2012.

[875] "More and Better Science in Antarctica Through Increased Logistical Effectiveness," Report of the U.S. Antarctic Program Blue Ribbon Panel, July 23, 2012, p. 171. Available at

http://www.nsf.gov/od/opp/usap_special_review/usap_brp/rpt/antarctica_07232012.pdf, accessed August 2, 2012.

[876] "More and Better Science in Antarctica Through Increased Logistical Effectiveness," Report of the U.S. Antarctic Program Blue Ribbon Panel, July 23, 2012, p. 169. Available at http://www.nsf.gov/od/opp/usap_special_review/usap_brp/rpt/antarctica_07232012.pdf, accessed August 2, 2012.

[877] "Executive Summary: More and Better Science in Antarctica Through Increased Logistical Effectiveness," Report of the U.S. Antarctic Program Blue Ribbon Panel, July 23, 2012, p. 3. Available at http://www.nsf.gov/od/opp/usap_special_review/usap_brp/rpt/antarctica_brochure_final.pdf, accessed August 2, 2012.

[878] "More and Better Science in Antarctica Through Increased Logistical Effectiveness," Report of the U.S. Antarctic Program Blue Ribbon Panel, July 23, 2012, p. 169. Available at http://www.nsf.gov/od/opp/usap_special_review/usap_brp/rpt/antarctica_07232012.pdf, accessed August 2, 2012.

[879] The report states that savings from reducing contractor labor would fund 60 grants at about $125,000 each, totaling $7.5 million. "Executive Summary: More and Better Science in Antarctica Through Increased Logistical Effectiveness," Report of the U.S. Antarctic Program Blue Ribbon Panel, July 23, 2012, p. 3. Available at http://www.nsf.gov/od/opp/usap_special_review/usap_brp/rpt/antarctica_brochure_final.pdf, accessed August 2, 2012.

[880] Cost of the contract depends on the year it is maintained. Website of Lockheed Martin, "Lockheed Martin Wins Contract Worth up to $2 Billion to Support the U.S. Antarctic Program," Press Release, December 28, 2011. Available at http://www.lockheedmartin.com/us/news/press-releases/2011/december/1228-antartic-program.html, accessed August 3, 2012.

[881] "Executive Summary: More and Better Science in Antarctica Through Increased Logistical Effectiveness," Report of the U.S. Antarctic Program Blue Ribbon Panel, July 23, 2012, p. 10. Available at http://www.nsf.gov/od/opp/usap_special_review/usap_brp/rpt/antarctica_brochure_final.pdf, accessed August 2, 2012.

[882] This figure represents the $15 million net present value minus the $1.8 million investment needed. "Executive Summary: More and Better Science in Antarctica Through Increased Logistical Effectiveness," Report of the U.S. Antarctic Program Blue Ribbon Panel, July 23, 2012, p. 22. Available at http://www.nsf.gov/od/opp/usap_special_review/usap_brp/rpt/antarctica_brochure_final.pdf, accessed August 2, 2012.

[883] "Executive Summary: More and Better Science in Antarctica Through Increased Logistical Effectiveness," Report of the U.S. Antarctic Program Blue Ribbon Panel, July 23, 2012, p. 20. Available at http://www.nsf.gov/od/opp/usap_special_review/usap_brp/rpt/antarctica_brochure_final.pdf, accessed August 2, 2012.

[884] "Gillibrand Announces Nearly $50,000 in Value-Added Producer Grant for Long Island Farm," Website of US Senator Kirsten Gillibrand, Press Release, February 8, 2012, http://www.gillibrand.senate.gov/newsroom/press/release/gillibrand-announces-nearly-50000-in-value-added-producer-grant-for-long-island-farm, accessed August 20, 2012.

[885] Gustavson, Jennifer. "North Fork Potato Chips awarded $50,000 marketing grant," *The Suffolk Times*, February 9, 2012. Available at http://suffolktimes.timesreview.com/2012/02/29564/north-fork-potato-chips-awarded-50000-marketing-grant/, accessed August 20, 2012.

[886] "Order Our Chips," Website of North Fork Potato Chips, https://www.northforkchips.com/order.html, accessed August 20, 2012.

[887] "A Chip Off the Old Block – North Fork spud + slicer + frying = saving the farm," Website of North Fork Potato Chips, http://www.northforkchips.com/EdibleEE_summer09.htm, accessed August 20, 2012.

[888] "A Chip Off the Old Block – North Fork spud + slicer + frying = saving the farm," Website of North Fork Potato Chips, http://www.northforkchips.com/EdibleEE_summer09.htm, accessed August 20, 2012.

[889] "Value Added Producer Grants Announced," Press Release, February 3, 2012, US Department of Agriculture website, http://www.rurdev.usda.gov/STELPRD4014692.html, accessed August 20, 2012.

[890] Martin Sidor Farms, Inc., http://www.rurdev.usda.gov/SupportDocuments/rd-vapg012012.pdf, p. 6

[891] This information was provided by the National Endowment for the Humanities to the Congressional Research Service, April 25, 2012.

[892] This information was provided by the National Endowment for the Humanities to the Congressional Research Service, April 25, 2012.

[893] The Website of the Modernist Journals Project, http://www.modjourn.org/, accessed October 15, 2012.

[894] The sum of the grant awarded in 2012 covered in this report, and those that follow in the paragraph: the grants awarded between 2003 and 2010, and the grant awarded in 2009 for a four-week seminar to study the golden age of magazines.

[895] Website of the National Endowment for the Humanities, Grant no. PW-50516-10, PM-50084-07, PA-50026-03, https://securegrants.neh.gov/publicquery/main.aspx?q=1&a=0&n=0&o=0&k=1&kv=modernist+journals+project&kj=phrase&w=0&f=0&s=0&p=0&d=0&y=0&prd=0&cov=0&prz=0&wp=0&pg=0&ob=year&or=DESC, accessed October 15, 2012.

[896] "National Endowment for the Humanities, Awards and Offers, August 2009," National Endowment for the Humanities website, http://www.neh.gov/files/press-release/awards_09aug_pt3_nctowy.pdf, accessed August 29, 2012. These grants awarded to the University of Tulsa were highlighted in Dr. Coburn's July 2011 exposé on unnecessary federal spending in his home state, "Oklahoma Waste Report".

[897] Thomson Reuters, "Cooper Tire Receives $6.9 Million U.S. Department of Agriculture Grant," July 11, 2012, http://www.reuters.com/article/2012/07/11/idUS104284+11-Jul-2012+HUG20120711, accessed August 31, 2012. Cooper Tire is listed on the New York Stock Exchange (NYSE: CTB) and reported nearly $4 billion in revenue in 2011.

[898] Ray, D.T. "Guayule: A source of natural rubber." p. 338-343. In: J. Janick and J.E. Simon (eds.), New crops. Wiley, New York. Available at http://www.hort.purdue.edu/newcrop/proceedings1993/v2-338.html, accessed September 24, 2012.

[899] Yulex Corporation, "Cooper Tire and Yulex Announce Joint Development Agreement," http://www.yulex.com/news/news_window.html?/news/Yulex_Cooper_Tire_Release_Final.pdf, accessed September 24, 2012.

[900] Yulex Corporation, "Medical and Sexual Health," http://www.yulex.com/markets/medical.php, accessed September 24, 2012.

[901] Ray, D.T. "Guayule: A source of natural rubber." p. 338-343. In: J. Janick and J.E. Simon (eds.), New crops. Wiley, New York. Available at http://www.hort.purdue.edu/newcrop/proceedings1993/v2-338.html, accessed September 24, 2012.

[902] Bridgestone Corporation, "Bridgestone Launches Research Project to Develop a Sustainable Source of Natural Rubber," http://www.bridgestone.com/corporate/news/2012030801.html, accessed September 24, 2012.

[903] "Deficient Bridges by State and Highway System; As of December 2011," Federal Highway Administration website, http://www.fhwa.dot.gov/bridge/nbi/defbr11.cfm, accessed October 3, 2012.

[904] Jamison, Tim. "Lou Henry Hoover sculpture is about to get some company," *Waterloo Cedar Falls Courier*, December 12, 2010; http://wcfcourier.com/news/local/lou-henry-hoover-sculpture-is-about-to-get-some-company/article_dacdaa17-f111-5a76-9dec-cf21b187a745.html, accessed October 3, 2012.

[905] Jamison, Tim. "Lou Henry Hoover sculpture is about to get some company," *Waterloo Cedar Falls Courier*, December 12, 2010; http://wcfcourier.com/news/local/lou-henry-hoover-sculpture-is-about-to-get-some-company/article_dacdaa17-f111-5a76-9dec-cf21b187a745.html, accessed October 3, 2012.

[906] Jamison, Tim. "Downtown Lou Henry Hoover project ready to start," *Waterloo Cedar Falls Courier*, August 11, 2012, http://wcfcourier.com/news/local/downtown-lou-henry-hoover-project-ready-to-start/article_04f87e12-8e82-5c76-a162-baef76594ff1.html, accessed October 3, 2012.

[907] Jamison, Tim. "Lou Henry Hoover sculpture is about to get some company," *Waterloo Cedar Falls Courier*, December 12, 2010; http://wcfcourier.com/news/local/lou-henry-hoover-sculpture-is-about-to-get-some-company/article_dacdaa17-f111-5a76-9dec-cf21b187a745.html, accessed October 3, 2012.

[908] Jamison, Tim. "Downtown Lou Henry Hoover project ready to start," *Waterloo Cedar Falls Courier*, August 11, 2012, http://wcfcourier.com/news/local/downtown-lou-henry-hoover-project-ready-to-start/article_04f87e12-8e82-5c76-a162-baef76594ff1.html, accessed October 3, 2012.

[909] "Lou Henry Hoover Memorial Sculpture Garden Request for Proposals," Waterloo Center for the Arts, 2010, http://www.waterloocenterforthearts.org/PDF/Lou_Henry_Hoover_RFP-2010.pdf, accessed October 13, 2012.

[910] "Lou Henry Hoover Memorial Sculpture Garden Request for Proposals," Waterloo Center for the Arts, 2010, http://www.waterloocenterforthearts.org/PDF/Lou_Henry_Hoover_RFP-2010.pdf, accessed October 13, 2012.

[911] "Lou Henry Hoover Memorial Sculpture Garden Request for Proposals," Waterloo Center for the Arts, 2010; http://www.waterloocenterforthearts.org/PDF/Lou_Henry_Hoover_RFP-2010.pdf, accessed October 13, 2012.

[912] Jamison, Tim. "Hoover project draws no bids," *Waterloo Cedar Falls Courier*, July 17, 2012, http://wcfcourier.com/news/local/govt-and-politics/hoover-project-draws-no-bids/article_394f25cb-81d0-521a-b82c-ad0987acc5b8.html, accessed October 3, 2012.

[913] Jamison, Tim. "Downtown Lou Henry Hoover project ready to start," Waterloo Cedar Falls Courier, August 11, 2012, http://wcfcourier.com/news/local/downtown-lou-henry-hoover-project-ready-to-start/article_04f87e12-8e82-5c76-a162-baef76594ff1.html, accessed October 3, 2012.

[914] "GALLERY EIGHT: An Uncommon Woman," The Herbert Hoover Presidential Library and Museum website, http://www.hoover.archives.gov/exhibits/Hooverstory/gallery08/index.html, accessed September 28, 2012.

[915] "Art in Public Places," The City of Whittier website, http://www.cityofwhittier.org/depts/prcs/arts/aipp.asp, accessed October 4, 2012.

[916] "Media Arts: Film/Radio/Television: FY 2012 Grants," Website of the National Endowment for the Arts, http://www.nea.gov/grants/recent/disciplines/Media/12media.php?CAT=Art%20Works&DIS=Media%20Arts&TABLE=2, accessed June 1, 2012.

[917] Games for Change website, http://www.gamesforchange.org/2012/01/g4c-12-call-for-talks-presentations/, accessed October 11, 2012.

[918] "Zombie Yoga," Games for Change website, http://gamesforchange.org/festival2012/?game=zombie-yoga, accessed August 29, 2012.

[919] "Playforward: Elm City Stories," Games for Change website, http://gamesforchange.org/festival2012/?game=playforward-elm-city-stories, accessed August 29, 2012.

[920] "Yourturn! Designing a Music Game for Social Impact," Games for Change website, http://gamesforchange.org/festival2012/?event=yourturn-designing-a-music-game-for-social-impact, accessed August 29, 2012.

[921] "Game-O-Matic: A Tool for Generating Journalistic Games on the Fly," Games for Change website, http://gamesforchange.org/festival2012/?event=game-o-matic-a-tool-for-generating-journalistic-games-on-the-fly, accessed October 11, 2012.

[922] "Deepak Chopra's Leela – Creating a Video Game to Connect People with Themselves," Games for Change website, http://gamesforchange.org/festival2012/?event=deepak-chopras-leela-creating-a-video-game-to-connect-people-with-themselves, accessed August 29, 2012.

[923] Games for Change website, http://www.gamesforchange.org/2012/01/g4c-12-call-for-talks-presentations/, accessed October 11, 2012.

[924] Games for Change website, http://gamesforchange.org/festival2012/, accessed August 29, 2012.

[925] Ninth Annual Games for Change Festival website, http://gamesforchange.org/festival2012/attend/ (page no longer exists here). However, registration fees can be found here: http://www.nyuskirball.org/calendar/gamesforchange, accessed October 12, 2012.

[926] "Report on Costs of Treatment in the President's Emergency Plan for AIDS Relief (PEPFAR)," *Office of the US Global AIDS Coordinator*, February 2012, http://www.pepfar.gov/documents/organization/188493.pdf, accessed September 10, 2012.

[927] Alexander, Brielle Valyntin. "Ogden City Corporation invests $1 million towards Mobile App Lab," KSL-5, June 11, 2012, http://www.ksl.com/?nid=148&sid=20790861, accessed September 27, 2012.

[928] "U.S. Economic Development Administration Announces $1 Million Investment to Establish Mobile Apps Lab in Ogden, Utah," U.S. Economic Development Administration website, June 7, 2012, http://www.eda.gov/news/pressreleases/2012/06/07/ogden_ut.htm, accessed October 11, 2012.

[929] Alexander, Brielle Valyntin. "Ogden City Corporation invests $1 million towards Mobile App Lab," KSL-5, June 11, 2012, http://www.ksl.com/?nid=148&sid=20790861, accessed September 27, 2012.

[930] Alexander, Brielle Valyntin. "Ogden City Corporation invests $1 million towards Mobile App Lab," KSL-5, June 11, 2012, http://www.ksl.com/?nid=148&sid=20790861, accessed September 27, 2012.

[931] "Port of Los Angeles Gets Final Approval from Coast Guard to Create First Harbor Vessel Retrofitted with Hybrid-electric Propulsion System," The Port of Los Angeles website, Press Release, February 2, 2012, http://www.portoflosangeles.org/newsroom/2012_releases/news_020212_angelina.asp, accessed August 21, 2012.

[932] Goldstein, David. "Taxpayer Money Used to Maintain Million-Dollar Yacht," *CBS-2 Los Angeles*, February 6, 2012. Available at http://losangeles.cbslocal.com/2012/02/06/taxpayer-money-used-to-maintain-million-dollar-yacht/, accessed August 21, 2012.

[933] "Insurance," National Marine Bankers Association website, http://www.marinebankers.org/index.php?option=com_content&view=article&id=19&Itemid=13, accessed August 21, 2012.

[934] "Port of Los Angeles Gets Final Approval from Coast Guard to Create First Harbor Vessel Retrofitted with Hybrid-electric Propulsion System," The Port of Los Angeles website, Press Release, February 2, 2012, http://www.portoflosangeles.org/newsroom/2012_releases/news_020212_angelina.asp, accessed August 21, 2012.

[935] "Oversight Committee Reviewing Port of L.A. Grant for Port-Owned Yacht," Website of the House Committee on Oversight and Government Reform, February 7, 2012, http://oversight.house.gov/release/oversight-committee-reviewing-port-of-l-a-grant-for-port-owned-yacht/, accessed August 21, 2012.

[936] "Port of Los Angeles Gets Final Approval from Coast Guard to Create First Harbor Vessel Retrofitted with Hybrid-electric Propulsion System," The Port of Los Angeles website, Press Release, February 2, 2012, http://www.portoflosangeles.org/newsroom/2012_releases/news_020212_angelina.asp, accessed August 21, 2012.

[937] Goldstein, David. "Taxpayer Money Used to Maintain Million-Dollar Yacht," *CBS-2 Los Angeles*, February 6, 2012. Available at http://losangeles.cbslocal.com/2012/02/06/taxpayer-money-used-to-maintain-million-dollar-yacht/, accessed August 21, 2012.

[938] "Port of Los Angeles Tour Boat," document provided by Mr. Jim Olds, Departmental Audit Manager for the Port of Los Angeles.

[939] Goldstein, David. "Taxpayer Money Used to Maintain Million-Dollar Yacht," *CBS-2 Los Angeles*, February 6, 2012. Available at http://losangeles.cbslocal.com/2012/02/06/taxpayer-money-used-to-maintain-million-dollar-yacht/, accessed August 21, 2012.

[940] Reynolds, Kevin. "Fullerton Installs $35,000 Book Vending Machine," *The Orange County Register*, June 20, 2012, http://www.ocregister.com/articles/machine-359831-books-library.html, accessed September 18, 2012.

[941] "Library Services and Technology Act (LSTA) Projects, 2011/2012," http://www.library.ca.gov/grants/lsta/docs/LSTAProjectAbstracts1112.pdf, accessed September 18, 2012.

[942] Reynolds, Kevin. "Fullerton Installs $35,000 Book Vending Machine," *The Orange County Register*, June 20, 2012, http://www.ocregister.com/articles/machine-359831-books-library.html, accessed September 18, 2012.

[943] "Library expansion named '2011 Facility of the Year,'" *Fullerton Stories*, November 2, 2011, http://fullertonstories.com/library-expansion-named-%E2%80%982011-facility-of-the-year%E2%80%99/, accessed October 5, 2012.

[944] Google maps, http://maps.google.com/maps?hl=en&bav=on.2,or.r_gc.r_pw.r_qf.&biw=1680&bih=906&um=1&ie=UTF-8&q=fullerton+library&fb=1&gl=us&hq=fullerton+library&hnear=fullerton+library&cid=0,0,16962019063076370950&sa=X&ei=VC5vUPn9LYaB0QGOoYGgDQ&ved=0CJQBEPwSMAA, accessed October 5, 2012.

[945] "Transportation Center," City of Fullerton website, http://www.ci.fullerton.ca.us/visitors/downtown_fullerton/transportation_center.asp, accessed October 5, 2012.

[946] Prices from Amazon.com and BestBuy.com, accessed October 5, 2012.

[947] Chip Carter, "Watermelon queen program creating industry ambassadors," The Produce News, June 4, 2012; http://www.theproducenews.com/index.php/what-s-new/7966-watermelon-queen-program-creating-industry-ambassadors.

[948] Information provided by the U.S. Department of Agriculture to the Congressional Research Service, October 5, 2012.

[949] Information provided by the U.S. Department of Agriculture to the Congressional Research Service, October 5, 2012.

[950] "Fruit and Vegetable Programs: Specialty Crop Block Grant Program; Fiscal Year 2012 Description of Funded Projects," USDA Agricultural Marketing Services, accessed October 3, 2012; http://www.ams.usda.gov/AMSv1.0/getfile?dDocName=STELPRDC5100734.

[951] "Welcome to the Alabama Watermelon Association!," The Alabama Watermelon Association website, accessed October 3, 2012; http://www.alwatermelon.org/#!.

[952] "Queen Program," The Alabama Watermelon Association website, accessed October 3, 2012; http://www.alwatermelon.org/#!queen-program.

[953] "Alabama Report," The Vineline, National Watermelon Association, page 19, Spring 2012; http://www.nationalwatermelonassociation.com/pdfs/spring_2012.pdf.

[954] "Queen Program," The Alabama Watermelon Association website, accessed October 3, 2012; http://www.alwatermelon.org/#!queen-program.

[955] Chip Carter, "Watermelon queen program creating industry ambassadors," The Produce News, June 4, 2012; http://www.theproducenews.com/index.php/what-s-new/7966-watermelon-queen-program-creating-industry-ambassadors.

[956] "Alabama Report," The Vineline, National Watermelon Association, page 19, Spring 2012; http://www.nationalwatermelonassociation.com/pdfs/spring_2012.pdf.

[957] Chip Carter, "Watermelon queen program creating industry ambassadors," The Produce News, June 4, 2012; http://www.theproducenews.com/index.php/what-s-new/7966-watermelon-queen-program-creating-industry-ambassadors.

[958] "Fruit and Vegetable Programs: Specialty Crop Block Grant Program; Fiscal Year 2012 Description of Funded Projects," USDA Agricultural Marketing Services, accessed October 3, 2012; http://www.ams.usda.gov/AMSv1.0/getfile?dDocName=STELPRDC5100734.

[959] Malinda Geisler, "watermelon," Agricultural Marketing Resource Center (AgMRC) at Iowa State University in AmesApril 2011; http://www.agmrc.org/commodities_products/vegetables/watermelon/.

[960] Chip Carter, "Warm winter bringing heavy volume of high-quality watermelons," The Produce News, April 19, 2012; http://www.theproducenews.com/index.php/news-dep-menu/test-featured/7610-warm-winter-bringing-heavy-volume-of-high-quality-watermelons.

[961] "Award Abstract #0905127: HCC: Medium: Collaborative Research: Improving Older Adult Cognition: The Unexamined Role of Games and Social Computing Environments," Website of the National Science Foundation, http://nsf.gov/awardsearch/showAward.do?AwardNumber=0905127, accessed April 11, 2012. The grant was funded through the American Recovery and Reinvestment Act.

[962] "Award Abstract #0904855: HCC: Medium: Collaborative Research: Improving Older Adult Cognition: The Unexamined Role of Games and Social Computing Environments," Website of the National Science Foundation, http://nsf.gov/awardsearch/showAward.do?AwardNumber=0904855, accessed April 11, 2012.

[963] Netburn, Deborah. "Can playing World of Warcraft make you smarter?" *Los Angeles Times* Tech Now blog, February 23, 2012, http://articles.latimes.com/2012/feb/23/business/la-fi-tn-world-of-warcraft-boosts-cognitive-ability-20120223, accessed April 11, 2012.

[964] "Playstation 2, World of Warcraft, Most Playedi n January," Nielsenwire, March 12, 2009, http://blog.nielsen.com/nielsenwire/media_entertainment/playstation-2-world-of-warcraft-most-played-in-january/, accessed October 13, 2012.

[965] Netburn, Deborah. "Can playing World of Warcraft make you smarter?" *Los Angeles Times* Tech Now blog, February 23, 2012, http://articles.latimes.com/2012/feb/23/business/la-fi-tn-world-of-warcraft-boosts-cognitive-ability-20120223, accessed April 11, 2012.

[966] Netburn, Deborah. "Can playing World of Warcraft make you smarter?" *Los Angeles Times* Tech Now blog, February 23, 2012, http://articles.latimes.com/2012/feb/23/business/la-fi-tn-world-of-warcraft-boosts-cognitive-ability-20120223, accessed April 11, 2012.

[967] Amazon.com, "Boom Blox," http://www.amazon.com/Boom-Blox-Nintendo-Wii/dp/B000YDIYFG/ref=pd_sim_sbs_vg_1, accessed August 23, 2012.

[968] Louisiana Land Trust, Current Property Listings as of October 12, 2012, http://www.lalandtrust.us/index.php?option=com_content&view=article&id=47&Itemid=49, accessed October 12, 2012.

[969] Minutes of the Road Home Corporation, DBA Louisiana Land Trust, Board of Directors Meeting, April 16, 2012, p. 3. Available at http://www.lalandtrust.us/RFP/4-16-12LLTBoardMeetingMinutesASapproved5-21-12.pdf, accessed August 7, 2012.

[970] Minutes of the Road Home Corporation, DBA Louisiana Land Trust, Board of Directors Meeting, October 10, 2011, p. 6. Available at http://www.lalandtrust.us/RFP/10-10-11LLTBoardMeetingMinutesasApproved12-10-11.pdf, accessed October 12, 2012. Funding for LLT comes from the federal Department of Housing and Urban Development: see "FAQs," Louisiana Land Trust website, http://www.lalandtrust.us/RFP/10-10-11LLTBoardMeetingMinutesasApproved12-10-11.pdf, accessed October 12, 2012.

[971] Hammer, David. "Officials hope to put sale of Road Home properties on the fast track," *The Times-Picayune*, August 4, 2011, http://www.nola.com/politics/index.ssf/2011/08/agency_short_on_money_unveils.html, accessed October 12, 2012.

[972] Louisiana Land Trust, Current Property Listings as of October 12, 2012, http://www.lalandtrust.us/index.php?option=com_content&view=article&id=47&Itemid=49, accessed October 12, 2012.

[973] Burdeau, Cain. "Millions spent on upkeep of empty Katrina lots," Associated Press, July 16, 2012. Available at http://news.yahoo.com/millions-spent-upkeep-empty-katrina-lots-165405007.html, accessed September 24, 2012.

[974] Hammer, David. "Officials hope to put sale of Road Home properties on the fast track," *The Times-Picayune*, August 4, 2011, http://www.nola.com/politics/index.ssf/2011/08/agency_short_on_money_unveils.html, accessed October 13, 2012.

[975] Burdeau, Cain. "Millions spent on upkeep of empty Katrina lots," Associated Press, July 16, 2012. Available at http://news.yahoo.com/millions-spent-upkeep-empty-katrina-lots-165405007.html, accessed September 24, 2012.

[976] Burdeau, Cain. "Millions spent on upkeep of empty Katrina lots," Associated Press, July 16, 2012. Available at http://news.yahoo.com/millions-spent-upkeep-empty-katrina-lots-165405007.html, accessed September 24, 2012.

[977] Burdeau, Cain. "Millions spent on upkeep of empty Katrina lots," Associated Press, July 16, 2012. Available at http://news.yahoo.com/millions-spent-upkeep-empty-katrina-lots-165405007.html, accessed September 24, 2012.

[978] Burdeau, Cain. "Millions spent on upkeep of empty Katrina lots," Associated Press, July 16, 2012. Available at http://news.yahoo.com/millions-spent-upkeep-empty-katrina-lots-165405007.html, accessed September 24, 2012.

[979] The Chief Legal Counsel of the Miami-Dade County Health Department provided this information via email, May 10, 2012.

[980] Murphy, Samantha. "High-Tech School Vending Machines Serve Up Fresh Lunches," *TechNews Daily*, August 12, 2011. Available at http://www.technewsdaily.com/3036-vending-machines-for-healthy-foods.html, accessed July 10, 2012.

[981] Murphy, Samantha. "High-Tech School Vending Machines Serve Up Fresh Lunches," *TechNews Daily*, August 12, 2011. Available at http://www.technewsdaily.com/3036-vending-machines-for-healthy-foods.html, accessed July 10, 2012.

[982] "Miami-Dade School Cafeterias Get High-Tech, Healthy Makeovers," CBS4-Miami, August 19, 2011. Available at http://miami.cbslocal.com/2011/08/19/miami-dade-school-cafeterias-get-high-tech-healthy-makeovers/, accessed July 10, 2012.

[983] "Miami-Dade School Cafeterias Get High-Tech, Healthy Makeovers," CBS4-Miami, August 19, 2011. Available at http://miami.cbslocal.com/2011/08/19/miami-dade-school-cafeterias-get-high-tech-healthy-makeovers/, accessed July 10, 2012.

[984] "Miami-Dade School Cafeterias Get High-Tech, Healthy Makeovers," CBS4-Miami, August 19, 2011. Available at http://miami.cbslocal.com/2011/08/19/miami-dade-school-cafeterias-get-high-tech-healthy-makeovers/, accessed July 10, 2012.

[985] "Miami-Dade School Cafeterias Get High-Tech, Healthy Makeovers," CBS4-Miami, August 19, 2011. Available at http://miami.cbslocal.com/2011/08/19/miami-dade-school-cafeterias-get-high-tech-healthy-makeovers/, accessed July 10, 2012.

[986] The Chief Legal Counsel of the Miami-Dade County Health Department provided this information, May 10, 2012.

[987] The Chief Legal Counsel of the Miami-Dade County Health Department provided this information, May 10, 2012.

[988] Recovery.gov, Award Number 1U58DP002406-01. Available at http://www.recovery.gov/Transparency/RecipientReportedData/pages/RecipientProjectSummary508.aspx?AwardIDSUR=88940, accessed September 6, 2012.

[989] Miller, Michael. "Miami-Dade Health Squanders $15 Million From Feds Meant to Bring Farmers' Markets to Town," *Miami NewTimes* blog, February 13, 2012, http://blogs.miaminewtimes.com/riptide/2011/08/vending_machines_replacing_lun.php, accessed October 13, 2012. The Miami-Dade County Health Department verified that the grant recipients listed in the article are correct, in correspondence with the Congressional Research Service and sent to the Office of Senator Tom Coburn, April 20, 2012.

[990] Tuttle, Brad. "Cheers! Increase in Liquor Sales Bodes Well for Economic Recovery," *Time* Moneyland blog, January 31, 2012, http://moneyland.time.com/2012/01/31/cheers-increase-in-liquor-sales-bodes-well-for-economic-recovery/, accessed August 20, 2012.

[991] Tuttle, Brad. "Cheers! Increase in Liquor Sales Bodes Well for Economic Recovery," *Time* Moneyland blog, January 31, 2012, http://moneyland.time.com/2012/01/31/cheers-increase-in-liquor-sales-bodes-well-for-economic-recovery/, accessed August 20, 2012.

[992] Fox, Craig. "County Planning Board reviews Clayton distillery plans," *Watertown Daily Times*, May 30, 2012. Available at http://www.watertowndailytimes.com/article/20120530/NEWS03/705309830, accessed June 7, 2012.

[993] Booker, Ted. "Developer says grant-funded Clayton business jeopardizes distillery plans," *Watertown Daily Times*, May 31, 2012. Available at http://www.watertowndailytimes.com/article/20120531/NEWS03/705319835, accessed August 31, 2012.

[994] Block, Gordon. "Three rural economic development organizations receive grant funding," *Daily Courier-Observer*, May 5, 2012. Available at http://www.mpcourier.com/article/20120505/NEWS03/705059916/0/news04, accessed October 10, 2012.

[995] Fox, Craig. "County Planning Board reviews Clayton distillery plans," *Watertown Daily Times*, May 30, 2012. Available at http://www.watertowndailytimes.com/article/20120530/NEWS03/705309830, accessed June 7, 2012.

[996] Fox, Craig. "County Planning Board reviews Clayton distillery plans," *Watertown Daily Times*, May 30, 2012. Available at http://www.watertowndailytimes.com/article/20120530/NEWS03/705309830, accessed June 7, 2012.

[997] Booker, Ted. "Developer says grant-funded Clayton business jeopardizes distillery plans," *Watertown Daily Times*, May 31, 2012. Available at http://www.watertowndailytimes.com/article/20120531/NEWS03/705319835, accessed August 31, 2012.

[998] Booker, Ted. "Developer says grant-funded Clayton business jeopardizes distillery plans," *Watertown Daily Times*, May 31, 2012. Available at http://www.watertowndailytimes.com/article/20120531/NEWS03/705319835, accessed August 31, 2012.

[999] Fox, Craig. "Plans for two area distilleries are fermenting in the north country," *Watertown Daily Times*, August 31, 2012. Available at http://www.watertowndailytimes.com/article/20120831/NEWS03/708319882, accessed August 31, 2012.

[1000] Information provided by 100-year Starship to the Office of Senator Coburn, May 31, 2012.

[1001] Foust, Jeff. "Building a starship's foundation," *The Space Review*, September 24, 2012, http://www.thespacereview.com/article/2161/1, accessed September 28, 2012.

[1002] "2012 100YSS Symposium Proceedings," Website of the 100-Year Starship Symposium, http://symposium.100yss.org/symposium-proceedings, accessed August 8, 2012.

[1003] Foust, Jeff. "Building a starship's foundation," *The Space Review*, September 24, 2012, http://www.thespacereview.com/article/2161/1, accessed September 28, 2012.

[1004] Foust, Jeff. "Building a starship's foundation," *The Space Review*, September 24, 2012, http://www.thespacereview.com/article/2161/1, accessed September 28, 2012.

[1005] Foust, Jeff. "Building a starship's foundation," *The Space Review*, September 24, 2012, http://www.thespacereview.com/article/2161/1, accessed September 28, 2012.

[1006] Foust, Jeff. "Building a starship's foundation," *The Space Review*, September 24, 2012, http://www.thespacereview.com/article/2161/1, accessed September 28, 2012.

[1007] Foust, Jeff. "Building a starship's foundation," *The Space Review*, September 24, 2012, http://www.thespacereview.com/article/2161/1, accessed September 28, 2012.

[1008] "2012 100YSS Symposium Proceedings," Website of the 100-Year Starship Symposium, http://symposium.100yss.org/symposium-proceedings, accessed August 8, 2012.

[1009] "2012 100YSS Symposium Proceedings," Website of the 100-Year Starship Symposium, http://symposium.100yss.org/symposium-proceedings, accessed August 8, 2012.

[1010] "2012 100YSS Symposium Proceedings," Website of the 100-Year Starship Symposium, http://symposium.100yss.org/symposium-proceedings, accessed August 8, 2012.

[1011] Foust, Jeff. "Building a starship's foundation," *The Space Review*, September 24, 2012, http://www.thespacereview.com/article/2161/1, accessed September 28, 2012.

[1012] Foust, Jeff. "Building a starship's foundation," *The Space Review*, September 24, 2012, http://www.thespacereview.com/article/2161/1, accessed September 28, 2012.

[1013] Moskowitz, Clare. "100 Year Starship Symposium Kicks Off to Ponder Interstellar Travel," LiveScience.com, September 13, 2012, http://www.livescience.com/23172-100-year-starship-symposium-kicks-off.html, accessed October 11, 2012.

[1014] "Special Events," Website of the 100-Year Starship Symposium, http://symposium.100yss.org/special-events, accessed August 8, 2012.

[1015] "Special Events," Website of the 100-Year Starship Symposiu,. http://symposium.100yss.org/special-events, accessed August 8, 2012.

[1016] Foust, Jeff. "Building a starship's foundation," *The Space Review*, September 24, 2012, http://www.thespacereview.com/article/2161/1, accessed September 28, 2012.

[1017] Information provided by DARPA to the Congressional Research Service, June 18, 2012.

[1018] Information provided by DARPA to the Congressional Research Service, June 18, 2012.

[1019] McVey, John. "Queen Street Rising," *Martinsburg Journal*, June 28, 2012. Available at http://www.journal-news.net/page/content.detail/id/581047/Queen-Street-rising.html?nav=5011, accessed October 11, 2012.

[1020] McVey, John. "Lego Queen Street: Streetscape model will be on display at children's museum," *Martinsburg Journal*, June 23, 2012. Available at http://www.journal-news.net/page/content.detail/id/580825/Lego-Queen-Street.html?nav=5006, accessed August 9, 2012.

[1021] McVey, John. "Queen Street Rising," *Martinsburg Journal*, June 28, 2012. Available at http://www.journal-news.net/page/content.detail/id/581047/Queen-Street-rising.html?nav=5011, accessed October 11, 2012.

[1022] McVey, John. "Queen Street Rising," *Martinsburg Journal*, June 28, 2012. Available at http://www.journal-news.net/page/content.detail/id/581047/Queen-Street-rising.html?nav=5011, accessed October 11, 2012.

[1023] "Project: WV: Washington Heritage Trail for the kids, by George, an Exhibit," Department of Transportation Federal Highway Administration website, http://www.bywaysonline.org/grants/funded/detail.html?id=55117, accessed July 10, 2012.

[1024] "Deficient Bridges by State and Highway System," Department of Transportation Federal Highway Administration, http://www.fhwa.dot.gov/bridge/defbr06.cfm, accessed July 10, 2012.

[1025] "GSA Announces Plans to Modernize Schedules," General Services Administration, Press Release, June 7, 2012, http://www.gsa.gov/portal/content/136647, accessed September 11, 2012.

[1026] "GSA Announces Plans to Modernize Schedules," General Services Administration, Press Release, June 7, 2012, http://www.gsa.gov/portal/content/136647, accessed September 11, 2012.

[1027] In March 2012, 83 summer stipends were awarded, worth $6,000 each totaling $498,000. "National Endowment for the Humanities Grant Awards and Offers, March 2012," National Endowment for the Humanities website, http://www.neh.gov/files/press-release/march2012statebystatefinal.pdf, accessed June 8, 2012.

[1028] "National Endowment for the Humanities Grant Awards and Offers, March 2012," National Endowment for the Humanities website, http://www.neh.gov/files/press-release/march2012statebystatefinal.pdf, accessed June 8, 2012.

[1029] "Faculty," Website of Kalamazoo College, https://reason.kzoo.edu/history/faculty/, accessed June 8, 2012.

[1030] "National Endowment for the Humanities Grant Awards and Offers, March 2012," National Endowment for the Humanities website, http://www.neh.gov/files/press-release/march2012statebystatefinal.pdf, accessed June 8, 2012.

[1031] "National Endowment for the Humanities Grant Awards and Offers, March 2012," National Endowment for the Humanities website, http://www.neh.gov/files/press-release/march2012statebystatefinal.pdf, accessed June 8, 2012.

[1032] "National Endowment for the Humanities Grant Awards and Offers, December 2011," National Endowment for the Humanities website, http://www.neh.gov/files/press-release/december2011statebystatefinal.pdf, accessed June 8, 2012.

[1033] This study was funded from part of two FY2012 NIH grants: "Alcohol and Adult Development: Understanding Etiology and Consequences," National Institutes of Health, project no. 5K05AA017242-05, http://projectreporter.nih.gov/project_info_history.cfm?aid=8137213&icde=12672567, accessed May 31, 2012. "Psychology of Alcohol Use and Dependence Training," National Institutes of Health, project no. 5T32AA013526-10, http://projectreporter.nih.gov/project_info_history.cfm?aid=8101007&icde=12672359, accessed May 31, 2012. Grants are attributed in Winograd, RP, AK Littlefield, KJ Sher. (2012) "Do People Who 'Mature Out' of Drinking See Themselves as More Mature?" *Alcoholism: Clinical and Experimental Research*, 36(7):1212-1218.

[1034] Wall, Timothy. "To feel more mature, cut back on booze," *Futurity.org*, April 17, 2012, http://www.futurity.org/society-culture/to-feel-more-mature-cut-back-on-booze/, accessed May 31, 2012.

[1035] Wall, Timothy. "To feel more mature, cut back on booze," *Futurity.org*, April 17, 2012, http://www.futurity.org/society-culture/to-feel-more-mature-cut-back-on-booze/, accessed May 31, 2012.

[1036] Wall, Timothy. "To feel more mature, cut back on booze," *Futurity.org*, April 17, 2012, http://www.futurity.org/society-culture/to-feel-more-mature-cut-back-on-booze/, accessed May 31, 2012.

[1037] Wall, Timothy. "To feel more mature, cut back on booze," *Futurity.org*, April 17, 2012, http://www.futurity.org/society-culture/to-feel-more-mature-cut-back-on-booze/, accessed May 31, 2012.

[1038] Wall, Timothy. "To feel more mature, cut back on booze," *Futurity.org*, April 17, 2012, http://www.futurity.org/society-culture/to-feel-more-mature-cut-back-on-booze/, accessed May 31, 2012.

[1039] Information provided by the Department of Agriculture to the Congressional Research Service, April 17, 2012.

[1040] "Idaho Firearms and Accessories Manufacturer's Association," *Idaho Press-Tribune* calendar, http://www.idahopress.com/calendar/idaho-firearms-and-accessories-manufacturer-s-association-conference/event_55289bf2-d974-11e0-bfd2-0019bb2963f4.html, accessed September 10, 2012.

[1041] Dutton, Audrey. "Fircarms big business in Idaho," *Idaho Statesman*, October 1, 2011, http://www.idahopress.com/news/state/firearms-big-business-in-idaho/article_e0fa2037-1ae6-50f8-b088-c760099fe558.html, accessed October 11, 2012.

[1042] "BRFSS Survey Results 2001 for Nationwide," North Carolina State Center for Health Statistics website, September 20, 2002, http://www.schs.state.nc.us/SCHS/brfss/2001/us/firearm3.html, accessed August 30, 2012.

[1043] Miniter, Frank. "What the Left Won't Tell You About The Boom In U.S. Gun Sales," *Forbes*, August 23, 2012, http://www.forbes.com/sites/frankminiter/2012/08/23/what-the-left-wont-tell-you-about-the-boom-in-u-s-gun-sales/, accessed August 30, 2012.

[1044] Miniter, Frank. "What the Left Won't Tell You About The Boom In U.S. Gun Sales," *Forbes*, August 23, 2012, http://www.forbes.com/sites/frankminiter/2012/08/23/what-the-left-wont-tell-you-about-the-boom-in-u-s-gun-sales/, accessed August 30, 2012.

[1045] "Idaho Firearms and Accessories Manufacturer's Association," *Idaho Press-Tribune* calendar, http://www.idahopress.com/calendar/idaho-firearms-and-accessories-manufacturer-s-association-conference/event_55289bf2-d974-11e0-bfd2-0019bb2963f4.html, accessed September 10, 2012.

[1046] "Idaho Firearms and Accessories Manufacturer's Association," *Idaho Press-Tribune* calendar, http://www.idahopress.com/calendar/idaho-firearms-and-accessories-manufacturer-s-association-conference/event_55289bf2-d974-11e0-bfd2-0019bb2963f4.html, accessed September 10, 2012.

[1047] USASpending.gov, federal award IDS: 4979995001, 5379375004, 5076645005, 5360225005, 5076605004, 5176615004, 4974405000, 4998355003, 4917705000, 4914545005, 5085325005 (search for "cupcake" restricted to fiscal year 2012).

[1048] All loans were part of the 504/CDC or 7(a) programs managed by the Small Business Administration. Taxpayers are on the hook for a percentage of the loans if the businesses fail to repay them. See Dilger, Robert Jay. "Small Business Administration 504/CDC Loan Guaranty Program," Congressional Research Service, R41184, March 20, 2012.

[1049] USASpending.gov, federal award IDS: 4979995001, 5379375004, 5076645005, 5360225005, 5076605004, 5176615004, 4974405000, 4998355003, 4917705000, 4914545005, 5085325005 (search for "cupcake" restricted to fiscal year 2012).

[1050] Dilger, Robert Jay. "Small Business Administration 504/CDC Loan Guaranty Program," Congressional Research Service, R41184, March 20, 2012.

[1051] USASpending.gov, federal award IDS: 4979995001, 5379375004, 5076645005, 5360225005, 5076605004, 5176615004, 4974405000, 4998355003, 4917705000, 4914545005, 5085325005 (search for "cupcake" restricted to fiscal year 2012).

[1051] USASpending.gov, federal award IDS: 4979995001, 5379375004, 5076645005, 5360225005, 5076605004, 5176615004, 4974405000, 4998355003, 4917705000, 4914545005, 5085325005 (search for "cupcake" restricted to fiscal year 2012).

[1052] USASpending.gov, federal award IDs: 5076605004, 4914545005, 5176615004.

[1053] "Cupcake Station of Birmingham: Bursting with Flavor and Booming with Business," *PositiveDetroit*, February 4, 2009, http://www.positivedetroit.net/2009/02/cupcake-station-of-birmingham-bursting.html, accessed August 20, 2012.

[1054] Website of Heavenly Cupcake, http://www.heavenlycupcake.com/flavors.html, accessed August 20, 2012.

[1055] "One-of-a-kind Smartphone Lab Takes Shape at UB," *University of Buffalo*, News release, August 30, 2012, http://www.buffalo.edu/news/13631, accessed September 14, 2012.

[1056] Website of PhoneLab, http://www.phone-lab.org/info/, accessed September 14, 2012.

[1057] "NSF Award Abstract #1205656: CI-ADDO-NEW: PhoneLab: A Programmable Participatory Smartphone Testbed," Website of the National Science Foundation, http://nsf.gov/awardsearch/showAward.do?AwardNumber=1205656, accessed September 14, 2012.

[1058] "One-of-a-kind Smartphone Lab Takes Shape at UB," *University of Buffalo* news release, August 30, 2012, http://www.buffalo.edu/news/13631, accessed September 14, 2012.

[1059] "One-of-a-kind Smartphone Lab Takes Shape at UB," *University of Buffalo* news release, August 30, 2012, http://www.buffalo.edu/news/13631, accessed September 14, 2012.

[1060] Website of PhoneLab, http://www.phone-lab.org/info/, accessed September 14, 2012.

[1061] Website of PhoneLab, http://www.phone-lab.org/info/, accessed September 14, 2012.

[1062] Website of PhoneLab, http://www.phone-lab.org/join/, accessed September 14, 2012.

[1063] "Your Vote Counts for Kossuth County Ag & Motorsports Museum," DirtTrackRadio.com, March 1, 2010, http://chadmeyermotorsports.blogs.com/dirt_racing_blog/2010/03/your-vote-counts-for-kossuth-county-ag-motorsports-museum.html, accessed September 24, 2012.

[1064] Algona Municipal Utilities, "AMU Receives Grant for County Ag/Motorsport Museum," *The Wire* [newsletter], July 2012, http://2006.netamu.com/company/AMUNewsletterJuly2012.pdf.pdf, accessed September 24, 2012.

[1065] Website of KLGA-92.7FM, http://www.radiop1.com/stationrss/viewpost.aspx?id=25706, accessed August 15, 2012.

[1066] "Rural Economic Development Loans," US Department of Agriculture, June 26, 2012, http://www.rurdev.usda.gov/SupportDocuments/RD_Economic_Dev_Jun_2012.pdf, accessed September 24, 2012.

[1067] "Stamp Manufacturing and Inventory Management," United States Postal Service Office of Inspector General, Report Number MS-AR-12-006, July 23, 2012, p. 12. Available at http://www.uspsoig.gov/foia_files/MS-AR-12-006.pdf, accessed September 24, 2012.

[1068] "Stamp Manufacturing and Inventory Management," United States Postal Service Office of Inspector General, Report Number MS-AR-12-006, July 23, 2012, p. 2. Available at http://www.uspsoig.gov/foia_files/MS-AR-12-006.pdf, accessed September 24, 2012.

[1069] Keane, Angela Greiling. "D'oh! USPS Stuck With 682M Unsold Simpsons Stamps," *Bloomberg Businessweek*, August 21, 2012. Available at http://www.businessweek.com/news/2012-08-21/d-oh-usps-stuck-with-682-million-unsold-simpsons-stamps, accessed August 22, 2012.

[1070] "Stamp Manufacturing and Inventory Management," United States Postal Service Office of Inspector General, Report Number MS-AR-12-006, July 23, 2012, p. 2. Available at http://www.uspsoig.gov/foia_files/MS-AR-12-006.pdf, accessed September 24, 2012.

[1071] "Stamp Manufacturing and Inventory Management," United States Postal Service Office of Inspector General, Report Number MS-AR-12-006, July 23, 2012, p. 13. Available at http://www.uspsoig.gov/foia_files/MS-AR-12-006.pdf, accessed September 24, 2012.

[1072] "Stamp Manufacturing and Inventory Management," United States Postal Service Office of Inspector General, Report Number MS-AR-12-006, July 23, 2012, p. 2. Available at http://www.uspsoig.gov/foia_files/MS-AR-12-006.pdf, accessed September 24, 2012.

[1073] "Stamp Manufacturing and Inventory Management," United States Postal Service Office of Inspector General, Report Number MS-AR-12-006, July 23, 2012, p. 2. Available at http://www.uspsoig.gov/foia_files/MS-AR-12-006.pdf, accessed September 24, 2012.

[1074] Ross, John. "Stamps – What an Idea!" *Smithsonian*, January 1998. Available at http://www.smithsonianmag.com/history-archaeology/object_jan98.html?c=y&page=2, accessed August 22, 2012.

[1075] "Stamp Manufacturing and Inventory Management," United States Postal Service Office of Inspector General, Report Number MS-AR-12-006, July 23, 2012, p. 13. Available at http://www.uspsoig.gov/foia_files/MS-AR-12-006.pdf, accessed September 24, 2012.

[1076] "Stamp Manufacturing and Inventory Management," United States Postal Service Office of Inspector General, Report Number MS-AR-12-006, July 23, 2012, p. 13. Available at http://www.uspsoig.gov/foia_files/MS-AR-12-006.pdf, accessed September 24, 2012.

[1077] "Stamp Manufacturing and Inventory Management," United States Postal Service Office of Inspector General, Report Number MS-AR-12-006, July 23, 2012, p. 2. Available at http://www.uspsoig.gov/foia_files/MS-AR-12-006.pdf, accessed September 24, 2012.

[1078] "Stamp Manufacturing and Inventory Management," United States Postal Service Office of Inspector General, Report Number MS-AR-12-006, July 23, 2012, p. 3. Available at http://www.uspsoig.gov/foia_files/MS-AR-12-006.pdf, accessed September 24, 2012.

[1079] "Stamp Manufacturing and Inventory Management," United States Postal Service Office of Inspector General, Report Number MS-AR-12-006, July 23, 2012, p. 13. Available at http://www.uspsoig.gov/foia_files/MS-AR-12-006.pdf, accessed September 24, 2012.

[1080] "Stamp Manufacturing and Inventory Management," United States Postal Service Office of Inspector General, Report Number MS-AR-12-006, July 23, 2012, p. 12. Available at http://www.uspsoig.gov/foia_files/MS-AR-12-006.pdf, accessed September 24, 2012.

[1081] The House and Senate Ethics Committees both held no hearings in 2012 and are not included in this analysis since their role is not legislative in nature.

[1082] Hearings held by congressional committees in 2012, as of August 20, 2012, provided by the Congressional Research Service and compiled by the ProQuest Congressional database.

[1083] This analysis omits committees that typically do not legislate such as House and Senate Ethics Committee and the Senate Special Committee on Aging.
See appendix. "Browse Committees & Subcommittees with Legislative Action; The 112th Congress," Congress.gov website, http://www.congress.gov/billsumm/vwList.php?&lid=1#notes, accessed August 22, 2012.

Made in the USA
Lexington, KY
13 October 2013